Paul Bryers

Coming First

BLOOMSBURY

First published 1987
Copyright © 1987 by Paul Bryers
This paperback edition published 1988

Bloomsbury Publishing Ltd, 2 Soho Square, London W1V 5DE

British Library Cataloguing in Publication Data

Bryers, Paul
Coming first.
I. title
823′.914[F]   PR6052.R94

ISBN 0-7475-0153-X

Designed by Newell and Sorrell Design Limited
Printed in Great Britain by
Richard Clay Ltd, Bungay, Suffolk

Preston Moody was miserably aware of his failings as a 'New Man'. A born-again feminist, his was a complicated endeavour to re-model himself along the lines apparently preferred by the women in his life. His wife Polly – who had frankly become irritated by Preston's anxious concern over her sexual needs – had banned him from the bedroom ever since he unwisely confessed to an affair with BBC *Shrews at Ten* presenter, Carla. Carla disapproved of *penetration* on political grounds. It was a situation pregnant with irony, speaking of which there was also Miranda whom he accompanied to natural-childbirth classes on Tuesdays for reasons best known to themselves. Preston sometimes wondered if any of these women really knew what they wanted. What if they just *thought* they wanted the 'New Man'? What if what they really wanted was Oliver Reed? Search with Preston Moody for guidelines to a peaceful life. Follow his quest through Lime Grove Studios, Toxteth and Suffolk marshes for the Right Attitude. Preston's plight may be your own. Or perhaps you are a woman whose man is always just getting it wrong. *Coming First* is the hilarious antidote to many of natures's little niggles – salutary, and a grand entertainment.

CONTENTS

CONTENTS

1 IN THE BEGINNING
Start Here

'Men,' wrote Eva Eichler, 'cannot relate to other people without hiding behind a mask of Purpose. They may call it work or sport, politics or war but they need some Object between themselves and others. This is why men are always doing things.'

This criticism, as it may be taken, was much quoted against Ms Eichler when her own political ambitions became known but she argued, quite convincingly, that she had not meant to imply that women should be excluded from having a purpose, or doing things. As one of America's leading feminist writers, she wished them to do a great deal more.

'Women,' wrote Eva Eichler, 'if they are to compete with men, must learn to overcome their natural reluctance to draw blood. Lady Macbeth came to a bad end, but remember, the writer was a man.'

This gave more ammunition to Ms Eichler's critics, particularly within the Democratic Party, and when she, too, came to a bad end there were those who drew the moral. Even when the rumours began and it became clear that suicide was not the only explanation.

'Men,' she had written, 'have developed a peculiar form of tunnel vision which permits them to see only the direction they wish to travel.

'They also have little capacity for humour when it is directed against them, particularly in a sexual context.'

Men, said some women when she died, were not likely to take that kind of thing lying down and in her writing Ms Eichler had been characteristically trenchant on the violent nature of the beast.

'Men,' wrote Eva Eichler, 'find violence a useful basis for social contact, hence the nature of the games they play ... among which one must include work, sex and war.'

2 MEET NAUGHTY BOYS
Miss a Go

There was a game Preston used to play as a child called Right Roads and Wrong Roads. It was one of those Victorian board games, heavy on moral dilemma and light on the intellect. The idea was you had to find your way through a maze of pathways designated Good Boy's Avenue and Bad Boy's Drive, Probity Pass, Prudence Passage, Ruination Row and so on until you reached The Cottage of Content. Or a dead end, depending on who or what you encountered along the way. Preston usually came to grief on The Naughty Boys Who Led You Astray. He remembered them as scruffy little brats who lounged around with their hands in their pockets, smirking. The instruction read: Fall into Bad Company. Miss a Go.

Preston looked at the American and recognised the same degenerate charm.

He was sitting across the table from Preston, waving his fork at him and talking. He had been talking almost incessantly for the best part of two hours and Preston, who should have been at natural childbirth classes, was hanging on to every word, wherever it led.

'Writes a book on male inadequacy,' he was saying now, 'then walks into the sea and drowns herself. Can you explain the logic in that, Preston? Is there some superior intellect at work here which I, as a poor inadequate male, cannot interpret?'

A passing waitress told him to eat up his greens like a good boy.

'We know what happens to naughty boys who don't eat up their greens, don't we?'

Preston knew. They got spanked by the waitress. There was a note about it on the menu and Preston had seen it happen to one of the other diners. He had appeared to enjoy it but Preston didn't want it to happen to him.

All around them, middle-aged boys in grown-up suits were stuffing themselves with meat and two veg as if their lives depended on it. The waitresses wore a skimpy parody of the English school uniform: tight little gym slips, striped ties, black stockings and suspenders. They frisked between the crowded tables dispensing ribaldry, mashed potatoes and occasional beatings. Preston lowered his eyes to his plate and ate his shepherd's pie and peas like a Good Boy, temporarily diverted from his route to the Cottage of Content and determined to blame it on the Americans.

They were watching the English at play. That was what the American had said and that is what Preston would tell his wife, Polly, if she asked, which was unlikely given the current state of their marriage, but Preston always liked to have a story to hand just in case.

He was still talking.

'This woman taught at a reputable university. She wrote books, albeit of a feminist nature. She was, we have to say, though we may not agree with her presumptions, a Serious Person. A person with friends in high places. A contender for the Democratic nomination for Vice-President. Smile though you may.'

Preston smiled dutifully, though not amused, nor particularly interested. It was another country and besides he'd been drinking rather a lot. He listened not because of what was being said, but because of who was saying it. Dr Milton Mahlzeit was a Serious Person. He, too, wrote books, taught in universities and had friends in high places. He was an authority on terrorism and US foreign policy. He knew the President. He appeared on serious television programmes on both sides of the Atlantic talking about serious things. They had only just met and he had told Preston to call him Milton.

'Maybe it was sharks,' said Preston.

'Off Felixstowe?'

Preston was jolted out of the Milton-and-alcohol induced haze that had descended somewhere between Soho and Covent Garden.

'Felixstowe?' he queried. 'Not Felixstowe, England?'

'Is there another?' enquired Milton.

Preston supposed not. He had been to Felixstowe only once, a few years back, for a conference of Conservative Women. He remembered an Edwardian sea-front, frowsty and faded, and a mist over the sea and the women, stiff with cold and the effort of holding the country together. As far as he was aware it was not a place you went to kill yourself, particularly not if you were an American with friends in high places.

'Why Felixstowe?'

'I believe that is an unsolved mystery of our times,' said Milton.

He smiled, almost leered, over a great mound of mashed potatoes. 'Perhaps you should look into it, given your current preoccupation with the sisters.'

Preston wondered what he'd been saying.

He dredged the murky waters of the evening and came up with ... Gus Petrell.

Of course.

At precisely 5.35 p.m., six minutes after a very fraught production meeting and five after opening time, Preston had entered the BBC club in search of alcohol and sympathy.

Instead he had found Gus Petrell, the Boy Wonder.

Petrell was, unlike Preston, a success. Also an old rival. A long time ago they had been junior researchers together on a children's series which aimed to answer every question that had ever been asked about the health and general welfare of hamsters, gerbils and white mice.

From these small beginnings Petrell had gone far. After directing a string of award-winning documentaries he had quit the BBC for more lucrative employment and had come back to crow, though he said it was to collect his expenses.

Milton had been in tow – part of the display process – introduced as his programme consultant for a Channel Four epic on Anglo-American relations.

Mercifully, Petrell hadn't stayed long. But Milton had. He seemed to like an audience and, as an audience, Preston was miles ahead of the Boy Wonder. Unfortunately, before leaving, he had treated Milton to a less than flattering description of Preston's new series which, he said, attempted to bridge the gap between the women's movement and pet care.

This was presumably what Milton meant by Preston's preoccupation with the sisters. Or at least Preston hoped it was.

'You mean *Shrews at Ten*?' he said, to make sure.

Milton nodded, frowning. 'What did Gus say it was – an extreme form of self ...'

'It's a chat show,' said Preston, not wanting to be reminded of what Gus had said.

'But what do you *chat* about?' Milton persisted.

Preston considered. The programme publicity said it was about modern women, their hopes and aspirations, their fantasies and their fears, their views about themselves, men, and the world they lived in.

'Orgasms mostly,' he told Milton. 'Well, female orgasms, anyway.'

Milton beamed. He put down his knife and fork and sat back in his chair. Preston began to worry. There was a lot of broccoli left on his plate.

'I like you, Pres,' Milton said.

Preston was pleased. He was glad Milton liked him. He wanted to be like Milton. A Serious Person.

'I have a theory I wish you to consider,' said Milton.

Preston inclined his head respectfully.

'I have a theory that a nation's decline is invariably associated with the Female Orgasm.'

Preston, a trained historian, nodded wisely, though it was a new concept to him and he was not altogether sure that it was flawless. But the power of Milton's voice and the authority of his name inclined him to go along with it, whatever theoretical rapids lay ahead. At least the journey was exciting.

'Look at the English,' Milton said. Preston stopped eating for a moment and looked at the English. They were not looking their best. On a neighbouring table a fat young man was bending over to have his bottom smacked. He was beaming with delight, or it may have been embarrassment. His friends were cheering and banging their cutlery on the table. It was not dignified.

'Lost an Empire,' said Milton. 'Know the reason why?'

Preston knew all sorts of reasons, all boring. He shook his head hopefully.

'I will tell you why. Because the English male, who had devoted his genes and his genius to the expansion of Empire, began to pay disproportionate regard to the requirements of the opposite sex.'

Preston wondered when precisely this had happened and had anyone noticed.

'They lost the Spartan touch. They embraced the encumbrances of civilisation. Household gods replaced the laws of the jungle.'

Milton was pleased with the sound of this. He closed his eyes, the better to appreciate it, and drank some wine. Preston thought there was something of W. C. Fields in Milton. His voice had the same well-rounded texture. His words swelled with self-importance until the last, which usually expired with a croak. His face was comfortably corrupt. He looked like an avuncular Mephistopheles. His thick white eyebrows rose to twin points, his eyes darted mischief. It was a powerful face for all its well-fed benevolence. Preston felt he would not like to be the cause of that face ever losing its amiability. Not that there was the slightest chance of that, thought Preston, as he smiled and filled the glasses.

'They tamed a wilderness for the comfort of Woman,' said Milton. 'And why? Guilt, that is why. Guilt and obligation. Because the English male could not give the English female what she most desired – an orgasm.'

He paused to let Preston take this in. Preston took it in, wishing there was something appropriate he could say, but there was nothing. Nothing he could think of, anyway. Fortunately most of the time he didn't have to say anything. Just listen and eat up his greens.

'That sort of thing takes time, Preston.' Milton gazed earnestly across the table. 'Time and patience and much application.'

Preston was aware of this.

'You cannot maintain an Empire while having regard to the exigencies of Woman.

'And may I say this, Preston, as an aside to the general line of argument, the English male ... and I mean no disrespect here ... '

Preston made a gesture of reassurance.

' ... the English male, I think, did not have the inclination.'

Oh dear, Preston thought, rapids.

'Gordon, Lawrence, Rhodes ... these are but the most prominent examples of an imperial trait.' The brows grew fierce, the points drawing together. 'A certain preference for the company of one's own sex, a certain delight in native culture, if you comprehend.'

Preston did, and thought it was going a bit over the top. A few of the great Victorian imperialists had, it was true, indulged in sexual practices which would not have pleased their sovereign, had she understood them, but not with the natives, surely? Not Rhodes, at least.

'And it was a not ineffectual means of ruling an Empire – until the women recalled them to a sense of their domestic responsibilities.'

Preston felt a stirring of latent patriotism. He was also aware of a definite lowering in the level of background noise. He was suddenly recalled to a sense of his own domestic responsibilities, but too late.

'Er, excuse me, sorry to butt in an' all that, but I think yer talkin' a loada crap.'

It was the voice of Preston's youth, unadulterated by elocution lessons or prolonged contact with Southern gentry. Preston had heard it increasingly of late as it deserted its neglected homeland for the bright lights and the black economy. He turned, smiling reassuringly. The owner of the voice smiled back but Preston was not reassured. He wore a suit and tie but there was a small scar just above his right eyebrow and a gap in his teeth.

'Christ,' said Preston. 'Natural childbirth.'

They looked at him.

'I've got a class,' he explained to Milton. 'About having a baby. The natural way.'

For once Milton said nothing.

'Just remembered. I'll be late.' Preston put his hand out and Milton took it, confusedly. 'Safe trip back,' he said. 'Give us a call when you're next over. Always get me at the Beeb.'

He deposited a tenner towards the bill, but there was a restraining hand on his shoulder.

'Yer've left yer greens,' said the voice, in tones of scandalised outrage. 'You can't come to this place and leave yer greens. They'll go barmy.'

Preston forked peas with frantic haste.

'Remember t' breathe deeply,' said the man, 'but if it starts t' hurt, don't let 'em fuckyer about. Demand an epidural.'

He acknowledged Preston's surprise with satisfaction.

'Useter work in the maternity wing,' he explained. 'As a porter.'

When Preston turned and looked back from the comparative safety of the door, he was seated in the chair Preston had just vacated and Milton appeared to be listening intently, though with a patronising smile that suggested he had a lot more to say on this and any other subject and would do so very soon, whatever the consequences. Preston experienced a momentary twinge of conscience, but filed it away for future reference and cleared the mental decks for the next exercise in guilt and obligation.

3 ATTEND NCT CLASS
Throw Again

The Tooting branch of the Natural Childbirth Trust met in a large terraced house in the gentrified back streets near the common. Preston could hear the screams as he walked up the path. The door was opened by a tall, gaunt man with a beard and an air of weary resignation. He let Preston in and said if he wanted the circus it was upstairs.

Preston gathered he was not a New Man.

The class had split into its family units, each of which appeared to be indulging in a form of sado-masochism involving the use of an ordinary kitchen chair and a lot of physical and vocal effort. The women were doing the screaming. They were squatting on the chairs, holding the backs for support and the men were clinging to their shoulders and baying.

Miranda, the perpetual wallflower, sat on a couch in the window watching this performance with an expression of earnest wonderment. When she saw Preston her lips formed a bright smile of welcome.

'You're late, Mr Moody, find a chair.'

This was Barbara Barnes-Warden who ran the class and owned the house. A small woman, but fierce. Preston, mumbling his apologies for being late, looked for a chair, but couldn't see one that wasn't having things done on it.

'Fetch one from the kitchen,' she ordered. Preston and Barbara Barnes-Warden had a difficult relationship. She came originally from Melbourne and combined a naturally abrasive disposition with the assumed authority of the English hyphenocracy into which she had married. The class called her Barb or, some of them, privately, the Australian Knee-Capper. She was not the sort of person you argued with, especially not if you were Preston.

He trudged back down the stairs like a little boy sent on some mysterious errand by the teacher. The house was, in fact, reminiscent of his first school, a private kindergarten in the Sefton Park area of Liverpool. It had the same Victorian solidity, the same atmosphere of the nursery, at once both reassuring and overwhelming. There was evidence of infant occupation – scribble marks on the walls (unthinkable in Preston's kindergarten), wellies on the landing and the cage of some small animal, empty, at the bottom of the stairs. Preston seemed to recall there had been a reference to 'the sprogs' in a previous session. He wondered how many there were and whether they all looked like the Australian Knee-Capper. Her own more mature influence was evidenced by the framed posters hanging in the hall. They portrayed Women confronting Peril in its many guises. But whatever the guise, Peril was invariably a man. Thus, Poverty took the form of a rascally landlord casting a pregnant woman into the street. War a charging marine, all teeth and bayonet. Famine a fat capitalist snatching the wooden bowl from the hands of a skeletal young girl. But the one Preston liked least was of Oriental origin and showed a woman with ten arms. The arms on the right had been hacked off at the wrist and a small caption beneath them read, Woman Enslaved. The arms on the left were intact and equipped with an armoury of potentially lethal weapons – a sword, an axe, a spear, a bow and arrows – and the head of a man, recently severed. The caption on this side read, Woman Empowered. Preston got the message and considered it unfriendly. He felt threatened by the ten waving arms, as much by the ones hacked off at the wrist as by the ones that were whole.

He proceeded to the kitchen where he found the man with the beard cutting up women's tights with a large pair of scisssors. Doubtless there was some rational explanation but even if there was not Preston sympathised. He explained what he wanted.

'Help yourself,' said the man. Preston picked up the nearest chair and felt his hands sink into something soft and gooey. His dismay must have showed.

'I'm afraid Ben and Rosie are rather into jam butties at present,' said the man, wearily.

Ben and Rosie were presumably 'the sprogs', or at least two of them, and the man one of those responsible for inflicting them on the world. If so he looked as if he had been punished enough. Preston was prepared to believe there was a small colony of Barb's drones distributed through the honeycomb cells of the house, all – except this one – headless. He accepted a cloth to wipe his hands with and carried the chair back to the Room Upstairs.

Thankfully the screaming had stopped and Barb was conducting the women in deep breathing exercises while the men practised being supportive, quietly. Preston remembered his compatriot's advice but thought it best to keep to himself in the circumstances. He gave Miranda a weak smile meant to express apology and encouragement and climbed over the heaving, panting bodies to her side. He was beginning to feel a bit unwell.

'Right, now that everyone has a partner,' said their team leader, 'we'll do the Singing Exercise.'

Preston's stomach took a turn for the worse. With the same weak smile on his face but murder in his heart, Preston crouched behind the chair and held it steady for Miranda to climb on top of. The Singing Exercise was for Preston the single most ludicrous and demoralising of the various stunts he was obliged to perform in the interests of natural childbirth and the Knee-Capper's psychotic condition. He tensed as she gave them their starting orders.

'One, two, three ... '

'Some sing of Alexander, and some of Hercules ... ' Preston was off. Marginally ahead of the field.

'Adeste fideles,' sang the couple on his right. 'Born the king of angels ... '

'Feed the worrhurld ... '

'Pad-dee McGinty was an Irishman of note ... '

The room echoed to diverse rhythms, though none quite so diverse as Preston's.

'Of Hector and Lysander and such great names as these.'

He sang without hope of redemption, his eyes half closed, filling his lungs with air at whatever intervals seemed appropriate and shaking his head to what he understood to be the beat. He was vaguely aware of Miranda's voice, sweeter and softer than his own, and doubtless in tune, joining in halfway through the first verse. The couples closest to Preston seemed to be faltering. Several had already corpsed.

'Louder, Mr Moody, louder,' screamed his tormentor.

'But of all the world's great heroes,' yelled Preston.

It was the only song he knew more than a few lines of. He had been taught it by his Auntie Ethel at the age of seven for a concert. Lacking encouragement he had never bothered to learn another. Preston had once been told by his school choirmaster that he had a voice almost scientifically designed to derange anyone with a love of music.

The theory behind the Singing Exercise, as expounded by the Knee-Capper, was that it took the woman's mind off her immediate problems. This might have been true, but Preston was sufficiently self-obsessed to believe that its sole purpose was to humiliate and embarrass him in public. Besides, the hysteria induced by his performance was sufficient, in Preston's opinion, to bring on a multiple miscarriage if some people weren't careful.

'There's none that can compare, with a ta-ra-ra-ra-ra-ra-ra for the British Grenadiers.'

Miranda's trusting child eyes stared into Preston's with an expression of melting ambiguity. There was pain, certainly, but also, he thought, compassion and, yes, gratitude. She seemed to be saying, I don't know why you're doing this, Preston, but thanks anyway. On the other hand, they might just be watering with the effort of keeping in tune, no mean feat when singingalongaPreston.

When it was over Preston stood up, carefully avoiding looking at anyone but Miranda. The woman was quite mad of course if she expected people to do things like that in a public hospital. What would people think? The doctors, the nurses, the other patients? The baby?

'Now then,' she clapped her hands to call them to order. 'Question time. Mr Moody ... '

Preston smiled good-naturedly, his soul shrieking for vengeance. Of course it had to be him. The entire object of the exercise was, after all, the abasement of mankind in general and him in particular. Doubtless they had run out of small animals to torture in the Barnes-Warden household. The empty cage in the hall should have alerted him. He sensed the expectancy of his classmates.

'Assuming your wife is having the baby in hospital and supposing ... ' a fierce look around the room ... 'just supposing, she has ignored my advice to be prepared for any eventuality ... ' Everyone smiled, except Preston who didn't have the faintest idea what she was talking about, ' ... and goes into contractions before she's had time to pack, what do you take in with you?'

Breathless hush. Anticipatory smirks. Preston, on the spot. What would he take in with him? He might be hours. A bottle of wine? A sandwich? No. That's what she wanted him to say. It was a trick question to catch him out. Preston, thinking of his stomach while the poor woman was lying there suffering.

'A book,' he said. General hilarity. Good old Moody, form clown, done it again. He grinned amiably, wondering what was so bloody hysterical.

'Mr Moody,' said Barb with terrible patience, 'your wife is in labour. It is *her* needs you should be thinking about, not your own.' She looked at Miranda pityingly. Preston knew Miranda would be smiling with embarrassment. 'You pack her nightie, you pack her wash-bag, you pack massage cream to rub in her back, a hot water bottle for her cold feet. Got it. Hoo-ray.' She raised her eyes to the flaky ceiling. Preston wished it would fall in on her.

'Somebody else,' she said. 'Mr Knowsley. What is a breech birth and what should you do about it?'

Preston listened, miserably aware of his failings as a New Man, especially when compared directly with the Knowsleys of this world, who knew everything, read all the right books and would have the babies themselves given half the chance. Preston was currently engaged in a complicated attempt to remodel himself along the lines apparently preferred by the women in his life. Research indicated that he should aim for something between a cuddly left version of Dr Spock and the latter-day John Lennon, deep into homebaked bread and domestic bliss. But there were problems.

In the first place it was felt by these same women that Preston's attempts to be a New Man lacked conviction, or 'gut feeling'. Preston denied this, but entertained private doubts. What if it was just guilt? Guilt and obligation.

But the real problem was that Preston wasn't at all sure that the women in his life, or anybody else's, really knew what they wanted. Research could be misleading. What if they didn't want a cuddly left version of Dr Spock or even John Lennon up to his arms in a loaf? What if they just *thought* they wanted the New Man for the same reasons Preston was trying to *be* one? What if what they really wanted was Oliver Reed?

'Mr Moody, are you still with us?' Barnes-Warden was glaring at him again and Preston became aware of surrounding activity, more climbing on chairs, squatting, gripping and grunting. He sighed and wished he hadn't had so much to drink.

The exercises continued for another quarter of an hour or so before they were dismissed with a cheery reminder to keep up 'The Breathing' at home. Preston wondered if it was worth it.

He was halfway down the stairs when he heard the forceful Antipodean tones summoning him back. He bumbled apologetically into the room anticipating a bollocking for being late and a peremptory order to stack chairs as punishment.

'I wanted a quiet word with you,' she said, 'about Miranda. She seemed to be a bit worried. Is she like that at home?'

Preston, not having the slightest idea what Miranda was like at home, said he hadn't noticed anything, which was true.

'Not anxious about the baby!'

'I don't think so. Should she be?'

She looked at him with contempt. Men, she was thinking. Preston knew she was thinking that because he'd seen the same look accompanied by the same scornful expletive from his wife and his mistress. In fact the only woman who didn't look at him like that most of the time was Miranda.

She was waiting for him downstairs. 'Everything all right?' she enquired. Preston said it was. 'How's Polly? And the twins?'

'Twins are fine,' said Preston. 'Polly sends her love.'

He was pleased with that. Neatly handled, he thought. They beamed at each other, rigid with embarrassment. Miranda had her hair tied in bunches, increasing the pre-natal look, but Preston wasn't fooled. At least he hoped he wasn't.

'Recognise the smock?' Preston dropped his gaze a few inches and raised it hastily when he realised he was staring fixedly at her breasts. 'Sorry?'

'It was Polly's.'

'Ah. Yes. Suits you.' He blushed furiously. He still couldn't come to terms with the one time he had seen Miranda naked. Not that he'd been looking closely. They walked to her car and Preston declined the offer of a lift home.

'But it's ever so far for you to come,' she protested. 'Right across London.'

'Nonsense,' he said, nobly, holding the door for her. There was the usual moment of intense anguish when they both wondered if they were going to kiss. This time Preston actually leaned forward just as she ducked her head to get into the car. He stood hastily to attention hoping she hadn't noticed. 'Well. Bye.' She waggled her fingers at him and pulled the door shut. He watched miserably as the little green Deux Chevaux chugged off into the night.

Only two bloody changes on the tube, he thought.

He walked alone through the silent streets of Tooting, ignoring the lurid invitations of the video shop and the chemists and the Late-night Kebab House, shuffling through the assorted rubbish on the pavement, noting the day-old headlines on the poster outside the newsagents: SENATOR SHOT IN SARAJEVO, or was it somewhere else?

On the stairs down to the Underground there was another poster, warning against a gang of muggers who had been robbing passengers at knife point on late evening trains. Dismally, expecting the worst, Preston took the escalator to the north-bound platform. It was empty. He stood opposite an advertisement for Smirnoff. It showed a youngish couple standing at the bar of a restaurant drinking vodka. Behind them you could just glimpse a few crowded tables and a haughty head waiter standing beside a sign saying Restaurant Full. The young man was holding a small clockwork mouse in his hand and a large key. The caption read, Reserving a Table – With a Dash of Pure Smirnoff.

Preston viewed this hoarding, and the couple depicted, with a disfavour that verged on malice. The man wore a modern, gold-flecked jacket and a red open-necked shirt with the *shirt* collar folded over the *jacket* collar and a tie knotted loosely at the level of the second button. He had a long firm jaw, squared at the edge like a screwdriver, and he was smirking. The designer of the hoarding probably thought it was a mischievous grin but as far as Preston was concerned it was a smirk. The woman was smiling too, open-mouthed displaying perfect white teeth. She wore a Grecian-style dress with a plunging neckline and her hand with its red-painted finger nails rested lightly but possessively on the man's shoulder. Preston glow-ered at them both, feeling increasingly malevolent. The man rep-resented almost everything he hated about modern society, the pushy assertiveness extolled in every other TV commercial, the man who always came first, who always knew the answers, who had the right bit of plastic, the man with all the advantages, everything thought out, the man who cheated and not only got away with it but was universally admired and envied for his cool. Especially, Preston thought savagely, by women.

The train, when it finally arrived, was almost as empty as the platform. Preston chose the compartment containing the most people – a young woman and an old man – on the grounds that there was safety in numbers. They both looked up briefly and anxiously when he got on and then quickly away again. Preston knew how they felt. Sooner or later it would happen to one of them, perhaps all three. They'd be on a train like this, going back into the city late at night when most people were going the other way, and They would get on. The sociopathic hoodlums from *A Clockwork Orange*, the dwarf from *Don't Look Now*, with six more just like him, all dressed in red plastic macs and meat cleavers in every pocket. Hey ho, Hey ho, smash, gouge, spurt. The horror of their daily imaginings suddenly unleashed, Neanderthal Man on the rampage in the London Underground.

Preston worried about this frequently. He worried about the inner cities. He was never going to be king but he worried about them all the same. He worried about riots and no-go areas and rapists and the architecture. He worried about education and housing and bombs in crowded restaurants and dog shit on the pavements.

He opened his briefcase and took out a magazine. His briefcase was in fact full of magazines, mostly women's, but the one Preston selected was not. He had begun to buy women's magazines some weeks previously when he had first started the new job. For a while he had found them educational and absorbing. He discovered things he had never known before. He discovered, for instance, that women worried about shaving their legs. That there was a big international debate on the subject and that it wasn't just about hair, it was about women's perception of themselves and the male-dominated society they lived in. Similar debates raged about orgasms, menstrual sex, contraceptives and body odour. They were unashamedly personal. They were not about the direction of US foreign policy, or the problems of the debtor nations, they were about things you could do something about. They were about ʾ ɔu. It was incredible. You could just read the articles, weigh up the pros and cons and act on them. You could shave your legs or leave them unshaven, you could invite 'the man in your life' to have sex while you were menstruating or you could tell him to sod off. It was all so easy. Except that it wasn't, Preston eventually discovered. It was all so depressingly complicated, and, more to the point, it was usually his fault. And so he had started taking *Time* and *Newsweek* again in an attempt to escape into things over which he had no control whatsoever, and for which someone else was to blame.

So he read, without hope but with no sense of personal responsibility, about the breakdown of the latest arms talks in Geneva, the increased tension in Central America and the Mediterranean, about hot wars and cold wars and Star Wars. He changed trains at Stockwell and again at Victoria where he was joined by late-night revellers, on their way, by the look of some of them, to more and later revels in the privacy of their bachelor boy/girl apartments, and finally, as was invariably the case, having failed to meet the Beast from Balham, or the Woman in the Smirnoff Ad, he was deposited, in a fine drizzle and without an umbrella, at Chiswick Park, a mere ten minutes' walk from his own home.

When he arrived, wet but not quite dripping, Polly was still up, in her dressing-gown and slippers, making a hot drink in the kitchen.

4 GO HOME

'I'm making some herb tea,' said Polly. 'Want some?'

Preston did not want herb tea. He wanted a brandy and, somewhat to his surprise, sex. But he'd already had far too much drink for one evening and any more would banish what little hope he had of the other. So he said, Yes please, and observed her covertly as she dispensed tea bags, wondering if she was wearing anything under the dressing-gown and whether there had been a recent Change of Attitude.

'How's Miranda?' she said.

'Fine,' said Preston, carefully. He sat down in a kitchen chair. It was not covered in the residue of jam butty, or any other goo. Polly's children did not eat jam butties. Whatever they did eat went straight into their tiny mouths and any that didn't was promptly removed by a J-cloth. Polly was good about things like that. Within seconds of putting them both to bed she would have started to tidy, throwing their toys into a big wicker basket, clearing away dishes, wiping surfaces. In theory Preston approved of this but in practice, for reasons he couldn't quite put his finger on, it sometimes depressed him.

'But how does she seem mentally?' asked Polly.

Preston was instantly alert. Did she know? Had Miranda told her? Had she guessed?

'What do you mean?' he demanded.

'Well, Preston,' Polly began in the tone of voice he hated, like the tone she used with the children when she was explaining things, but not quite as kind, 'when women are having babies they sometimes feel a bit tense, a bit nervy, you know what I mean?' She observed him critically. 'No. I don't suppose you would.'

Preston didn't know whether to feel relieved or disappointed. 'She's fine,' he said again. 'Thanked you for the smock.'

That put paid to Conversation for the time being. Preston slumped in his chair and listened to the ticking of the clock on the wall, the hiss of the gas-ring, a high-pitched whine from somewhere indeterminate, possibly his head. He felt he had somehow lost the initiative with Polly, but then he couldn't remember when he'd last had it. They had known each other for six years, been married for just a few months less. They had two children. They were joint holders of a mortgage endowment policy. Once, a long time ago, they had made love standing up against the wall of a cottage in the New Forest.

Polly handed him his herb tea. 'I'm taking mine up to bed,' she said. 'Good-night.'

'Good-night,' said Preston. He meant it to sting.

'Something the matter?' Polly enquired, in nothing like the tone she used for the children. More like the tone she might have used on a store detective who was about to accuse her, falsely, of shop-lifting.

'Oh no,' said Preston. 'Nothing's the matter.' He meant that to sting too.

'Good,' said Polly, proceeding with a small, tight smile to what had once been their bedroom.

'I just think,' said Preston, reckoning that if he wasn't going to have sex or sympathy he might as well have a row, 'that all things considered I deserve a little bit of credit for what I've put into Miranda, that's all.'

Unfortunate phrase, that, he reflected, in the circumstances, but at least he'd got the ball over the net.

Polly had stepped back a pace the better to see him for the worm that he was.

'Credit, Preston? I'm sorry, I didn't realise you expected some kind of payment, otherwise I'd have taken her to a sperm bank.'

Love fifteen. Preston picked the ball up from the back of the court and tossed it thoughtfully into the air.

'All I'm asking for is a little less hostility,' he said, reasonably. 'After all, it wasn't my idea about Miranda, was it?'

'But Miranda is not the issue here, is she, Preston? The issue is Something Else Entirely.'

They never used her name. It was always Something Else Entirely, either Your Friend with a faint sneer beginning on the letter 'F', or That Ridiculous Woman, with a pronounced sneer all the way through, or, more delicately, by Preston, The Situation.

'Are you sure about that?' said Preston. It was a phrase that particularly infuriated Polly who described it as a slightly more subtle version of 'I think you'll find I'm right, my dear.'

'Yes, I believe I am sure of that.' Polly poured the words slowly over crushed ice. 'No matter how much you try to use Miranda as your smoke-screen.'

'If it hadn't been for you and Miranda and your wonderful ideas . . .' began Preston.

'Balls,' said Polly. 'It is nothing to do with me, or Miranda, or what Happened. It is You, Preston. You alone. Though I concede,' she conceded, 'that you might have had a little help from Your Friend.'

'I'd never have even thought of it,' Preston persisted, not entirely truthfully.

'My God, you really must learn to take responsibility for your own actions, Preston. I'd say you were behaving just like a spoiled teenager, except that I rather suspect you've leaped straight from adolescence to the male menopause.'

'Oh yes?' said Preston, provoked. 'I suppose that's why I go along to those bloody classes . . . I suppose that's not responsible.'

'Those bloody classes,' repeated Polly, with satisfaction. 'Now we're coming out in our true colours.'

Blast, thought Preston.

'You go to those bloody classes, Preston, because I make you go to them.'

'Yes, and why?' Preston thought he saw an opening. 'Not because you believe in them. It's just revenge, you just want to see me suffer.'

'Oh grow up. How do you know what I believe in?'

'We didn't have to go through this with the twins,' Preston pointed out. This was a mistake. Polly put down her herb tea with a restrained force that made Preston cringe and caused a small amount to spill on to the table.

'*We*, Preston? If I remember rightly, *we* did not go through anything with the twins. Not together, anyway. *I*, first person singular, might have gone through a great deal, but you wouldn't know very much about that, would you? You didn't even notice they existed until they were about six months old and you suddenly found you had a receptive audience who'd clap hands whenever you did a trick.'

Oh foul! Oh linesman, umpire! And now she was leaning forward over the table, revealing that she was, indeed, naked under the dressing-gown, or at least from the waist up.

'But far be it from me to force you to do this, Preston. Or even shame you into doing it. If you want to leave Miranda to cope with this on her own, then go ahead, that's your business, it's no more than I'd expect. But I would have thought that the very least you could do in the circumstances is offer a little moral support when she needs it. She doesn't ask for much for God's sake.'

'She didn't ask for this,' Preston howled. 'She doesn't ask for anything. It's you. Playing your stupid games. And look where it's got us.'

Polly picked up her herb tea. 'Good-night, Preston,' she said again, 'I'm going to bed.'

And isn't that just typical of a girl, Preston thought, marching off when she was losing, and taking the ball with her. He listened to her steps receding up the stairs and sank into chronic depression. After a while he got up and poured his herb tea down the sink. He looked for some brandy but there wasn't any. They only bought it duty free and they hadn't been away for over a year. There was only some left-over wine. He drank that anyway and then, when he knew Polly would be well clear, trudged upstairs to the bathroom.

When he'd washed and cleaned his teeth he looked in on the twins. They slept at opposite ends of the same bottom bunk, having piled all their furry animals into the top one. Preston sneaked up to administer good-night kisses and check they were still breathing. He couldn't be sure with Daniel so he shook him until he almost woke up and started hitting out.

'All right, darling, it's all right,' Preston murmured. 'No tiger. Only Daddy.'

Daniel moaned and turned to face the wall.

Preston sat next to the bed for a while, feeling sorry for himself. It was true he hadn't put a lot into Polly's pregnancy. But that was before he became a New Man. He'd thought it was something women just got on with. Preston had been brought up almost exclusively by women, and they'd got on with everything by themselves. Men, if you needed them at all, were useful for humping heavy things about, delivering coal and the like, and even then you had to watch them or they'd diddle you out of a sack or two.

Preston twitched the curtain outside and looked out on the night. He saw roof-tops, attic rooms, the bare branches of trees against the sky, a blue haze of cloud across the moon. There was a book Preston often read to the twins at bedtime. It was called *I Want to See the*

Moon. In the story, a little boy wakes up in bed with his room full of moonlight. 'I want to see the moon,' he shouts. His Daddy comes up to him. His Daddy wears slightly scruffy clothes. He has a solid, trustworthy face. He looks happy in his role. Preston wanted to be that kind of Daddy, but the image was spoiled for him by the fact that the Daddy in the story wore slippers. Tartan slippers. Preston wanted to be a good father to the twins but he did not want to compromise his image of himself, he did not want to wear tartan slippers.

Preston gave Daniel a last pat, more to comfort himself than the child, and crept downstairs to make up the sofa-bed in the sitting-room.

He did not expect sleep to come easily and it didn't. He was tormented by thoughts of Polly in the bed upstairs. They were mostly erotic thoughts which puzzled him slightly as he had not experienced them much when he had shared it with her. He had always found her attractive. Well, striking. Slim and fair and raunchy in that trendy Home Counties way, but she'd never exactly turned him on. He fancied rounder, coarser women, like the plump, cuddly Scousers of his youth whom he'd never got around to groping, not even in the dark.

Maybe he was changing at last, and, as usual, too late.

Preston tried to find a more comfortable position on the bed and reflected dismally on the particular cause, or symptom, which had resulted in his instant ejection from the one upstairs.

The Affair. The first, as it happened, of his married life. Inevitable, he supposed, given the circumstances, but none the less disastrous for that. But then everything was disastrous, everything he touched: his marriage, his work, his adulteries – the one he'd had, anyway – and if he ever had any more, which God forbid, he anticipated that they would turn out disastrous too. He tossed and turned, tormented by a sense of failure and self-pity. He was thirty-six years old and going nowhere. Leaping ungracefully from adolescence to the male menopause. Next stop . . .

He thought of Milton and his story about The Woman who had Walked into the Sea. The story bothered him and he suspected the reasons had more to do with himself than with the woman. Preston had always feared The Tower more than any other card in the Tarot. The fall from Grace – and Power and Position. In his case, of course, it wouldn't be very far, but it had to be a lot further for her. All the way to Felixstowe.

He turned once more in the bed and doubled up the pillow. It had been a mistake to finish off the wine in the fridge. He was dehydrated from all that drink. But he didn't have the energy to get up and fetch some water. He embarked on a deliberate exercise in sleep inducement. It was an original method he had developed and refined over the years and despite its almost total lack of success Preston persisted in regarding it as foolproof if only he could do it right. It involved thinking himself into a situation where sleep comes naturally and the situation he had evolved was that of the skipper of an old sailing ship, becalmed off a tropical island, who settles himself into the netting below the prow for a quiet midday snooze.

Preston would imagine the soft slap of the waves against the hull, the gentle creak of rope on wood, the warm sun on his face ... but his brain was incapable of taking all this at its face value. It wanted to know where the ship was, what was it doing there, who was this captain, what was his background? Preston had been obliged to invent a story to explain it all. But complications kept arising. The present state of play was that the captain, an Elizabethan sea-dog who had worked his way up from cabin-boy, was trying to make contact with a small fleet of English privateers that had been dispersed by a storm off the Azores. He didn't know whether they were still on their way to join him, or whether they'd pressed on ahead leaving him behind. He suspected that they despised him for his humble origins and planned to take the treasure ship without him. Moreover, he was beginning to have serious doubts about the ethics of priva-teering. Stripped of its romantic overtones, it seemed as indefensible as highway robbery, but with more chance of drowning. And that was another thing. The sea was calm now, yes, but how long would it stay that way?

And now there was another problem. The last time he had tried this he had picked up a beautiful Spanish condesa, just to give him something to think about while he was in the netting. She'd been shipwrecked. Or else they'd sunk the ship carrying her to her fiancé in the New World. Someone she didn't really want to marry, of course. This was an entirely reasonable addition to the story, but the condesa had been accompanied not only by her duenna but by her confessor, a spidery, sinister individual called Don Miguel. Preston couldn't figure why he'd let Don Miguel get into the act at all. Possibly something to do with being a lapsed Catholic. Don Miguel was his conscience. Crabbed and twisted and arthritic. And there he was lurking in the scuppers while Preston tossed and turned in the netting trying to get to sleep.

Don Miguel, Preston realised now, was waiting to hear his confession.

It would be worth waiting for, too. Father forgive me for I have sinned. It is ... God, how many years was it? Twenty? ... Twenty years since my last confession. The sheer enormity of what would have to come next overwhelmed him. Twenty years of extended adolescence. Never mind the first nineteen, how could he begin to confess the goings on of the past year? And to a celibate priest?

Preston writhed and Don Miguel thrust his spidery fingers deep into his soul and brought them out black and dripping.

'Look,' he said, and mysteriously turned into Preston's grandmother. 'Just look at that. Dirty little tyke. I'd a good mind to rub your nose in it.'

And silently, a long way from the Azores, a long way from Liverpool, alone in the storm-tossed rigging of his Habitat sofa-bed, Preston howled for pity and absolution. *Mea culpa, mea maxima culpa*.

But not quite all mine. Not entirely. Oh no. One must not overlook – God are you listening to this? Don Miguel, don't look at me like that – one must not overlook the significant contribution made by a handful of very determined women. Preston began to count them, one by one, instead of sheep, starting with his grandmother ...

5 POLLY'S SPACE

While, upstairs, alone in her big brass bed, Polly nursed her cup of herb tea and brooded on men, and revenge.

Polly's grandmother, who was not acquainted with Preston's, had once told Polly in a rare burst of clarity: 'Men are such a nuisance, dear, best avoided.'

It seemed to Polly now, some twenty years later, that this just about summed it up. You could be more eloquent about it, more analytical, you could couch it in all sorts of sociological terms, but what it came down to was that they were a nuisance.

She looked around the room with something approaching satisfaction. She had chosen the colours herself, a very pale primrose with slightly darker woodwork and an oatmeal carpet and curtains. There was a fitted wardrobe filled with her clothes, all neatly hung away, and a bookshelf by the bed, filled with her books, in each of which she had written her name and the date. Polly's neatness and her possessiveness went back to the small private school run by nuns where Polly, though not a Catholic, had spent her adolescence. Each of the girls had been allowed one small locker by her bed for her possessions which had to be neatly arranged and jealously guarded, not so much because someone might steal them, but because they were yours, and you didn't have much that was. Sometimes, when he still shared the room with her, Preston would pick one of Polly's books up and hum and hah over it and while it was in his hands Polly would experience a sharp feeling of discomfort, bordering on actual pain. She felt as she imagined a flower must feel when some great clodhopping gardener comes along and pulls you about.

Polly hadn't liked to say so at the time but she didn't think Preston really went with the room. He didn't improve its appearance. Even if he could be prevailed upon to put the rest of his clothes away he invariably left his socks lying around like a dog marking territory. Once she had counted three pairs in various corners of the room, like sly turds. She had removed them to the dustbin and then, on second thoughts, retrieved three single, odd socks and put them back in his drawer. It seemed to her now that this had been her first positive act of protest.

Polly had not been raised to protest. The nuisance remark had been Gran's best, coming towards the end of her span when she might have been feeling a bit liverish. She had spent most of her life trying to please Polly's grandfather and passing the lessons on to an eager brood of daughters and granddaughters, all waiting for a Mr Right to come along to be honoured and obeyed till death do us free. Polly remembered another of Gran's remarks, more in character: 'Never marry out of your class, dear, it always leads to misunderstandings.'

Polly had not taken much notice of that at the time. She was only seven and had better things to think about: four-legged things, mostly, with long manes. The first time she did give serious thought to marriage it was not her own but somebody else's and the chances of its continuing into the foreseeable future, thus leaving Polly in the invidious role of what her gran would have called His Bit of Fluff. After five years, one abortion and a lengthy period under analysis, she had concluded that the marriage had a better chance of surviving than she did and married Preston instead.

In revenge?

Polly wondered.

Was she a vengeful person? Was that why she had packed Preston off to NCT classes with Miranda? Polly frankly doubted it. If she was honest with herself, and she tried to be nowadays, The Situation suited her. For the time being, at least. It induced in Preston a healthy feeling of guilt. And he didn't seem to be enjoying himself as an adulterer, which was satisfactory. Besides, even if she had wanted to be revenged on him, she would hardly use poor Miranda as the instrument. No, that was how Preston *would* feel, forever relating things to himself.

He was so bloody self-conscious. It was like a disease. Gran, of course, would have said it was because he was from the lower classes. Gran was very class conscious, like Preston. Perhaps because, like Preston, she wasn't sure precisely what her class was, or where she stood in it. Gran's own origins were rooted in careful obscurity but Grandad had been something fairly modest in Customs and Excise. Polly's own father had joined the Air Force and ended up a Squadron Leader, though they'd never quite got around to giving him a squadron. He'd retired on a good pension and Polly supposed he and Mummy lived in some comfort, but they were so broadly middle class the term seemed meaningless to her, whatever Preston liked to make of it. It was one of his *things*, her family, one of the many.

She had realised, of course, quite early on that Preston's background was different from hers. She knew he was from The North and that his family probably had to struggle a bit when he was young, but she'd never reckoned he was 'working class', even though he liked to pretend he was. He said it was just the elocution lessons that fooled her – as it did everyone else he encountered – but it was more than that. The trouble with Preston was he came from a family that wasn't so much working class as frantically trying not to be and he couldn't come to terms with it. He was desperately afraid of being lower middle class and that was exactly what he was, of course, thought Polly, with satisfaction, as she finished the last drop of herb tea and put down the empty cup and turned out the light.

It was a comfortable bed with nice clean sheets and she felt pleasantly tired. She'd put in a full day at the abortion clinic while the twins were with the childminder and then taken them out to the park on their bikes. They were at an exhausting age, forever asking questions. She smiled, recalling some of the things they'd said. Then sighed, thinking about her and Preston. They'd have to have a reconciliation, she supposed, as much for the twins' sake as anything. But . . .

But what?

But she didn't love him?

She thought about this carefully. Even if it was true she was not at all sure that it mattered. She hadn't really loved him when he'd asked her to marry him and it hadn't stopped her. The way she'd looked at it then, she was a few months off her thirtieth birthday and she'd had one nasty experience with love and didn't care to repeat it and she wasn't doing anything else worth speaking of. *And he'd asked her*.

She was a bit puzzled about why he'd asked her, really. She'd never been terribly convinced that he loved her. But that wasn't the problem either. At least she didn't think it was. After all, you could never be sure about something like that – who could? – and he wasn't actively unpleasant to her, not much of the time. He didn't appear to have a violent streak, he was quite a good father when he put his mind to it, and he was quite good-looking, not that Polly cared much about appearances, but at least you didn't feel embarrassed about him in front of your friends. Not until he started to talk to them, anyway.

That was the real problem, of course. His mind. He was so *irritating*. He was so full of clutter. Cluttered thinking, cluttered behaviour. He could never feel something or do something naturally. He always had to have an Attitude to it. It was just too wearying. It was like having another child about the place, a pubescent teenager, dripping around, peering into mirrors, worrying about its hair or its spots. She couldn't be bothered with it. If he was going to stay he'd have to sort himself out, he'd have to get rid of that ridiculous woman and smarten himself up. Mentally, at least.

Having tidied Preston away for the time being, Polly put him out of her mind and thought about nice things instead. The twins on their bikes, the sound of their voices across the park, herself walking, tired and content after a long day, the satisfaction of giving advice and not needing it, the smell of Spring in the air, the damp earth . . .

She remembered a boy she had known once, a long time ago. He *had* been working class. Polly's bit of rough. God, she must have been about eighteen, just out of school, staying with the family of posh friends. He was the gardener. Classic. Really good-looking. She remembered the way he smelled. Clean earth. Mushrooms. Or was it sex? And the feel of his hands, sort of capable and workmanlike and calloused. Her own hand moved down to her vagina. It had been great sex, even though he'd never made her come. Not then. He could now though.

6 WAKE UP
Look Around

Preston awoke early and, for no explicable reason, erect. Though this phenomenon had been common in his youth it had not occurred for some time and he had assumed it was no longer feasible. He felt it and confirmed that it was substantial. He had no clear recollection of his dreams but he did not think they had been erotic. He rather thought the Australian Knee-Capper had figured in them somewhere, along with some terrifying creature, possibly also she, who had been pursuing him through a swamp. He could remember his feet sinking into it and a sense of panic. The sea was involved somewhere, and something else. Mud flats. That was it. He'd been running along by the sea and sinking into the mud and the tide was coming in and the creature was closing on him.

None of which explained the erection, though he had read somewhere that it happened to people at times of extreme danger. Or maybe that was ejaculation. Some primitive desire to spread one's seed, even uselessly, before it was too late. So was this a warning, then? Sleepily, and more to comfort himself than from any erotic desire, or creative impulse, Preston began to move his hand up and down, mentally flipping through his selection of masturbation fantasies to find one that fitted the mood of the moment. The most reliable, when he didn't want to make any particular effort, was The Fancy-Dress Party.

The Fancy-Dress Party had its origins in a trivial event of Preston's early adolescence when a neighbour had invited him to celebrate the New Year (Preston doubted if it had been fancy-dress. He thought that had probably been one of the later embellishments. Preston's neighbours didn't go in for fancy-dress parties) and among the guests was a woman Preston's grandmother always referred to, scathingly, as Mrs Gladrags.

Mrs Gladrags lived a few doors down from Preston with her husband, who Preston's grandmother called The Layabout. She was small and plump. She wore tight, flower-pattern dresses with buttons up the front. She wore high heels with peep-toes, even when she was putting out the washing. She never wore curlers in her hair, certainly not in public, and she often smiled at Preston or waved cheerily at him when he came home from school. Preston lusted after her desperately and hopelessly.

He wasn't sure precisely what she'd been wearing at the party. He had incorporated her into so many fantasies over the years that the original Mrs Gladrags and the clothes she wore were obscured by time and imagination. But in the original version she wore a cowgirl outfit. This consisted of a tight see-through blouse, a stetson, a short fringed leather skirt and high-heeled buckskin boots. After all these years and all the embellishments, Preston could not swear that this was fact or fantasy. All he knew for certain was that at some stage in the evening she had asked him to dance with her, taking off her boots so she could move better. Preston could remember his excitement when she had held on to him to pull them off and his feeling of manly pride when it was revealed that in her stockinged feet she was slightly shorter than he was.

He suspected that this was all that happened. Even had he not been hopelessly inept, there was little else that *could* have happened with his grandmother and his mother and his aunt there to keep an eye on him, and presumably The Layabout lurking in the background, too. But the experience had fuelled Preston's fantasies for many years and caused him to come more often in one night than at any time before or since.

In the fantasies, later that same evening Mrs Gladrags required Preston to escort her home, The Layabout having mysteriously but conveniently vanished. They went round the back way and Mrs Gladrags asked Preston to help her over the fence. So Preston filled his arms full of warm, round, cuddly Mrs Gladrags and felt the warm, round cuddliness of her body through the cowgirl outfit, and when they reached her home Mrs Gladrags felt the bulge in his trousers and pulled him down on to the couch and did amazing things to him.

Thus the modest dreams of Preston's adolescence.

Experience had made him more imaginative, but the basic storyline remained more or less intact. Over the years a number of women had played the role of Mrs Gladrags, some of whom he had known and loved in reality, though not in cowgirl outfits, and the scene had shifted from the suburbs of Liverpool to more exotic locations.

With the passage of time, the cowgirl outfit, too, had succumbed to more sophisticated tastes. Mrs Gladrags now wore a succession of daring costumes. The two most adventurous were The Vamp and The Queen of Hearts.

In her role as The Vamp, Mrs Gladrags wore a slinky, silver, thirties creation, just about hanging on to the end of her nipples and slit up to the waist. Preston, in this version, was dressed as a pirate, not a comic-opera pirate with a patch over one eye and a parrot and a crutch, but a dashing Errol Flynn/Clark Gable pirate with chest hairy and breeches rampant. After the dance routine and the carrying home, which was more often in a Porsche, she invited Preston in for a drink. There was a snooker table in the 'games room' – presumably The Layabout's influence – and they started to play. When she leaned over the table her breasts popped out of the top of her dress. When she reached for a shot she lifted one leg on to the table and revealed to the enchanted Preston that The Vamp costume did not include knickers. At which point he dropped his cue and reached for more appropriate equipment.

That was The Vamp, but the most daring was The Queen of Hearts.

In the Queen of Hearts Preston, instead of being Preston, the man she dances with, had become Preston, the layabout husband. And Mrs Gladrags, though still varying with taste and inclination, had increasingly become associated with his wife, Polly.

It began with Preston, dressed as a clown, waiting for her to get ready. When she appeared she wore a coat over her costume. They drove to the party, sometimes at a friend's house, sometimes in a larger establishment with hundreds of guests and an orchestra. In the entrance hall the unsuspecting Preston helped her off with her coat. Underneath she was wearing red high-heeled shoes, red lace gloves and a red G-string in the shape of a heart.

Preston spent the rest of the evening in a state of shock and excitement watching his wife dance with other men. In the most outrageous version of the fantasy she removed the red lace gloves and the red G-string, kicked off the red high-heeled shoes and announced, to general acclaim and some pursing of the lips, that she was now the ace of spades.

Preston was dimly aware that as a New Man he should not entertain such fantasies. They contained elements that were definitely suspect. On the other hand he didn't know what kind of masturbation fantasies a New Man should have, or even if you were supposed to masturbate at all. He lacked guidelines. It wasn't the sort of thing you could ask anyone about, not even another New Man. So he tended to stick to the old and tried formula and feel guilty afterwards. He was at the point where his wife accepts the first request for a dance and starts to gyrate wildly to Ry Cooder when a small voice from the foot of the bed said, 'What's Daddy doing?'

Preston froze.

He raised his head from the pillow and peered over the top of the hump in the duvet. The twins stood, pensively, in their matching Mr Men pyjamas, at the foot of the bed.

'He-he-he is playing rocking-hortheth,' announced Anna.

'Can we play wocking-horses?' demanded Daniel.

Preston let go of his penis and groped for his watch. It was five to six.

'Oh God,' he said.

They began to climb on to the bed.

'Make a rocking-horthe, Daddy,' said Anna.

'Make a wocking-horse for me,' said Daniel.

The twins, who were alike only in perversity, had managed to develop their own distinctive speech defects. It rendered communication doubly difficult. Preston began to plead.

'It's only five to six.'

'Ith a thunny day,' said Anna.

'Not waining,' added Daniel.

'It's not a sunny day.' Preston articulated carefully. 'The sun isn't up yet.'

'Yeth it ith, Daddy, I can thee.'

'That's moonlight,' lied Preston. 'Go back to bed.'

'The thun hath got hith hat on,' sang Anna joyfully, 'well hip, hip, hip hooray . . .'

'Wide a cock horse to Banbury Cwoss,' yelled Daniel.

'The thun hath got hith hat on and ith coming out to play.'

'Wiv wings on her fingers and bells on her toes . . .'

Preston began to have some idea of how his music teacher might have felt.

'Have you been to kiss Mummy good-morning?' he asked, cunningly.

The twins had no trouble with Preston and Polly's sleeping arrangements. It was utterly natural to them that Daddy should sleep downstairs and Mummy upstairs. The trouble would come, Preston suspected, if they ever started sleeping together again.

'Mummy ith thleepy,' said Anna, doubtfully.

'Let's wake her up,' said Daniel.

That's my boy, thought Preston, but his conscience put its foot down.

'Better not,' he said. He sighed. 'Come on in and keep warm.'

They clambered in under the duvet, one on each side.

'Cuddle, Daddy,' said Anna.

But Preston had had experience of Anna's cuddles. 'Only if you promise not to kick me in the balls,' he said, firmly.

'I promith I won't kick you in the ballth, Daddy,' said Anna.

Preston turned towards her, keeping one hand over his genitals, which was now possible.

'I wanna cuddle, too,' wailed Daniel, predictably.

Preston rolled over on to his back and reached out an arm for his son. At the precise moment that he removed the hand from his balls and before he had completed the turn, Anna's foot lashed out with deadly precision.

At eight o'clock, feeling he'd reached the end of a long day, Preston sat in the kitchen, still in his dressing-gown, watching the twins, still in their pyjamas, having breakfast. He should really have got them dressed but he didn't have the energy and he felt he could justify leaving it to Polly as she wasn't working today. He had a studio in the afternoon and he liked to be in the Right Attitude for studio. Dressing the twins would not induce the Right Attitude.

Preston had not quite come to terms with his role as father. Again, he lacked guidelines. His own father had been a distant figure, literally at sea. Home on leave he would be playful and teasing, teaching Preston how to box and play football, taking him to the pictures to see *The Cruel Sea* and *The Malta Story*, but then he would disappear again, leaving Preston to his mother and his grand-mother and his aunt. When he'd come home for good he'd been a sick man, dying, though Preston had not known it then, of leukaemia. He no longer boxed with Preston, or played football, but sat in a chair downstairs, alternately gloomy or sentimental, until he was moved by stages to the bedroom, where he watched television all day, and then to the hospital where he died. The process had been mercifully short and the mother and the grandmother and the aunt had coped, as they always did, and compensated, perhaps over-compensated, to Preston for the father-figure he'd been denied.

But Preston remembered the playful, teasing sailor forever sailing away again and he remembered the old man in the armchair and he wanted to have the Right Attitude to the twins, whatever it was.

So he watched them at the table and tried to work it out. They sat at opposite ends with their dolls flanking them. Anna had a scruffy red-haired rag doll called Mop, Daniel a simpering golden-haired doll of a doll which he'd chosen himself and called, for reasons best known to himself, Weewee. Preston had problems with Weewee but his son's affections were firmly attached and Preston did not want it to come to a choice between him and Weewee in case he lost.

He took the orange juice out of the fridge and poured it into two tall glasses and took it up to Polly. She was reading the paper, which he'd sent up earlier with Anna.

'What's this?' she said.

'Orange juice,' he said.

She looked at it without moving, duvet up to her chin, eyes narrow with suspicion.

'What's the bits in it?'

'Orange,' said Preston. 'It's *real* orange juice.'

He handed one of the glasses to Polly. She was careful to keep the duvet over her breasts.

'Didn't the milkman leave a carton?'

'I was up before the milkman came,' said Preston, 'making the kids their breakfast.'

'What did they have?'

'Muesli.'

'You mean you had to pour it out of the jar into their little bowls.' Polly registered shock, horror. 'And then pour milk on top. Poor love, you must be exhausted.'

Preston would not rise to this. He sat, carefully, on the edge of the bed, near the end. Polly looked at him.

'Did you want something, Preston?'

'Just a chat,' he said.

'Oh,' she said.

'Room looks nice,' he said.

'Thank you,' she said. 'What about?'

33

He got up and mooched around the room. It looked different, somehow, from when he'd slept here, but he couldn't quite work out what it was. He studied the bookshelves, pretending to read titles while he thought of what to say. Then he saw something.

Men – the Second Sex by Eva Eichler.

Eva Eichler was the woman Milton Mahlzeit had told him about. The woman who'd walked into the sea.

Preston took it from the bookshelf and looked at the back cover.

'What are you doing?'

Preston turned. She seemed in some distress.

'Have you read this?' he asked.

'Yes,' she said. 'What about it?'

'Is it any good?'

'It's educative,' she said. 'I don't know about a good read.'

'D'you know anything about the woman who wrote it?'

'Not much. Will you put it back, please.'

'Can I borrow it?'

There was a pause.

'I thought you were still reading *Biggles Flies East*.'

'Ha, ha,' said Preston. 'Go on, it might do me some good.'

'Preston,' said Polly. 'If you want to do yourself some good I suggest you start with something a little less advanced than that. Go and ask Anna if you can borrow *The Paper Bag Princess* or *Topsy Slays the Dragon*.'

Preston kept the book and returned to the bed.

'Don't you think you'd better keep an eye on the twins,' she said.

'Polly,' he said, 'while I do respect your approach to The Situation . . .'

'It's no good, Preston,' she informed him reasonably, 'I'm not having you back in here.'

Preston felt like a bit of furniture that had been removed for aesthetic reasons.

'I understand that,' he said, 'but I do think we can behave like civilised human beings.'

'I'm being perfectly civilised, Preston. Anyone less civilised would have had you out in the street.'

Preston swallowed to keep his voice normal, but it still came out squeaking slightly.

'I know,' he said, 'I know. I appreciate that. But, as you haven't,

I think, well, why not make the best of it. I mean, all right, you up here, me down there, I don't mind that, but perhaps we could just be a bit more relaxed with each other.'

'I'm not having sex with you, Preston,' said Polly, agreeably, 'if that's what you mean.'

Preston stood up and left the room with what he hoped was quiet dignity.

Downstairs, in an attempt to feed Weewee, Daniel had emptied his bowl of muesli on the floor.

7 GO TO WORK

Preston arrived at the studio late and with the Wrong Attitude. As if from a distance, as if on the monitor of some hidden security scanner, he saw himself scurrying along the corridor with his anxious expression and his battered briefcase and his soul deep inside his Nike trainers ... One day Preston wanted to arrive at Television Centre with the Right Attitude. Positive, raring to go, *confident*. Same old exterior but inside, Mick Jagger. Prancing into the gallery, all hips and mouth, up on the stage, Hey look at me, *I can do this*.

'Sorry I'm late,' said Preston, sidling into the studio. The designer and the lighting director were standing in the middle of the set, talking. About him, judging from their expressions when they saw him.

'Hello, Preston,' said the designer. 'We were just talking about the set.'

Preston looked at the set. His soul tried to get out of the trainers and dig a hole in the floor.

'What about the set?' said Preston.

The designer and the lighting director looked at each other as if to say, Well, if you don't know ...

But Preston did know. It was a mess. It was the worst set he had ever commissioned. It was a cross between a seedy pub off the Caledonian Road and a tart's boudoir. It contained a large couch, a bar, a dressing-table, a juke-box, a Victorian screen, a formica-topped kitchen table with three chairs, a darts-board, a piano and a life-size statue of Apollo with a leaf over his genitals and a plastic inflatable parrot on his left shoulder. Viewed as a bit of a joke, in the right mood, it could have been considered fun. That was how Preston had tried to consider it some time ago. But it was not fun. It didn't work. It looked what it was, artificial, contrived.

'I know it breaks a few rules,' said Preston.

'Like taste?' suggested the designer. It was not her design. She had been brought on to the programme after the last designer had left. After a row about the set.

'It's supposed to look anarchic,' Preston pointed out.

'I don't necessarily object to anarchy,' said the designer who looked as if she objected to anarchy very much. She had short dark hair and she wore a white tunic belted at the waist over tight black trousers with elasticated straps at the bottom. She looked neat, efficient, organised. 'But does it have to be quite so lacking in *style*. I mean . . .' she screwed up her face as if in severe pain . . . 'The Couch.'

The Couch, whatever its politics, was difficult to defend. It was a lurid, almost luminous, green in hue and five people could sit on it, not comfortably. If you sat well back your legs stuck out straight in front of you, so people tended to perch on the edge. Preston had a lot of trouble getting the eyelines right in close up and if there were only two people sitting on it they looked like goalkeepers at either end of a football pitch.

'Yes,' Preston conceded. 'I suppose the couch is a bit of a problem.'

'Can't we just sort of lose it?' the designer wondered.

'Oh, I don't think we want to do that, do we?'

This was not Preston's voice. It was female, and quite loud, and it came from the gallery. They all looked up knowing what they would see.

'Hello, Carla,' said Preston, brightly.

Carla. The presenter. His Friend. The Situation.

Preston marvelled at how Carla had this way of homing in on any conversation that remotely affected, could be said to be even marginally critical of, her. She reminded him of a little girl who had attached herself to the (until then) exclusively male gang he had knocked around with as a small boy. You'd think you'd got rid of her once and for all, you'd think she was three blocks away in someone's backyard, locked in the coal shed with the spiders, and you'd get the Lucky Bags out and she'd be there with one hand crushing your balls and the other removing the largest stick of liquorice. One of Preston's friends had tried to pull her hair once but she'd fought dirty and sent him howling back to his mum.

Preston watched her as she came down to the floor. She wore some kind of kaftan thing like a tapestry or an oriental carpet over a pair of loud check trousers, rolled up at the bottom to reveal red socks and a pair of sensible men's shoes, slightly military in style, with laces. Like the set, which was entirely her inspiration, she suggested fun and excitement. The zany, mixed-up, laid-back approach. And like the set it didn't come off. It was an Act. It was an unconvincing

Act. Especially if you knew Carla who was, in Preston's estimation, about as zany and laid back as a dalek on a mission to exterminate.

'What d'you think, Preston?' she said, when she reached floor level.

'Oh, I think it's all right,' said Preston, avoiding the eye of the designer. The lighting director had already distanced himself from the encounter. He was halfway up the rostra where the studio audience would sit and though Preston couldn't see him he knew he would be taking in every word for future reference and pretending he wasn't.

Carla flung herself down on the couch, stretching one arm along the back and holding the other up in front of her eyes as she surveyed the designer.

'What don't you like about it?'

The designer shrugged. 'It's not exactly my style,' she said, 'but if *you're* happy . . .'

Preston smiled at them both desperately but they ignored him.

'Oh, I'm quite happy,' said Carla. Preston, still smiling, doubted this. Whatever else Carla was, she was not, in his opinion, happy.

'You don't think it's a bit overstated?' said the designer. 'A bit boudoir-ish?'

Preston held his breath. Carla had explained her theories about the set to Preston when they had first started work on the show. Women like corner spaces, she had said. You watch men at a party, they head straight for the middle of the room and stand there, holding forth. Women go for the corners. They have their most intimate conversations off stage, in bathrooms, kitchens, cloakrooms . . . They're off-stage people. That's what I want the set to be like, Preston, an off-stage area, intimate, with lots of clutter. Carla did not use this argument on the designer. Possibly because the designer was a woman. All she said was, 'Well, if I knew what a *boudoir* was, dear, perhaps I could tell you.'

The designer sucked in her cheeks and nodded slowly to herself, gazing around at nothing in particular. Then she went to join the lighting director who was examining his light-meter very carefully. Carla gave Preston a look which seemed to involve him in her victory, though he was not sure what role he had been allocated. Collaborator, helpless witness, or victim? Carla was the most unashamedly competitive person Preston had ever encountered. She thought people were either for her or against her, they were never neutral, and practically everything she did, almost every human contact, was measured in terms of victory or defeat.

'Coffee?' she beamed at him, and as they left the studio she remarked, loud enough for it to carry, 'I can't stand pastelly people, can you?'

There weren't many people Carla *could* stand, Preston reflected, as he followed, blushing. The wonder was she could stand *him*, let alone sleep with him. They had about as much in common as a vixen and a rabbit. Perhaps that was the attraction, though, the age-old association of predator and prey. But he was being unduly romantic. Carla probably felt she needed an ally with so many people hating her. The real question was, why was *he* sleeping with *her*?

Carla is a very talented person, he told himself as they waited for the lift. She is interesting. She is Going Places. It is possible she will take me places. Already I am being noticed. She is making me more enemies every day than I've made in the last eleven years.

The lift was empty. They got in. The doors shut. Carla grabbed him round the neck and put her tongue in his ear. Preston tried to climb up the wall.

'For God's sake, Carla, this is the BBC.'

Carla fell about.

'Preston, you never fail me.'

Preston was well aware that the assault had not been motivated by passion. This was poking sticks through the bars.

'Go on,' she said. 'Give us a kiss.'

'Good Lord,' said Preston, provoking more hilarity. He was tempted on such occasions, which were not rare, to call Carla's bluff and give her what for. But he wasn't absolutely sure it *was* bluff. He wasn't absolutely sure his nerve wouldn't crack before hers did.

'Tonight, then?'

The lift stopped. The doors opened. People got in.

'I thought the Nicaraguan child with the artificial legs was a bit unnecessary though,' one was saying. 'I mean, one knows what they look like.'

Carla threw her head back and feigned paralysis until they all got out. Everyone pretended not to notice.

Preston shook his head at her as they walked towards the canteen. Her clothes hung loosely on her sparse frame and she walked with a

39

slightly rolling gait, like a sailor. It was her 'tough' walk, meant to put off rapists. So far as Preston knew it was a hundred per cent effective, at least in the BBC. He felt a rare gush of affection. Whatever he thought of Carla personally he was forced to admire her Attitude.

'OK for tonight,' she said.

It wasn't really a question.

Preston felt depressed again. Carla always liked to see him after a recording. She liked to talk about it for most of the evening, while Preston just wanted to forget.

'I'll have to go home first . . .' He sounded like a kid. Young Preston with his mates.

Come on, Pres, let's go trespassing.

I'll have to go home first for me tea.

But Preston was grown up now, with different priorities.

'. . . to put the twins to bed,' he said.

'Can't Polly do that?'

Preston gave her a shocked glance, triumphant.

'Sorry,' she said. 'Didn't mean that. Damn.'

They entered the canteen.

'You get the coffee,' she said, 'I'll find a table.'

Preston did as he was told.

When he came away with the coffees, Carla was sitting at a table with the PA and one of the researchers. Carla and the researcher were having an argument.

'I don't understand the problem,' Carla was saying.

This was a favourite expression of Carla's. It usually meant someone was not doing things the way Carla wanted them doing. She used it a lot.

'I've spoken to them on the phone and they said no way,' the researcher said.

'*No way.*' Carla's thin lips curled. 'Were those the precise words?' Preston wished she wouldn't do this kind of thing. It was so unnecessary. He smiled sympathetically at the researcher, but the researcher ignored him. Her name was Andrea. She had recently transferred from the BBC's Glasgow studios and still had the armour on. Carla liked her at first because, she said, she wouldn't let men patronise her. But apparently she wasn't too keen on Carla patronising her either.

'No, those were not the precise words. The precise words were that

Her Royal Highness was not envisaging any television appearances in the near future.'

At last Preston knew what they were talking about. Carla wanted the Princess of Wales on the programme to discuss 'Her Kind of Music'. At least that was what they were telling the Palace. Actually Carla wanted to ask her about her infatuation with George Michael. And the Palace were saying, No Way.

'But does she know what I want to talk to her about?' demanded Carla. 'Do *They* know what I want to talk to her about?'

Any moment now Andrea was going to tell Carla to bloody well talk to them herself and then there'd be a real row.

'I think we're being a bit optimistic about this,' Preston said.

'Well, it's a damn sight better than being pessimistic,' Carla said, turning on him. 'You never get anywhere if you go in with that attitude. If you want something, you've got to go for it. Christ, you've got to expect to *get it*.'

Thus Carla's philosophy on life. Unlike Preston, Carla always expected to 'get it', and at the age of twenty-six she hadn't done badly.

Carla had made her name as a freelance journalist working for magazines like *Spare Rib* and *City Limits*. Her reputation was founded on controversy. She would pick a target and attack without mercy. Sometimes her victims fought back. This did her reputation no harm. At twenty-four she had become the editor of a 'respectable' downmarket women's magazine. It was a *controversial* appointment to 'give the magazine new life'. Six months later she had been sacked. For being too controversial, she said. For killing off a hundred thousand readers, said her bosses. This did her reputation no harm either. A few weeks later she'd been offered her own chat show by the BBC. The title had been her idea because the show went out on Thursdays at ten, opposite News at Ten on ITV. Preston had been amazed.

'*Shrew*,' he had quoted from the office dictionary. '*Noisy quarrelsome woman, scold, a termagant. Termagant: imaginary god of Saracens, of violent nature; small, aggressive mammal of spiteful intent; sometimes applied to a woman.*'

'Hardly appropriate,' he had said, 'for a programme with feminist aspirations.'

This was before he knew Carla very well.

'That's right,' Carla had said. 'It's controversial.'

Later, when he knew Carla better, Preston realised that being controversial was almost as important to her as being ruler of the universe.

'It seems,' said Carla, looking round the table, 'that if you want anything done on this programme, you've got to do it yourself.'

Preston had been working at the BBC for eight years. He had gone in from university and film school. He had wanted to make documentaries or drama, like everybody else. His first job had been as a researcher on a children's quiz programme. He had not been very good at it. After two years he had been given the chance to direct on a long-running series called *Animal Antics* ('more crazy carryings-on in the animal kingdom' – *Radio Times*). Preston had been on *Animal Antics* longer than any other producer. He did not regard this as an achievement. He feared that no one else at the BBC did either. It was not a programme for Serious Persons. Preston still received letters from an old lady in Worthing about the things her parrot got up to. Now he was producing a chat show aimed at the woman viewer, and what really bothered him, apart from his increasing lack of interest in programmes about children, animals and women, was whether he was going up or down the ladder. Was it going to be Men next or the God slot?

'They've got a problem with one of the cameras,' said the Production Assistant. 'Racks say can you cope with three.'

'I'd rather not,' Preston made a face. 'Not with an audience.'

She spoke into the phone.

'He says he'll see what he can do.'

Preston went back to marking the script. They were in the office, just him and the PA. Carla was off having a row somewhere.

'There's too much in this programme,' said Preston, not for the first time.

'Do you want to drop something?'

It was a tactful question. Everybody knew Carla made decisions like that, but the PA always deferred to Preston as if he was really in charge. He was touched.

'No. Not at this stage. If it starts to spread we'll just hold something over for next week.'

They always recorded the show on Wednesdays, leaving a day for editing before it went out. Invariably Carla wanted to put more into the programme than it would hold and invariably this led to rows about what should be cut. Thursdays were hell. Worse hell than every other day. Preston actually found studio days less fraught than most. He had his own territory up in the gallery and any tantrums on the floor could be left to the floor manager unless they got really bad. Besides, Carla tended to be a bit abstracted on studio days, thinking about her interviews and psyching herself up for battle.

Preston looked at the schedule again. They had five guests and a live band. The main interview was with the male director of a film which began with a lengthy sequence showing a woman being cut into small pieces by a chainsaw. Carla would want at least ten minutes to cut him up into even smaller pieces. Add fifty-two seconds for a clip of the film. Then there was the woman politician who wanted to ban Page Three girls and a former Page Three girl who had called her an interfering old bag with as much sex appeal as a cardboard box in an interview on the front page of the *Sun*. Carla wanted eight for that and the woman politician would probably want to come in on the chainsaw interview. Then there was a short piece with the resident agony aunt about jealousy and a song from the band on the same subject. Two minutes for the song, say, and they'd agreed four with the aunt. And finally, an interview with a doctor about thrush. Four minutes.

Preston did his sums. With titles and end credits it came to exactly thirty, which was the length of the slot, but they hadn't allowed for links, or a trail for next week's programme, or any one interview going particularly well. That was one of the basic problems with the show, Preston thought. They never allowed enough time for individual items. Four minutes for jealousy. It was ridiculous. It led to the kind of superficial treatment Preston hated.

'Do we really need four minutes for thrush?' said the PA.

Preston had just been thinking that.

'I mean, what can you say about it?'

Preston didn't know. Carla liked to do 'women's diseases' on the programme. She said there was a lot of interest and she was probably right. But four minutes for thrush seemed excessive in the circumstances.

'Maybe we should cut it to three and let jealousy go to five,'

Preston mused. It was an academic discussion and they both knew it. They both knew what would happen. There'd be a general punch-up involving Carla and the film director and the woman politician and the Page Three girl. Everyone would be shouting at once. Someone might even get violent. Carla would call this Good Television. It would run for three-quarters of the show. They'd have a quick song from the band and Jealousy and Thrush would be cut to a minute and a half each. Afterwards everyone would go into hospitality, even the doctor and the agony aunt who wouldn't know they were going to be cut, and they'd all congratulate each other on a great performance.

'I sometimes wonder why they do it,' said the PA.

Preston looked at her with some surprise, not because of what she had said but because she had said it. Usually the staff on shows like this kept their opinions to themselves, or else they didn't have any. It was like working on *Animal Antics*. On *Animal Antics* no one ever said, 'I just can't think why that monkey agreed to appear, just to make a fool of himself like that.' Or, 'There's going to be trouble from that lion when he's cut down to a minute and a half.'

And people were just the same. They knew they were just per-formers. They could be humiliated, exploited, ridiculed, taught to sit up and beg, roar, spit at the camera, anything, and they'd keep coming back for more. And why? Because of the lumps of sugar. Recognition. Notoriety. You couldn't be on a show like this unless you had some claim to fame, even if it was daft. They hardly ever had trouble persuading people to appear, unless they tried for people who were Really Famous. When those sort of people refused to appear Carla became very upset. It revealed to her that she was not yet Famous Enough.

The PA wanted to work on *Horizon*. She was a serious person. She had a degree in anthropology. It was typical of the BBC that they should put her on *Shrews at Ten*. But maybe she was learning something.

'Maybe it'll be better when we go out on the road,' said Preston.

Their ratings were down and Carla blamed this on the studio. She said it was stultifying. She wanted to go out and meet people, she said. Out of the studio she reckoned people would talk more freely. They'd still be cut down to one and a half minutes, but it would be a better quality one and a half minutes. And there'd be more action, too. Seeing people in Their Own Environment. Unfortunately the budget wouldn't allow them to do this more than one programme in three, but they were going to try it next week and if it worked Preston was going to try and wrestle more money out of the budget. According to Carla.

'If you've finished marking the script,' said the PA, 'I'd like to do the camera cards.'

Preston handed his script over.

'I'm going to the cuttings library,' he said. 'Keep on about that camera.'

There were only six cuttings on Eva Eichler and all but one were about the suicide.

'There might be more in the American papers,' the librarian said, 'but we don't take them.'

Preston found a quiet corner in the studio while everyone else was at lunch and started to read.

Eva Eichler was variously described as 'the 48-year-old commissar of Women's Lib', 'the blonde bruiser who took on American manhood – and made it bleed', 'the American author who won fame and recognition for her bestselling guidebooks on how to win the sex war' and 'the far-from-retiring academic who made a significant contribution to the feminist debate'. All agreed, however, that she had been convalescing in England after an illness. A woman called Bernadette McCarthy, described as either her secretary or her companion, was quoted as saying 'Eva had been very depressed and anxious. Her books had gone out of print and she was worried about the future direction of the feminist movement.'

Preston read this twice without coming to any concrete conclusions.

On the details of her death there was general agreement but little substance. Eva Eichler had simply walked into the sea at Felixstowe in the early hours of the morning of 11 May 1985, after leaving a suicide note in her hotel bedroom. It had been raining at the time, but the sea was calm.

The hotel overlooked the spot and was called the Blundell Towers.

The only cutting that was not directly related to the incident was from the *Daily Telegraph* dated three months before. It was about the Democratic candidates for the next Presidential election. Eva

Eichler was named as a possible running-mate. She had been closely involved with the Democratic Party since the McGovern campaign of 1972, the report said, and there was talk of her standing in a forthcoming gubernatorial election. The *Daily Telegraph* remarked that her 'strident feminism' might have some appeal on the East coast but was hardly likely to win votes in the Midwest. Many leading Democrats, it said, feared her nomination more than they feared the Republicans.

Preston folded the cuttings back into their envelope and took *Men – the Second Sex* out of his briefcase. It was a paperback edition preceding her death by several years and there wasn't much about the author on the jacket, just a few quotes from ecstatic reviewers. 'Remarkable for its insight into the male psyche,' said one. 'Ms Eichler strips men down to the bare essentials,' said another, 'and finds them drooping.'

Preston opened the book at Chapter One and started to read.

'One, two, three,' said Preston. 'Four.'

'Three minutes,' said the PA.

'Two,' said Preston.

Preston was happy doing what he did best, sitting in the control room, watching the monitors, calling the shots.

'Reaction on one?' suggested the vision mixer.

'One,' said Preston.

Camera one was on Carla. She was reacting. Sceptically. She heard him on the earpiece and looked more sceptical.

'Two,' said Preston.

'Tights,' said the doctor Carla was interviewing. 'Tight jeans. Terrible, my dear. The best thing is a loose cotton skirt and no knickers.' The vision mixer sniggered.

'Wouldn't men just love that,' said Carla.

'One,' said Preston.

'And what if you catch it anyway?'

'Two,' said Preston.

When Preston was directing he paid scant attention to what was being said on the floor. He moved the cameras around, he cut between faces. He painted the conversation, he didn't really hear it.

'Some people will tell you yoghurt is the answer . . .'

'But who wants to walk around with a cunt full of yoghurt?'

'Audience reaction on three,' said Preston.

The vision mixer was slower than usual. Preston looked at him sharply. It had been a long afternoon. The woman politician hadn't lost her temper, the film director had been frivolous, the ex-Page Three girl polite. No one had been violent. Carla would be in a filthy mood.

'What did she say?' said the vision mixer.

'Two,' said Preston.

'The best thing is to take a bottle full of water and pour it, like this.'

'Find it four,' said Preston.

'But let's face it, doctor,' said Carla, 'isn't the real problem Men?'

8 ENTER CLUB
Miss One Turn

'I hear you're about to make television history,' said Edward Cart-wright.

Preston didn't know what he meant.

'Cunt,' said Edward.

Several heads turned and the surrounding conversation faltered briefly and then picked up. They were in the BBC club where the language was normally more restrained, at least this early in the evening.

'Oh that,' said Preston, after a moment's thought, 'I think it's been said before hasn't it.' But he was uneasy.

'I'm bloody sure it hasn't,' said Edward. 'Not on the BBC anyway, I can't speak for Channel Four, of course.'

He said this with satisfaction.

Preston became more uneasy. Perhaps he should have stopped the interview and risked a row with Carla. Still, it wasn't too late.

'I can always cut it out in the edit,' he said.

'If she'll let you,' said Edward.

Preston wondered if Edward knew about him and Carla. He thought he probably did. Edward knew most things that happened at the BBC, and a lot that was just about to happen. After a long and distinguished career as a foreign correspondent he had settled himself firmly, if irascibly, into the presenter's chair at *Newsnight* and looked like staying there for life.

'Anyway, what can I do for you?' he said. 'If it's to further your career don't ask, my influence is on the wane. I've been found out.'

Edward claimed to be a mole for the KGB. He said he had been recruited as a young man in West Berlin after the war and that for years he had been revealing the secret workings of the BBC to the Kremlin. He said the trouble was that no one at the Kremlin would believe him. They can't believe it's that absurd, he said. In fact, Edward was that strange but by no means rare bird in the Lime Grove jungle, a conservative anarchist. He even looked like a bird. An ageing bird of prey with a great crest of grey-white plumage and sharp piercing eyes on each side of his beak. They watched Preston now over his gin and tonic while Preston told him about the woman who walked into the sea.

'I just wondered if you knew anything about it,' he said. 'I mean, whether you'd picked anything up in Washington.'

Edward looked arch.

'You know what I mean,' said Preston, 'anything in the press, talk, rumours?'

'Was I in Washington at the time?'

'You were running the bureau,' Preston pointed out, a little impatiently.

'Was that only last year? Good Lord.'

'Edward, are you going to tell me about this woman or aren't you?'

'Why the sudden interest – programme?'

'No. Just curious,' Preston said. 'I was having dinner with Milton Mahlzeit, last night,' he added, self-consciously, 'and he happened to mention it.'

'Milton Mahlzeit?' Edward looked satisfactorily impressed. 'I didn't know you moved in those kind of circles, Preston. What on earth has he got to do with women, their hopes and aspirations, their fears and fantasies?'

'Nothing,' said Preston crossly, 'that's the point.'

'Ah, trouble with the termagants?' Edward was enjoying himself, 'Do tell me.'

'Eva Eichler,' Preston persisted. 'What do you know about her?'

Edward shook his head and the feathers shook in the breeze. 'Very little. Never had the pleasure. Not sure that I wanted to. Bit of a termagant herself, wasn't she?'

'So it wasn't exactly big news over there when she died?'

'I seem to remember reading something about it, but it's not exactly my field. I mean, nude woman in sea death mystery. Tabloid territory, isn't it. Probably menopausal. What's Milton Mealtime doing in London, besides having dinner with you?'

'Making a series about Anglo-American relations with Gus Petrell for Channel Four,' said Preston, knowing it would upset him. 'How d'you know she was nude, then?'

'What? Petrell?' He pronounced it like the stuff that drives motor cars. 'What does he know about Anglo-American relations?'

'Thirteen-part series,' said Preston, with grim satisfaction. 'From the Boston tea-party to the raid on Libya. Co-production with WNET and a budget of six hundred thousand.'

Edward was shaking his head again.

'Why do they fall for it?'

'Come on, Edward, spit it out.'

'My dear fellow, I merely assumed she took her clothes off before she went for a swim.'

'She wasn't swimming.'

'Look, honestly, I didn't take much notice, Preston. More important things to think about. I can vaguely remember some talk at the time, that's all. It really wasn't a big story. Her books were out of print.'

'That's what her companion said. I heard she had political ambitions though.'

Edward pulled a face. 'Not taken seriously, not by serious people, anyway. Did Milton tell you all this?'

'Yes, and I got the cuttings out. I was wondering if you could find out what the American papers had about it.'

Edward frowned. 'Preston, if you want to move into current affairs, why not put in for a transfer ...'

'Because it wouldn't get me very far,' said Preston, recklessly, before he'd had time to think about it.

'Hmmm,' said Edward. They both knew why it wouldn't get him very far.

'Besides, I don't want a transfer,' he said, not even convincing himself.

'Well I should give it serious consideration,' said Edward, 'after today's performance.'

Preston started to worry again.

'*We're relying on you, Preston, to be a restraining influence,*' the head of network features had told him when he'd got the job, '*if you can control a studio full of performing seals, you can control one liberated female, ha, ha.*'

Ha, ha, thought Preston.

'Look, I'm just curious,' he repeated. 'It's nothing to do with work.'

Edward sighed. 'Very well, I'll make one or two phone calls,' he promised. 'But not today. I'm up to my neck in Nicaragua.'

Preston was alarmed. 'Why, what's happened.'

Edward tutted. 'You really must listen to the news, Preston, if you want to move in that direction. Washington says the Sandinistas were behind the assassination of Senator Sachs in Honduras.'

'Oh,' said Preston, 'and were they?'

'Possibly. He's had it coming for some time. Who knows. Anyway, it's the excuse they've been waiting for.'

'Excuse for what?'

'To send in the boys. Really, Preston.'

Preston always expected World War Three to begin with a conversation like this. It wouldn't be recorded in the history books, if there were any more history books, but it would be The Moment He Found Out About It, it would be The Moment He Started To Panic.

'Can I trouble you, Harry?' Edward waved his empty glass at the barman. 'Same again?' he asked Preston.

'No thanks,' said Preston, distractedly. 'I've got to pick up the kids from their childminder.'

'Now I come to think of it,' said Edward. 'There was some story about it being murder.'

But Preston was still in Central America.

'Your nude bather,' Edward explained. 'I seem to remember there was a suggestion that it wasn't suicide at all and she'd been bumped off, but I can't think why. Ah, thank you Harry, sure you won't have one?'

9 GO TO CHINA
Meet Willy

Preston picked the twins up from their childminder and walked them back along the side of the park. It was almost Spring but Preston smelt the damp, fungoid smell of Autumn in the air and was depressed.

The kids were foraging like a pair of puppies, but not so quick. Every few yards they stopped to examine something on the pavement. A dead wasp, betrayed by hope, a squashed slug punished for over-confidence, various unidentifiable droppings. Death and decay. Each time they stopped, they plagued Preston with questions: 'Is it a cat's, Daddy, is it a dogth, is-it-is-it-is a a a EWAAPHANTH!' Preston made brief reply. Progress was slow, but for once he didn't mind. He wasn't in a hurry to get anywhere. The evening and its inevitable complications stretched before him like a web, with the spiders in their corners waiting to pounce.

He was thinking about his conversation with Edward Cartwright. It had made him wonder why he was so interested in this woman when he'd never even heard of her until last night. A transfer to current affairs? Was that what this was all about? He tried to dismiss the suggestion. He'd felt irritated when it was made, and disturbed by the can of worms it opened. Edward had been very friendly with Polly. That was partly the reason he was friendly with Preston. He knew the score, probably better than Preston did.

Before she had married Preston, Polly had been secretary to the head of news and current affairs. Their relationship had been close, though Preston, coming from another department, had not known how close until some months after their marriage when Polly had told him, surprised he didn't already know. It was one of those office things that everyone knows about but is supposed to be secret. Later, and just as casually, she'd mentioned the abortion. And that when the affair had ended she'd 'gone to pieces a bit'.

Preston was not personally acquainted with the head of news and current affairs. He knew him only by sight. A youthful executive, overweight but darkly good-looking, who walked the corridors with a spring in his step and looked through Preston as if he did not exist. Preston did not think he minded this, or that Polly had been his mistress. What he did mind was that the man appeared to hold him in some contempt and that he had expressed this contempt, thinly disguised as professional criticism, at the Wednesday meeting of heads of department when a possible transfer of Preston to news and current affairs had been mooted.

Preston tried to puzzle this out. He overcame his reticence and talked to Polly about it.

'Maybe he's jealous,' she said. 'After all, darling, you did win me.'

'Hmmm,' Preston said.

A few days later, while preparing supper together, he asked her if the head of news and current affairs had ever wanted to marry her.

'Oh he said he did,' Polly shrugged. 'But he would, wouldn't he?'

'Hmmm,' Preston said, again.

'Did you want to marry him?' he asked her, affecting mild interest while scrubbing carrots.

'Preston what is this?' Polly said.

'Nothing. I'm just curious,' said Preston.

'Well of course I wanted to marry him.' She looked at Preston watching for a reaction. 'Well, I would, wouldn't I?'

And Preston said nothing.

Until a day or two later when he asked, 'Why didn't you?'

'Because Preston, as you very well know, he was married already. And married men do not marry their mistresses, whatever they may suggest to the contrary.'

'Sometimes they do,' said Preston.

'Well, this time they didn't.'

But this time it was she who reopened the subject, as if she couldn't let it go at that. There was always some problem, she explained. His wife was having problems with her au pair, the children were having problems at school, his career might suffer, his mother was ill, the kitchen ceiling had fallen in and they couldn't find a plasterer. Polly was cheerfully cynical and Preston tried to forget about it, until some chance remark at work brought him back, beating the same worn out old path to nowhere.

What about the abortion – hadn't she wanted the baby? Hadn't he wanted it? Who ended the affair, him or her? What happened next? How had she gone to pieces? To most of these Polly made evasive reply. She did, however, reveal that when the affair had ended she had, in quick succession, during one hectic month of June, indulged in a series of one-night stands with members of the news

53

and current affairs department. She had not kept an accurate record, she informed Preston, upon his inevitable enquiry, but she could assure him that they were all male and free of diseases. They included, so far as she could remember, a producer and a presenter on *Newsnight*, two reporters and a sub on the *Nine O'Clock News* and several assorted staff on *Panorama* during a special on the Irish elections.

'I was making up for lost time,' Polly told him. 'I was a virgin when I met Cliff.'

'Cliff' began to haunt Preston's imagination.

'You're obsessed,' Polly accused him. 'Obsessed with sexual and professional jealousy.'

'Don't be ridiculous,' Preston said.

He noticed details of the man's appearance which had formerly escaped him. The rather fleshy lips, the way his eyebrows met in the middle, the slightly obscene paunch. He transformed him into an overweight satyr who'd made it to the top of the forest, largely by trampling on people with his cloven hooves. A leering Pan viewing Preston's uphill struggle with the contempt of a superior being, dropping the occasional obstacle in his path. Like Polly, the ravaged nymph he'd left back on the road. For Preston to pick up and carry through life, the fool. Oh yes, Preston could explain that leer. Preston the plodder, stooping to retrieve a discredited cast-off, sullied by subsequent association with mere mortals, though none so mere as Preston.

'*A producer and a presenter on* Newsnight, *two reporters and a sub on the* Nine O'Clock News *and several assorted staff on* Panorama *during a special on the Irish elections.*'

How did these people find the energy, Preston wondered. How did they find the time? Had it been a slack period for news?

'What ith thith, Daddy?'

Preston stopped again and looked down.

'Thith' was the picture of a vagina, torn from a magazine and in sufficient close-up to confuse the less experienced observer. One way or another, Preston reflected dismally, he didn't seem to be able to get away from it.

'It's a cave,' he said. 'Come on.'

Daniel arrived. 'What's a cave, Daddy?'

Anna surveyed him pityingly. 'Ith a big hole with an ogre in it, ithn't it, Daddy?'

'Yes,' said Preston. 'Come on.'

But after a few yards they found another. Preston suspected kids from the local comprehensive. They were always littering the streets with their rubbish, though normally it was only crisp-wrappings. This was a wider illustration on the same theme.

'Why ith that man eating that lady?' demanded Anna.

'She spilt some yoghurt on her and he's licking it off,' said Preston, inspired.

'Off her china?' said Anna, mildly amused.

'Off her china,' repeated Daniel and fell about.

Preston needed a moment to interpret this.

'Who told you about . . . chinas?' he demanded.

'Mummy did,' said Anna. 'She-she-she hath got one and I-I-I have got one too.' She began to pull up her skirt. Preston stopped her.

'And I got a willy,' said Daniel, a bit on the defensive.

'That man hath got one, too,' Anna pointed at the illustration, 'and hith ith bigger than yourth.'

'Come on,' said Preston, dragging them away. 'We'll never get home at this rate.'

'Can I have some yoghurt?' asked Daniel.

'No,' said Preston, seriously alarmed. 'We haven't got any.'

Just as they arrived at the gate the Fischers rolled up in their Audi Quatro.

The Fischers were Preston and Polly's next-door neighbours. They weren't really called the Fischers, it was just Preston's name for them. Their real name was Manners. Preston called them the Fischers because of the television commercial for the Audi Quatro which featured a smooth, accomplished German family of that name who always reached their holiday villa before anyone else.

Mark Fischer – the one next door to Preston, not the one in the advert – was tall and lean and tanned, even in winter. He was director of a firm that sold computers and he was always flying to faraway places. His wife Sally designed kitchens. She actually looked like a German, or at least Preston's idea of a German. She was tall and blonde and wore a C-cup. Preston knew because he'd seen them hanging on the line and they looked like C-cups, but he'd have guessed anyway from looking at Sally Fischer.

The Fischers played tennis in summer and squash all the year round. They went sailing on their boat in the Solent. They wore expensive-looking clothes and they went out three or four evenings a week. They didn't have any children.

Preston loved his children but he wanted to be like the Fischers. He wanted to have their style. He wanted to drive an Audi Quatro and reach the holiday villa before anyone else.

Daniel ran to the gate while Preston fumbled for his front-door key.

'Hello, little man,' said Mark Fischer. 'How are you today?'

'I got a willy an' Anna got a china,' Daniel told him. 'Daddy sayth the man ith eating yoghurt off the lady'th china,' said Anna. 'Daddy sayth she hath spilled it over her and the man ith licking it off of her.'

Preston took hold of them in each hand and led them firmly away.

'Did you tell them about vaginas?' Preston asked Polly while she was giving the twins their bath before bedtime.

'What about vaginas?' Polly demanded.

'Did you tell them what they are?'

He was sitting on the lavatory seat, watching.

'I expect I did, yes,' said Polly. 'Do you have some objection or something?'

'Nnn-no,' said Preston doubtfully. 'Just seems a bit advanced, though, for someone who's only just three, don't you think, talking about vaginas?'

'As opposed to talking about willies, you mean?'

'Who talks about willies?'

'You and Daniel do, frequently.'

'I got a willy,' said Daniel.

'An' I got a china,' said Anna.

They both looked under the water.

'Why hant I got a china?' complained Daniel.

'Aaagh,' said Preston. 'I have a son with vagina envy.'

Polly turned on him. 'Preston, I realise you have problems but would you please not pass them on to the twins.'

'What problems?' Preston was indignant.

56

'Phobias, complexes ... problems. Jesus.'

'Daddy says I've got tadpoles in my willy,' announced Daniel on cue.

'And don't give them disinformation. I don't want them growing up like you.'

'Charming,' said Preston, but he knew what she meant. Preston had been given much disinformation as a child, largely of the stork and gooseberry bush variety. Chinas hadn't figured in it at all. He hadn't even considered what girls had under their skirts until the age of seven when his friend Billy Quirk had let it slip.

Billy Quirk went to the same prep school as Preston and they walked to the same bus stop together. One day, on the way to the bus stop, he asked Preston if Preston had ever seen a lady in the nude. Billy Quirk was a boy who, in the opinion of Preston's gran, was a bit too advanced for his age.

'Yes,' said Preston, as a matter of course, just as he would have said if Billy Quirk had asked him if he'd ever seen a ghost or a snake or a Sabre jet fighter. Preston was an honest boy, but not when it came to losing face in front of Billy Quirk.

'Which d'you like best?' Billy then asked. 'The front or the back?'

Preston suspected this was a trick question. He came from a very sheltered background, sexually speaking. His gran and his mum and his Auntie Ethel were all adamantly opposed to what they described as Smut. Preston had never seen a lady in the nude, neither in the flesh nor in the illustrations of a magazine. He made a wild guess.

'The back,' he said.

Billy Quirk looked at him pityingly.

'The front's much better than the back,' he said. 'The back's only got the bottom. The front's got two tits and a willy.'

That had been Preston's first definite piece of information on the opposite sex and like almost everything he'd learned since it had been totally misleading.

'Polly,' Preston said, when he'd read the twins their bedtime stories and been allowed into the bedroom to look for socks, 'do you think it's possible for you not to belittle me in front of the twins.'

'It's possible,' said Polly, 'if I work hard at it.'

'I know it's a difficult situation,' said Preston, 'and I know you're under a lot of strain, but I do think you might be a bit less hostile.'

He had a momentary doubt about the wisdom of this but it had been a hard day, he was feeling tense and guilty because he was on his way to meet Carla, and he couldn't seem to find two socks the same colour.

'I mean, don't you think you're a little bit po-faced about it sometimes?'

He opened another drawer and sprang back as it was slammed shut by Polly's foot.

'Get out of my knickers drawer,' she snarled.

Preston was shocked. 'You nearly had my hand off.'

'I'll have more than your hand off. You bastard. How dare you call me po-faced.'

'All I meant to say was ...'

'You're on your way out to meet your bloody girl-friend and you have the nerve to complain about *my* behaviour. God.'

'Look,' Preston prepared to be conciliatory, 'while I accept some responsibility for this situation it wasn't entirely my fault, you know.'

Polly stamped on his bare foot.

'Jesus, Polly ...' he hopped to the bed. 'That hurt.'

'Get off that bed.'

'It wasn't my idea about Miranda,' he said.

'We are not talking about Miranda,' she said. Polly really could talk through clenched teeth sometimes. Preston had practised this himself but had never been able to do it properly. He thought it was probably a class thing.

'But if you hadn't insisted ...'

She kicked him in the shin.

'Oh my God,' he said.

'Get off my bed.'

Preston got off the bed and sat on the floor.

'I will not discuss this under the threat of violence,' he said.

'Who's threatening?' she said, clipping him across the ear. 'And don't you dare throw Miranda at me.'

'You threw her at me,' he said. Irresistible, but a mistake, really, in the circumstances. If Polly had ever heard about kicking a man when he was down she'd taken it for advice.

Preston jumped up. The prevailing street philosophy of Preston's childhood was never to hit girls, but under extreme provocation you

58

could pull their hair until they cried. Preston seized a handful and yanked.

Polly wailed and burst into tears.

'I'm sorry,' Preston tried to put his arm round her.

'Get out,' she yelled.

Preston got out.

10 HERE BE CARLA
Throw Six or Be Eaten

'Preston, why aren't you wearing any socks?' Carla hissed at him as he sat down at a table in the corner with a plate full of nibbles and a glass of wine. It was the first time he had sat down all evening.

'I'll tell you later,' he said.

'You look like a wally,' she said. 'Stand up, so no one'll notice.'

Preston stood up resentfully, balancing his plate on top of his glass. 'I thought you scorned convention,' he said, quoting from a recent article in *Cosmo*.

'There's just some things I can't stand,' she informed him, complacently, 'and one is shoes without any socks. Another is socks without any trousers, if you're interested. There's nothing worse than a pair of thin nylon socks on the end of a pair of thin hairy legs. Yuk.'

'Perhaps I should wear a skirt,' said Preston, sulkily. He was in that sort of mood. He felt threatened. The room was full of women writers, women in publishing and women in the media. They all looked competent and assured and chic. Chins wagging in animated discourse, or held high, angle-poised between wine glass and cigarette, waiting to dart into the conversation. Preston felt like a frog, hopping in his sockless shoes between elegant storks, too well brought-up to bite, yet. Apart from that it was a very nice room. It was done up like an old wine cellar with sawdust on the floor and large casks for tables and old prints on the walls showing men drinking and plump, jolly women serving them. Left alone in a corner Preston might have been quite happy, but he hadn't been left alone, in a corner or anywhere else. He'd been forced to meet people and the experience had been, for the most part, demoralising.

The party was to launch a book by an American woman. It was about the break-up of her marriage to a famous film star. Preston had read a review. According to the woman the famous film star had used her as a public foil for his sardonic wit and a private crutch for his male insecurities. When he was feeling low he would weep and howl at every slight and humiliation. When he was feeling high he would slight and humiliate her before an invited audience. She had endured this for seven years until, while she was pregnant with their second child, he had indulged in a well-publicised affair with the wife of another famous film star. This had inspired her to leave him and write a book about it. The book was already a bestseller in America. The reviewer thought this was because the writer encapsulated the problems encountered by most women married to successful, but inadequate, men.

Preston had not met the writer. He had only seen her across the room. She looked like a film star herself, tanned and fit with blonde streaks in her brown hair. She drank with rapid gulps and nibbled gherkins and seemed to enjoy life and laughed a lot. Probably a lot more than her husband did at the moment, thought Preston, censoriously.

He had met other writers, though. He had met one writer who had written a book about her husband having AIDS. This had not been a bestseller but she was hopeful that it might take off if the epidemic got any worse.

He had met another writer who had written a book about her life as the mistress of an African dictator who beat his enemies to death with a golf-club and her problems reconciling this with a strict Catholic upbringing.

Both books and the one whose launch they were celebrating had been published by the same feminist publishing house. Preston had strong opinions, lengthily rehearsed, on what this revealed about modern feminism, but so far no one had asked him to express them.

Everyone he met emanated success, or insecurity disguised as success. It was not a place to come if you were feeling down, or if you'd just pulled your wife's hair and made her cry. It was not a place to come without any socks, not unless you dispensed with shoes also and pretended to be an ageing hippy. Preston had considered this but decided against it. His toes were still sore from the going over they'd got from Polly and a lot of women here looked fiercer and meaner than she was and wore sharper heels.

'Eat up your lentil pasty like a good boy,' said Carla, 'and shut up.'

She wasn't joking about the lentil pasty. All the food was vegetarian. The author insisted on it, someone had told Preston. Apparently there was a graphic description in the book of her feelings while watching her husband and assorted male carnivores devouring red meat at a barbecue. Preston could just imagine it.

'I thought I'd like to go soon,' said Carla, 'if that's all right by you.'

Preston looked at her, surprised.

'It depresses me,' she said, keeping her voice low. 'All this . . .' she waved a disparaging arm '. . . mediocre talent. In print.'

Preston understood. Carla had yet to write a book. She had probably come here hoping to be asked and no one had.

'I'm ready when you are,' he said, stuffing his mouth full of lentil pasty and knowing he'd get nothing at Carla's.

'When you've finished feeding your fat face,' she said, politely.

They were joined by a tall, thin woman who looked fiercer and meaner than anyone else in the room. She and Carla engaged in meaningful conversation. After standing to attention for a while in case they needed someone to hold their drinks or cigarettes, Preston wandered off in search of more food.

'Hello, Preston, what are you doing here?'

Preston turned, guiltily.

'Miranda,' he exclaimed, blushing.

'I didn't expect to . . . did you come with . . .' She began to blush, too.

'Some people from the programme,' Preston said quickly. 'What about you?'

'Well, I am in the same business. Well, sort of.'

Of course she was. He was inclined to forget. Miranda was an editor and illustrator of children's books. Preston had read some of them to the twins. They were about bizarre-looking animals like warthogs and armadillos and dinosaurs who were misunderstood and rejected by society until someone was King to Them and then they came Out of Their Shells and made Lots of Friends and were Universally Popular.

'But . . .' This is for grown-ups, he was going to say . . . 'I thought you were in a different field.'

'I am.' She dropped her voice. 'I'm only here for the beer and the vegetable samosas.'

She was wearing an orange jump suit with a zip up the front and a sign that said Blooming Marvellous. It seemed out of character, but then Preston couldn't quite pin Miranda down so far as character was concerned. She seemed so gentle and dreamlike and yet sometimes he wondered.

'Are you going to do something about it for the programme?' she asked.

'I'm not sure,' said Preston, cautiously. He wondered if Polly had told her about Carla. A few months ago it would have been impossible for her not to, but now he wasn't so sure.

He lowered his voice. 'I'm not sure I want to publicise something like this.'

Her lips formed a silent 'Oh'. 'Why's that?' she whispered.

'Well, I mean, it's all a bit sordid, isn't it? I mean, you know, like holding dirty linen up to the light so you can see the stains.'

She looked at him, puzzled.

'The book,' he said.

'Oh. I'm afraid I haven't read it myself,' she said.

'No? Well, I haven't exactly read it,' said Preston, 'but it's the subject matter, it speaks for itself, I mean ...' He launched into his rehearsed speech, keeping his voice down and his head bent towards her. She listened attentively, with a small frown of concentration. '... It's a pretty poor indictment of feminism,' he concluded, 'don't you think, if all you can write is books about men.'

'Has she written more books?' said Miranda. 'I thought this was the first.'

'Not just her.' Preston looked over his shoulder furtively. 'All of them.'

The frown deepened. 'Well, not all feminist books are about men,' she said hesitantly, 'I don't think, do you?'

'Name one that isn't,' he said recklessly.

She named several he'd never heard of, adding, in the same diffident manner, 'But I'm sure you're right. I suppose it's difficult writing a feminist book without mentioning men at all.'

'Ha,' said Preston. 'I wouldn't mind if they just mentioned them. Seems to me books like this leave their blood on every page.'

'Yes,' she agreed doubtfully, 'but I wouldn't really describe it as a feminist book, would you?'

Miranda's questions were never quite rhetorical. She always gave the impression she expected an answer. She held her face up to him, waiting for it with rapt attention, but Preston couldn't think of one. Again he had that momentary doubt about Miranda, but he stacked it up behind all the other worries.

'Ever read any Eva Eichler?' he demanded.

'Oh yes, well,' she said, with a small laugh.

Preston wondered what that meant. It occurred to him that Miranda might know something about Eva Eichler, being in the business herself, '. . . sort of'.

'So what kind of a writer would you say Eva Eichler was?'

'Well of course she did leave blood on every page, but not just men's. Quite a lot of it was her own.'

This was news to Preston. He was only three pages into *Men – the Second Sex* and finding it hard going. A bit of blood might liven things up a bit.

'Why do you think she killed herself?' he asked her.

She seemed taken aback. 'Oh. I suppose she wasn't very happy.' She smiled and tossed her head. 'That sounds terribly trite. I don't know. It was a bit of a mystery, wasn't it?'

'There was talk of it being murder,' he tried.

But she shook her head. 'I hadn't heard that. Why should anyone murder her. Oh – men, you mean?'

Preston hadn't meant that.

'No, well, no, I've no idea,' he said. 'Just something I heard. Some suggestion that it might have been political.'

'Well, I know she was involved in politics, but . . . I just read about her walking into the sea. I never realised there was any suggestion of . . . I just heard she'd gone a bit peculiar.'

'Peculiar? In what way?'

'Oh, just . . . a bit obsessive. About success and all that.'

Preston stared at her. For a moment he forgot he wasn't wearing any socks. He even forgot Carla was in the same room.

'Success and all that?' he said.

'Yes. She had this thing about Power. You know, that women needed power in order to change things. But, well, it seemed to me . . .' she gave a little self-deprecating smile . . . 'she was sort of so busy pursuing power she lost control. You know, of her own life. And that's not what feminism is about, is it?'

'No,' said Preston, who didn't know.

He realised it was the first time he had ever had a serious conversation with Miranda. He was startled, and also slightly embarrassed. He changed the subject quickly.

'How's the . . .' He nodded towards the jump suit.

'Oh, fine.'

Preston caught Carla's eye on him. She was pointing at her watch.

'I'd better be going,' he said, 'I'm with some people from the programme. Promised them a lift back.'

He broke into a cold sweat instantly, fearing she would ask if there was room for her, but of course, being Miranda, she wouldn't.

'Oh, of course.' She was blushing again. 'Bye. Take care.'

'And you,' he said, over-eagerly. 'See you Tuesday.'

The small furrow appeared between her brows. 'Are you sure? You don't have to, you know.'

'No, I know. Of course. No. No problem.'

'Well. We'll have to talk about it after the class,' she said, with unexpected firmness.

'Who was that?' asked Carla, when they were going up the stairs.

'Who? Miranda?' said Preston, vaguely. He was still thinking about Power and Control. 'She's an editor.'

'Editor of what?' Carla demanded, interested.

Preston told her. Carla's interest diminished.

'She looks pregnant,' she said.

'Does she? I didn't notice.'

'Friend of yours?'

'Well . . . -ish.'

'I thought I detected a certain *frisson*.'

'She's a friend of Polly's actually.'

'Oh.'

They loitered outside, looking for a cab. Preston hoped Miranda wouldn't come out.

'Let's walk to the lights,' he said.

'I've just been asked to write a book,' Carla announced. She looked pleased with herself. 'Isn't that great?'

'Great,' said Preston. 'What about?'

'It isn't definite, but we've arranged lunch to talk about it. About men.'

'It's not sour grapes,' said Preston, an hour or so later, 'I just wish someone would ask a man to write a book about men, that's all.'

'Who'd want to read it?' said Carla. 'It'd just be lies.'

Preston gave up and started to take his clothes off.

'That reminds me,' she said. 'Why aren't you wearing any socks?'

Preston considered lying. But it was too late, he couldn't think of a convincing story, and besides, after what Carla had just said, it seemed like letting the side down. He gave her the truth, or at least, an edited version.

She looked cross.

'I thought you said Polly was quite content with the situation, that she didn't mind.'

'I never said she was content,' Preston corrected her, 'I said she was reconciled. And sometimes she's less reconciled than at other times.'

'I hope you're not trying to make me feel guilty,' Carla said. She folded her arms sternly over her open dressing-gown.

'Gosh, no,' said Preston.

'Because if you are, can I just remind you that you told me there was no longer anything between you and Polly and that if you hadn't we would not be where we are now.'

Where they were now was on Carla's bed in Carla's bedroom with something raucous on the stereo and Carla's purple curtains drawn against the world, or what you could see of it from a basement flat in Islington shortly before midnight. Carla's room was like an extension of the set for *Shrews at Ten*. Red walls, purple curtains, a green bedspread. Lots of clutter. Fun.

'Shit, you always do this to me,' said Carla.

'What?' said Preston.

'Guilt,' said Carla. 'You lay it on me. Your own sense of guilt.'

'I don't feel any sense of guilt,' protested Preston.

But he did, and he wondered why he bothered to deny it. If he said 'Yes, I feel guilt' perhaps Carla would send him home. On the other hand perhaps they'd just have a row and Preston didn't think he could face another row. Besides, if she did send him home, chances were Polly had put the bolt on the door. Preston felt very tired suddenly.

'Oh come here,' said Carla.

Preston stretched out wearily beside her and composed himself mentally for sex. Incredibly, given the trouble he was taking and the mess it was getting him into, Preston found sex with Carla a bit of a problem, which was one of the reasons, besides drink, why he'd been arguing with her, pointlessly and repetitively, since they'd arrived at her flat. It wasn't that he found Carla unattractive. It was just that there was something wrong with their body chemistry. He found it very difficult to get interested.

The problem was not eased by Carla's Attitude. Carla had determined views on sex and the correct means of going about it. Being Carla she felt no inhibition about instructing Preston in the methods most conducive to orgasm, while maintaining a running commentary on the effect they were having on her. Not surprisingly, in the circumstances, Preston's prick had gone into a serious sulk.

Technically, this should not have mattered because Carla also had determined views on what she called 'penis penetration' which made Preston's prick, whatever its emotional state, entirely superfluous.

Carla regarded penis penetration as 'an act of imperialist aggression'.

She did not permit it, on political grounds.

Which should have made the entire business as easy as pie. Except that Carla, perversely, required Preston to have an erect penis throughout. Otherwise, she said, she didn't feel turned on.

It had taken Preston some time to come to terms with all this. Finally he had resolved the dilemma by leaning heavily on the Mrs Gladrags Solution.

While his hands and lips obeyed Carla's explicit instructions, Preston teased his reluctant member into a semblance of rigidity by concentrating hard on one or other of the Gladrags Fantasies and when he had brought Carla to a successful climax he lay back and thought Mrs Gladrags thoughts while Carla did it to him.

When it was over Carla mopped up the mess with some tissues from a box by the bed and they lay together for a while, not speaking.

Until Carla said, with affected lack of concern, 'Why did you and Polly stop making love together?'

This was dangerous ground and Preston proceeded with caution. In fact he and Polly had not stopped making love until, in a moment of breathtaking if not exactly unenforced honesty, he had confessed to his affair with Carla. Carla was, at least so far as Polly was concerned, the sole reason for the subsequent freeze. But Carla did not know this and Preston considered it unwise, at this stage, to tell her. He justified this small deception by telling himself that what he and Polly had been doing immediately prior to his encounter with Carla could not, accurately, be described as Making Love. More as Going Through the Motions, or Passing the Time Before Sleep.

An example sprang to mind. Polly had once remarked while he was engaged in stroking her clitoris that it was time he started looking at the price of things before he bought them.

Preston, who had been thinking about something quite different – a small problem with the car – was mildly incensed at this apparently ill-timed rebuke. Polly revealed that she had found a price tag on the lemons he had recently bought from the corner shop and that they had been fifteen pence a lemon, whereas she, Polly, normally bought three for twenty from Sainsbury's.

Shortly afterwards she had climaxed with apparent satisfaction, but the incident had rankled with Preston. He now saw it as a significant watershed in their relationship.

So Preston told Carla about the lemons as if it had been the last time they had Made Love and Carla turned towards him, supporting herself on one elbow and gave him an odd, speculative look that made Preston wonder what she thought about during sex.

'And on the strength of that,' she mused, 'you gave it up?'

Preston had a sudden impulse to tell her about Miranda, but he managed to control it. He did not trust Carla enough. He felt that on some future occasion, possibly at the Beeb and in public, she might be tempted to use it against him. So instead he said, by way of further explanation and to reinforce his case against Polly, 'And also, to be fair to Polly, I started to put pressure on her to have orgasms.'

'You mean she didn't have them?'

'Well not so I could be sure.'

For years he hadn't really thought about it. They had both been lazy in their lovemaking. Once or twice a week one or other of them would decide they wanted to and after a certain amount of what Preston described to himself as Foreplay, he would indulge in what Carla described to the world in general as An Act of Imperialist Aggression. And after a period of anything between one and five minutes they both came together.

At least that is what Preston had assumed.

For six years, while otherwise occupied in the production of *Animal Antics*, it had not occurred to Preston that Polly might not be coming when he did. Or indeed, even a few seconds before. His studies of animal and child behaviour, though superficial, had inclined him to the view that animals and children made sounds of pleasure when having a good time. Polly made sounds of pleasure. Ergo she was coming.

Having thus arranged their sex life to their mutual satisfaction, Preston and Polly got on with the important things in life: pursuing their respective interests, making programmes about children and animals, buying a different second-hand car every two years, decorating the house, doing the garden, envying the Fischers and producing the twins.

Then Preston moved to *Shrews at Ten* and discovered that inserting willies into chinas and waggling them about for one to five minutes did not automatically induce female orgasm.

And Preston's sex education made another quantum leap, equivalent to that memorable day when he had discovered that Billy Quirk's information was entirely erroneous and ladies did not, on average, have two tits and a willy.

'So how did you put pressure on her, Preston?' Carla enquired.

'Well,' Preston considered. Hours of anguished discussion came to mind.

'I just tried to cater to her needs a bit more – as a woman.' He didn't know why he added 'as a woman' but it was a phrase that came easily after working on *Shrews at Ten*. It was like saying, You know, or, I mean.

'And how did she react to this?'

Preston felt as if he was being interviewed for the chat show. Maybe he was.

'It pissed her off a bit,' Preston admitted. 'I think she'd rather have been left alone.'

It all sounded a bit thin, he thought, without the addition of Miranda, like explaining the causes of the First World War and missing out Sarajevo. He sensed that Carla was brooding on all this and in a bid to distract her he started to kiss her nipples. This had the desired effect – Carla's powers of recuperation being, in Preston's limited experience, formidable – but it obliged him to display similar signs of arousal. Anxiously, he sought to conjure up a Gladrags Situation but down below it felt not so much limp as numb. Carla was kissing his chest, his stomach, working her way down. Preston concentrated. He gave Sally Fischer the lead role and felt a faint stirring of, if not desire, at least curiosity. Then Carla said, 'What is that?'

Preston lifted his head and peered down the length of his body. Carla was holding his failed erection between finger and thumb in a way that reminded Preston of how his grandmother, while shopping, used to inspect a piece of fish which she suspected had been on the fishmonger's slab considerably longer than it should have been.

'I'm sorry.' Preston tried to think of a plausible excuse. He'd had too much wine. Eaten too many lentils. Was distracted by the situation in Central America.

'Those things there.' Carla pointed at something he couldn't see.

'What things where?' Preston panicked. The first signs of AIDS? Cancer of the genitals? Bubonic plague?

He shot up and grabbed it off her.

'There.' Carla indicated a row of tiny pink bumps along the underside of his penis. Preston sank back relieved. They'd been there so long he'd forgotten about them. He thought of them as nodules, distinctive little nobbly bits that were, if anything, an added attraction of the organ. Like the Durex you bought, rather more expensively, with rough bits For Added Sensation.

'They're nothing,' he said, modestly. 'They've been there ages.'

'They're not nothing,' said Carla. 'They're warts.'

'What?' Preston was outraged.

The word 'wart' was associated in his mind with the ugly, horny outbreaks of his youth, confined to hands, knees and occasionally the soles of the feet. These were nothing like that.

'Don't be ridiculous,' he said.

'Preston, those are genital warts. Would you like me to show you a book on the subject?'

Preston's indignation evaporated, leaving a brackish residue of doubt and dismay. Carla was invariably right about such things. If there was a book on the subject she would have it, she would almost certainly know the author and she might even have contributed a chapter on the subject.

'They're only small,' he said, defensively.

'Preston, we are not talking about pet gerbils,' she said. 'Those are genital warts. It doesn't matter how small they are. All the evidence suggests that they are a prime cause of cervical cancer.'

Preston reflected that in the present circumstances of his sex life there was precious little chance of anyone catching it from him, but he suspected this would carry little weight with Carla.

'You must see your doctor immediately,' she insisted.

Preston ventured to suggest that his doctor might not be too enthusiastic about attending him at such a late hour in an unfamiliar house on the far side of London for the treatment of alleged genital warts.

'Tomorrow, you ape,' Carla said, adding, with increased emphasis, 'Men,' the simian epithet doubtless being considered inadequate for the occasion.

She took herself off to the bathroom presumably to wash her hands and anything else that had been in contact with him, leaving Preston to reflect on this new problem in his life and decide what, if anything, to do about it.

There had been classic remedies for warts which Preston had practised as a child. He remembered one was to cut a nick in them with a penknife, drip the blood on to a piece of apple or potato peel and bury it in the garden at midnight. As the peel rotted so did the wart.

Preston glanced at the alarm-clock at the side of Carla's bed. The timing was almost right. He looked at the things he must learn to think of as warts. They were far too small and delicate to be nicked. He might do himself permanent injury. Besides, he didn't have a penknife.

There was another remedy, though, and it was much less drastic. What's more it worked, or at least it had done, once, when Preston was eleven, and the offending objects were on his hands. What you had to do was, you had to spit on them with the very first spit of the morning.

Preston wondered if five minutes after midnight counted as morning. Probably not, he thought, but it was worth a try. He twisted his penis round so he could see them and tried to summon up enough spit. His mouth was very dry and he had to pretend to chew something. He dribbled hopefully and missed.

'Preston, what on earth are you doing?'

Carla stood in the doorway with her hands on her hips and her mouth open. Preston, about to try for a second shot, swallowed and launched into a detailed explanation.

Carla stared at him for a moment, saying nothing.

'Well, that's the principle, anyway,' said Preston. He didn't like the expression on her face.

'And you seriously think it will do some good, do you?'

Preston admitted he had doubts about the timing. 'I think it's got to be when you wake up after a night's sleep,' he said. 'I think it's something to do with the acid content in the saliva. Maturing, as it were, overnight.'

'I see.' Carla sat on the edge of the bed, with the same thoughtful, slightly brooding look. 'Preston, sometimes I wonder if you're entirely sane,' she said, conversationally.

'Now listen to me,' she added, in the kindly but firm manner of a night nurse. 'First thing in the morning you will get up and you will go straight round to your doctor and you will demand proper treatment for those things . . .' Her voice became firmer and less kind . . . 'And if I wake up and I catch you spitting at them, Preston, I am going to be very, very cross. I shouldn't be surprised if I were to take you by the hair and rub your dirty little nose in it.'

Preston wondered why, sooner or later, almost every woman he met started to sound like his grandmother.

At least, he reflected, a little later, drifting into merciful sleep, he wouldn't have to go through the business of the Fancy-Dress Party for a while. The novelty was beginning to pall and it was proving less than a hundred per cent certain.

11 TROUBLE WITH CHINA
Miss a Go

'Murder by person or persons unknown,' said Edward Cartwright. 'That seems to be the general verdict.'

'But no one's done much about it?'

Preston kept his voice low because Carla was in the vicinity and for reasons he didn't like to think too much about he was anxious to keep Eva Eichler to himself for the time being. He was in the *Shrews at Ten* office, on the phone.

'Apparently not,' said Edward, drily.

'Lack of interest?' wondered Preston, detecting it in the voice on the other end of the line.

'Well, there are rather a lot of feminist writers in America,' said Edward, as if the loss of one or two wouldn't make much difference either way and might even improve matters, 'but Graham seemed to think it was just one of those things. Slipped under the mat. Something else cropped up.'

'Graham' had taken over from Edward in the Washington bureau. Preston knew him only as a face on the screen.

'Why is he so sure it wasn't suicide?'

He was reluctant to give up on the suicide theory. He wanted to know why a woman who had everything had walked into the sea. He wanted to know how, in pursuit of Power, she had lost Control. That is what spoke to him. That had been his original motivation. Murder might be more sensational, but somehow he felt cheated.

'I don't suppose he is. He got that from one of his police chums in Washington. Apparently some things didn't add up.'

'Are they still looking for someone?'

'Well, it wouldn't be them, would it? It would be the English police in wherever it happened.'

'Of course. Felixstowe.'

'Precisely. Doubtless there's some keen young constable on the trail even now, pedalling his bicycle for all he's worth.'

Edward had a somewhat restricted view of life outside the metropolis.

'One thing that might interest you, she had some woman travelling with her.'

'I know. Bernadette McCarthy. It was in the cuttings,' said Preston.

'And did you also know she came from your home town?'

'Liverpool?'

'That's right. I've asked Graham to send the cuttings over.'

Preston thanked him for his trouble.

'Not at all, m'dear,' said Edward, 'I'm fascinated to know what you're going to do with it.'

Preston put the phone down and caught Carla's eye on him.

'Ready for the conference?' she said.

It was an order, not a question, but Preston looked at his watch.

'OK,' he said. 'But we're due at the edit in half an hour.'

The production conference was a BBC ritual, like going to the canteen, but usually less productive. Curiously, Carla had quite taken to it and requested one on the slightest pretext. This was to discuss ideas for the insert they planned to shoot on location the following week. Carla had one or two ideas herself, she said, but first she'd like to hear what the researchers had in mind.

Andrea opened her notebook with distinct lack of enthusiasm. Preston thought he knew what she was thinking. She was thinking that if Carla had 'one or two ideas' the rest of them were wasting their time. He listened while the discussion ebbed and flowed around him, usually breaking on the rock of Carla's obduracy. In fairness to her they were not good ideas, mostly on the theme, woman in a man's job, which Carla rightly hated. The best of these, in Preston's opinion, was about a baronet's daughter who'd run off with a lion-tamer, learned to do it herself, and was now the star of the circus. For some reason this appealed to Preston. He imagined the original lion-tamer sulking in his caravan and taking to drink. He probably thought he was marvellous running off with a baronet's daughter. He probably thought she'd be watching him night after night while he set about the big cats with a whip and a bar-stool, biting her nails and exclaiming in her upper-class accent whenever he pulled off a particularly dangerous stunt, Oh do be careful, darling. Preston could have told him what would happen. He knew what would happen next. The baronet's daughter would get off with the circus owner and end up running the place while the original lion-tamer got more and more drunk until one night he wandered into the lions' cage to recapture his lost glory and they tore him to pieces.

'I used to work in a circus once,' he told everyone, 'I used to box a kangaroo.'

'Really,' said the PA, 'when was that?'

The PA's name was Jane. Preston decided he liked Jane.

'During my last university vacation,' he said, 'I was working as a circus hand, you know, just putting the tent up and things, and the bloke who boxed the kangaroo sprained his groin … '

'Preston, I hate to interrupt,' said Carla, 'but we've rather moved on from circuses.'

'Oh,' said Preston. 'Sorry.'

But it was on his mind now. He'd felt quite proud of working in a circus. It was a bit different from the usual run of vacation jobs. Not that he'd particularly liked animals, even then, long before he became the longest-running producer of *Animal Antics*, but when they'd asked for volunteers to box the kangaroo Preston was there with his hand in the air, waiting to be laced into a six-pound glove. It would be something to talk about when he went back to university for his final year.

'What did you do over the summer, Pres?'

'Oh, nothing much, boxed a kangaroo in a circus.'

The kangaroo's name was Cobber. Cobber the Boxing Kangaroo. It was six feet tall and it could leap thirty. Once it had leaped right out of the ring and terrified the audience with its forearm jabs. Only Preston and the man with the strained groin knew that a kangaroo is not to be feared for its forearm jabs. Even if it got the aim right a kangaroo's forearm jab would barely stun a mosquito. It was the legs you had to watch for. Used in the correct manner the legs could disembowel you.

Preston knew all there was to know about boxing a kangaroo. You had to go in close because a kangaroo is very short-sighted and if it can't see you it loses interest, and so does the audience. But you have to be careful when you go in close because of the hind legs. You can afford to ignore the arms with the claws sheathed in outsize boxing gloves, they're just for show, but the natural way for a kangaroo to fight in the wild is to drop back on to its tail and bring both legs up in a lethal gut-gouging kick. And in the heat of the moment, in the boxing-ring with the audience screaming for blood, a kangaroo will sometimes forget that it is only pretending to fight. It is possible that it does not know it is only pretending. Preston had spent many hours in the ring with Cobber and visiting him in his cage and poking raw carrots through the bars, which Cobber liked, but he had never been able to read the expression in Cobber's eyes and he never forgot how dangerous an animal Cobber really was. He always waited for the moment when Cobber dropped back on to his tail because he knew that was the moment when Cobber was preparing to disembowel him.

'What do you think, Preston?' asked Carla.

'Sorry?' said Preston. He realised that everyone was looking at him and hastily scanned that small part of his brain that had been logging the conversation. Something about a feminist poet who drove a bus in Newcastle.

'Bit of a trek,' he said. 'We've only got one travel day.'

'Well, I think we should do the band,' Carla said. 'It's only a four-hour drive to Liverpool.'

'Liverpool?' Preston was all attention.

'Where the band is,' said Carla, with heavy patience.

Preston groped in the fog, searching for clues.

'What's their music like?' Andrea wanted to know.

'I don't give a damn about their music,' said Carla, 'but they're all women and they've got lots to say for themselves.'

'Like what?'

'Like what it's like being an all-woman band in a place like Liverpool. For Christ's sake, Andrea.'

'I just don't see what's so special about Liverpool, or an all-woman band for that matter. There's plenty in London. I even know one or two in Glasgow.'

'The Beatles, Andrea, remember the Beatles, and all those other all-male groups? This is the place where it all happened. What's happening there now? Unemployment, the politics, the violence in the streets ... What's it like for them?'

'I think it's a great idea,' said Preston, with sudden decision, 'I think we should go to Liverpool.'

'I forgot you came from Liverpool,' said Carla in the lift on the way down to the editing room. 'Is that why you're so keen?'

'No, I think it's a good story,' said Preston, in case she changed her mind. He could go up there tomorrow on a recce, stay the weekend with his mum and shoot the band Monday night.

'How far in are we?' he asked the PA, to change the subject.

'Twenty-two minutes,' said the PA, 'with two more to do.'

'We'll have to get a move on,' he said, for Carla's benefit. 'Do a bit less talking.'

Until he met Carla, Preston had always enjoyed editing. He liked the functional masculinity of the cutting rooms. He liked being shut away down in the basement with only a VT editor between him and the finished product. Then Carla came along and spoiled everything.

Carla always insisted on sitting in on the edit and making her views known. It felt like being in a spaceship with the alien aboard.

The editor was waiting for them with the last shot up on the monitor. His greeting was less than cheerful. It had been a hard morning.

'What next?' he asked.

'The thrush interview,' said Preston.

'You interviewed a thrush?' said the editor. 'That's original.'

Carla looked at him.

The PA read out the time code and the editor bashed it out on the keyboard.

'How much do we have to lose?' asked Carla.

'Well, it was twenty-five seconds over,' said the PA, looking at Preston, 'but we're all right for time.'

They'd spent the morning hacking the film director to death and trimming a cliché here and there from the woman politician. The Page Three girl hadn't said enough to cut.

'If that's all, why don't we leave it as it is?' said Carla. 'I can think of at least one cut we can make in jealousy.'

'I want to look at something first,' said Preston. He asked the editor to fast forward for a couple of minutes, then play the interview through to the end. Carla asked why, but he pretended not to hear.

'What was that?' said the editor. He stopped the tape at the bit Preston was worried about and played it again.

'Exactly,' said Preston, making notes on a pad. It looked simple enough. They could cut Carla's question, *But what if, after all these precautions, you catch it anyway?* and come back on, *The best thing is to take a bottle full of water . . .*

He explained this to the editor.

'Why?' said Carla again, 'what are you doing?'

'Cutting out the cunt bit,' said Preston. 'It doesn't add anything to the discussion and we lose, what is it?'

'Seven seconds five frames,' said the editor.

'But why? Why do you want to cut it?'

Carla's voice had reached a familiar pitch. Preston knew he was going to have trouble. He asked the editor to run it again.

'Some people will tell you yoghurt is the answer.

'But who wants to run around with a cunt full of yoghurt?'

'What on earth is wrong with that?' Carla demanded.

Preston looked at the editor for support but the editor was saying nothing.

'I just think some people might object to the word Cunt,' he explained, 'and it's not an essential part of the argument is it, really?'

'I'm sorry, but I think it is.' Carla had her hands on her hips. 'If I conduct a serious interview I don't expect it to be hacked about because you object to part of a woman's anatomy.'

'Oh come on, Carla,' Preston was moved to protest, 'I don't object to anything.'

'So who else does?' She looked around the small room. The editor made a minute adjustment to the monitor. The PA studied her notes.

'Carla, you know very well what I'm talking about. It's nothing to do with anatomy, it's the use of language some people might object to. Using part of the female body as a term of abuse.'

He thought he'd got her there, but it was a mistake.

'But I didn't use it as a term of abuse, Preston, that's the point.'

Preston sighed, but there was no answer to that, none he could think of, anyway.

'Play it again,' he said.

The editor played it again.

'See, I use the word quite normally,' said Carla. 'There's no emphasis on it or anything. It's about time people realised that a woman's cunt is *not* a term of abuse. It's a very useful point we're making here.'

'But that's not what the interview's about.'

'Look, Preston,' Carla swivelled his chair round so he had to look her in the face, 'without that line this is a very ordinary interview about thrush. That line makes it controversial. It makes it worth watching. It also makes two valid points: one about thrush and one about the use of the word cunt. In a woman's programme that has to be a good thing.'

Preston wavered. Perhaps he'd allowed Edward to panic him. What was so awful about the word, anyway?

He turned back to the editor.

'OK, lay it down as it is. What's next?'

'Jealousy,' said the PA. 'Three and a half minutes.'

12 TROUBLE WITH WILLY
Miss Two Goes

Preston stood outside his local health centre and considered the names on the board. He was not a frequent visitor to the doctor's. He only went for something serious. In the past five years he had been to the doctor's three times, for leukaemia, heart disease and a brain tumour. Each time the prognosis had been reassuring, if mildly embarrassing. He tended to ask for a different doctor each time in case they remembered the last case of terminal neurosis and didn't take him seriously enough.

However, on his previous visit – with the suspected brain tumour – Preston had been treated with sympathy and understanding by a young woman doctor who had given him a complete going-over before pronouncing him one hundred per cent fit, at least physically. He might have been a bit tense, she had suggested, kindly, and the headaches of which he complained were probably a symptom. It had been a pleasant change from the gruff, please-don't-waste-my-time treatment he had received from the male doctor who'd examined him for suspected leukaemia. She was attractive and plump and she wore a rather old-fashioned looking frock in a flower pattern with buttons down the front. In the course of her examination she had made Preston strip to his underpants and lie down on her plastic couch where she had tapped him all over with a small rubber hammer. Testing for reactions, she said. When she had done this and taken his blood pressure she had remarked, 'Fantastic', in an admiring sort of way. Preston had been too worried about his brain tumour to say anything at the time, but afterwards he dwelt on the use of this word, Fantastic, and imagined what might have happened if he had responded with a suitable *bon mot*.

Such as, 'You're not so bad yourself.'

Perhaps not. But what if, while lying on her couch being hit all over with her little rubber hammer, he'd had an erection?

She'd have hit it with the little rubber hammer.

Not necessarily. This was Preston hammered down by experience and the women in his life. She might have been flattered. She might have stepped back and looked at him for a moment, saying nothing, her pink little tongue darting briefly to moisten her pouting lips, her hands, moving almost of their own accord, slowly undoing the buttons of her flower pattern frock to reveal that all she wore under it was a suspender-belt and stockings.

There *were* women like that. Preston had read about them in books. Or, at least, magazines. He imagined himself lying back on his couch, hands clasped behind his head, while she climbed on top of him. It was exactly what he wanted. A quick, uncomplicated fuck. An act of imperialist aggression in the clean, clinical environment of a doctor's surgery. No risk of catching anything and precious little chance of it developing into a relationship for fear the Medical Council got to hear about it. He wouldn't even feel guilty afterwards, he promised himself.

There were six names on the board. Five were prefixed by initials. The sixth was written out in full. Dr Emma Blackwell. That was her. Dr Emma Blackwell. The very name was redolent of old-fashioned flower-pattern frocks and stockings with suspender-belts. She probably didn't wear any knickers, he considered, because, as a doctor, she knew they encouraged thrush. Preston's heart began to pump wildly.

There was always the problem, of course, that she would be put off by the nature of his complaint, but on reflection he decided that this was unlikely. She was a doctor, after all. She might even be impressed by his sense of responsibility in bringing them to her.

'They don't really trouble me,' he would say, 'but I'm worried they might give someone cervical cancer.'

That 'someone' was useful, too. Implying a certain freedom from commitment. A certain buccaneer approach to sexual liaison. On the other hand, it might also be taken to imply that he put himself about a bit. He'd have to be careful about that. Still, once he'd got it out it was obviously up to her to make the first move.

The opening remark bothered him slightly. It could come out sounding a bit silly.

'Hello, Mr Moody, what can I do for you?'

'Hello, I've got warts on my penis.'

It was too direct. It introduced the word 'warts' too early in the scene, before she'd discovered how insignificant they were. Still, it was difficult to see how he could whip it out without warning and slap it on her desk.

'There, what do you reckon about that?'

The receptionist took his name and told him to take a seat. She was a young woman like Dr Blackwell but not so attractive. She peered out of her little window with her sharp nose and her hard eyes like a ferret making up its mind which rabbit was next for the chop.

There were eight or nine people in the waiting-room but with so many doctors Preston didn't expect he'd have to hang around too long. He was anxious to see the twins before they went to bed.

'*Hello, Mr Moody, what can I do for you?*'

'*Hello.*' Pause. Smile. The memory of their last encounter passing through the space between them like a shock wave. '*I've got a little problem with my penis. I wondered if you'd mind having a look at it.*'

How could he even think about this when only a second ago he'd been worrying about getting back to see the twins? Reading them a book before bedtime. Tucking them in, kissing them good-night. Preston sighed. Little white buttons, eight of them, or perhaps it was seven, starting just where her cleavage began and ending about three inches above the knee. He took out *Men – the Second Sex* and picked up where he'd left off.

Men, he read, are much more prone to obsessions and fantasies than women. They are much more obsessive about work and status because they are incapable and fearful of any other form of self-development. They are much more prone to sexual fantasy because they are incapable and fearful of any deeper emotional commitment.

Preston begged to differ. He had known women who were much more obsessive about work and status than the men he knew. Carla for one. And he knew women who fantasised all the time in preference to the real thing. Polly had as much as admitted it to him and she said she didn't think she was 'atypical'.

Preston had read six pages of *Men – the Second Sex* and he was beginning to get the hang of it. Men, not women, were the true second sex because of their inability to make deep emotional ties with other people. Men had few, if any, close friends. Men knew other men all their lives and the most profound thing they ever discussed with them was the advantage of four-wheel drive over any other form of propulsion.

Men felt like enemy aliens in their own homes. Men were essentially insecure, afraid to show their inner feelings, sheathing them in an armour-plating of roles: the role of man the provider, man the

82

father, man the warrior, man the over-achiever. Men were emotional cripples and social misfits. Men could not relate to other people except within work or some other organised pursuit, like sport or war.

Men were very dangerous animals. Men were a menace.

The door opened and a man walked in with an Alsatian. Preston gazed at him reflectively. He was not an ideal specimen of the breed. He looked mean and vicious. He looked repressed. Preston would not have used him as an example to refute the arguments contained in *Men – the Second Sex*. The Alsatian, by comparison, looked harmless. Preston wondered what was wrong with him. Probably just a bit tense.

'*Hello, I've got this small rash on my penis. I thought you might be able to give me something for it.*'

'Mr Moody,' the receptionist called, 'Dr Blackwell will see you now.'

Preston took his medical card and followed the corridor down to the room marked Dr Blackwell.

'Hello, Mr Moody, sit down, what's the problem?'

IT WASN'T HER.

Preston sat down, terrified. She looked like Barbara Barnes-Warden's big sister. She had the Barnes-Warden chin and her steely grey hair was cut like a helmet. She wore a kind of sports jacket in a dog-tooth pattern with shoulder pads that emphasised the resemblance to an ageing American footballer. Preston knew that beneath the desk she'd be wearing a skirt that matched the jacket and beneath that sensible underwear. Lots of it. Emma? Surely not.

'Would you like to tell me about it?'

She had a jolly hockey-sticks sort of voice, the sort of voice that slapped you on the back and told you to snap out of it. Preston realised he'd been staring at her, saying nothing. He blushed furiously and said the first thing that came into his head.

'I think I've got a brain tumour,' he said.

She looked at him for a moment, taking it in.

'May I see your cards?'

She took them out of the grubby, well-fingered envelope. His medical history from birth. His life story, written in the dry, unimaginative, matter-of-fact style of all the doctors he'd ever seen. The simple childhood complaints, the problems of pubescence, the more complicated ailments of manhood, the time he thought he was going bald, the time he thought he was verging on a heart attack, the last time he'd come here with a brain tumour. Ah, she'd found it. He could tell by the quick frown that crossed her face.

'I see you came to see my colleague, Dr Swann, with a similar complaint, about a year ago.'

Swann. That was it. How could he have forgotten? She'd been up on the board. Dr W. K. Swann. Why did she have to use initials. What woman's name began with a W? Wilma? Winnie? Wendy. She was a Wendy. Bound to be. Shit, he thought.

'I'm terribly sorry,' he said, 'but I haven't got a brain tumour. Actually, I was a bit embarrassed.'

She looked at him. He wondered if she was reaching surreptitiously and silently for the little button under the desk. Within seconds armed guards would rush into the room or an armoured-glass partition would drop down between them from ceiling to floor.

'Then what can I do for you?' she said.

'I think I've got warts on my penis,' he said.

She nodded as if she'd known all along.

'Would you like to show them to me?'

Preston stood up and unzipped his flies and took it out and lifted it up so she could see them.

'Ah, yes,' she said. Preston thought she sounded relieved. 'They're warts all right.'

Preston wondered if he should stay standing up or put it away or what. She slid back a drawer and took out a small bottle and a long brush.

'I'm going to put some of this on,' she said. 'It's very powerful so I'm afraid I can't let you administer it yourself.'

Preston was surprised she kept it in her desk. He wondered if many people suffered from the same complaint. And did she always use the same brush?

'If you'd just hold it up for a moment.'

Her manner was very professional, almost deferential, but Preston noticed she didn't look him in the eyes any more. He stretched it as far as it would go and she leaned across the desk with her long brush and painted them carefully.

'Just leave it for a minute or so until it dries,' she said.

It was a terribly long minute.

Preston tried to think of something intelligent to say but he thought he'd probably blown it with Dr Blackwell so far as intelligence was concerned. She busied herself screwing the top back on the bottle and wiping the brush on a piece of tissue. He wished she'd wash the brush. Maybe she would when he left. Maybe she'd throw it away. Maybe she just didn't want him to think she thought he was unclean.

He wondered if the minute was up. It seemed impolite to look at his watch, as if he was impatient. Preston had been brought up to believe that you mustn't make doctors cross, it was too dangerous. If you made them cross they chopped something off you. You had to be grateful to them for the time and effort they spent on you, even if they killed you sooner or later. If Preston had been a lamb, his mum and his gran and his Auntie Ethel would have taught him to smile at the slaughterer so the slaughterer would be nice to him.

He looked at his warts instead. They looked much more prominent with the stuff on, as if he'd been polishing them.

'After a few hours they'll turn black,' Dr Blackwell said.

'Oh, thank you,' said Preston, relieved to be able to say anything at all. 'And how long will it take for them to go?'

'I'm afraid it might take a while. You'll have to come back regularly for treatment. At least once a week.'

Preston was startled. He'd thought that was it.

'Does that present a difficulty?' she enquired.

'Well, it's not going to be easy,' Preston said. 'Can't I take it home?'

He meant the bottle.

'I'm afraid that's not advisable. It's a very strong medication. We've had one or two unfortunate accidents when we've given it on prescription, but if you prefer I can arrange for you to apply it yourself, provided you come to the surgery.'

Preston said he would prefer that. He didn't want to take up her time, he said. He wondered how bad the accidents had been.

'I'll speak to the receptionist,' said Dr Blackwell. 'I think it's probably dry now.'

'Oh, yes.' Preston put it away quickly and zipped himself up. She led him back to the waiting-room and left him there while she went round the back to speak to the receptionist.

Preston stood by the window of the reception desk, waiting. A few more people had come in. The man with the Alsatian was still there.

The Alsatian was lying across the middle of the room, asleep. Preston heard the doctor's voice. She was making an effort to speak quietly but it carried.

'Young man in there with warts on his penis,' she was saying. 'Told him he could come in any time and treat them himself.'

Preston fixed his eyes firmly on the Alsatian so he wouldn't have to look at anyone else. If he didn't blush they might not know it was him.

The Alsatian opened its eyes and lifted its ears and gazed back at him with the same expression he had seen in the eyes of Dr Blackwell when he'd told her about the brain tumour. It knows, he thought.

'That'll be all right.' Dr Blackwell leaned her square head through the window of the reception room. 'Just phone up and let her know when you're coming.'

13 REVIEW LIFE
Back Thirty Years

Preston walked home from the doctor's and wondered what he was doing with his life. If it hadn't been for Dr Emma Blackwell being who she was and not Dr W. K. Swann he'd have been walking home feeling even guiltier than he normally did. So why did he do it, what made him behave like this?

Sometimes, in a certain cold light, Preston looked at himself and was horrified. But that's not me, he'd scream silently to Whoever Was Listening Up There. I'm not like this. This is the behaviour of a bounder and a cad. Father, forgive me for I have sinned. Say three Hail Marys, my son, and make an act of contrition.

And the trouble with lust, so far as the Church was concerned, was that it was just as bad thinking about it as doing it. So he'd get it in the neck for Dr W. K. Swann even when it was Dr Emma Blackwell.

A vision of what might have been swam before his eyes and he looked hastily away. But it would have been so *nice*. That's what the priests couldn't understand, of course. They thought it was like rolling in pig swill, it was easy for them.

Between the age of seven and fifteen Preston had been sent once a week to a convent where he'd had Catechism and Instruction. This was because he did not go to a Catholic school and the priest told his mother he was in danger of losing his immortal soul to the Prods. For the first few years he had been taught by a nun called Mother Bernard. Mother Bernard was obsessed with two things: Martin Luther and something Preston hadn't quite grasped at the time. She called it Being Tempted in the Night. She said if he was Tempted in the Night he should say a quick Hail Mary and think about something else.

This puzzled Preston for a long time. He didn't know what could be so awful to think about that he should immediately say a Hail Mary and think about something else. And something you might do at night that you wouldn't think of doing during the day. He used to lie awake worrying about it. Then he'd give up and go to work on Mrs Gladrags and the Fancy-Dress Party. When it finally dawned on him that this was exactly what Mother Bernard meant by Being

Tempted in the Night, Preston was shocked and horrified. Though not as shocked and horrified as when he realised he was supposed to confess it.

He never did, of course.

It was far too embarrassing.

Imagine if the priest wanted details.

Imagine if he made him go round to Mrs Gladrags and apologise.

So Preston told himself that Mother Bernard had got her facts wrong and that this wasn't a Real Sin in the sense that not going to Mass was or biting the priest's hand when he gave you the Sacred Host, which was something Preston was very tempted to do, not out of any feelings of vindictiveness or anti-clericalism but just because he was so curious to know what would happen next.

Martin Luther was a different matter, though strangely related. Mother Bernard said there was conclusive evidence that Martin Luther had been mad. She explained that he had only become a monk because a tree had nearly fallen on his head and scared the shit out of him. She didn't quite put it like that but that was the gist of it. She said he'd been riding through the forest during a storm and a tree had come crashing down just in front of him and he'd become a monk out of fear. But Preston didn't think that was a sign of madness. He could understand it completely, even as a child. Being a monk was safe. It prevented trees from falling on your head, or, at least, it ensured that if they did you went straight to heaven, no messing about with a queue or years in purgatory or anything. And it stopped you being Tempted in the Night, or, at least, doing something about it.

Preston frequently considered becoming a monk. Or, failing that, a good husband and father. He wanted to surround himself with walls. Sometimes. When he was feeling particularly guilty or insecure.

Other times he was desperately afraid of being shut in.

Preston viewed the houses lining his route home. They were solid, Victorian semis, three storeys high, with attic windows and little turret roofs. They were built of red brick with elaborate mouldings around the windows and stone crenellations under the gutters. They had porches with tiled surrounds and doors with stained-glass windows. Some of them had little balconies with wrought-iron railings. They looked like miniature castles, or monasteries. You could imagine a good husband and father living in that kind of a house, or even a monk. What you couldn't imagine was an adulterer, or a philanderer or someone who went to the doctor's with genital warts hoping for a quick, uncomplicated fuck.

Preston looked up at the sash-windows and imagined the good fathers and husbands and monks in the rooms within, reading bedtime stories to their children before they went downstairs to join the wife for supper. He looked at the gardens and imagined the same solid, dependable men digging and planting during the weekend, preparing the soil for Spring, while the children played happily on the swings and slides and the wife watered the pot-plants in the conservatory. He could see green shoots coming up through the soil and tiny buds on the fruit-trees. In a week or two there would be daffodils and primroses and tulips, cherry blossom and apple blossom and lilac. Secure, tranquil, suburban.

A sanctuary, that was what he needed. He needed to escape to a monastery before a tree fell on his head.

Sometimes, of course, Preston wondered if it was all pretence and that, secretly, all those good fathers and husbands and monks were just like him. Adulterers and lechers and bounders and cads. But he knew that whatever they were they would handle it better than him. They might have a Carla somewhere – except that she'd be their secretary – but what they wouldn't have was a Miranda, too. And they wouldn't get found out.

He reached his own home and looked at it. It was the same as all the others but shabbier. They never had enough money to do anything about it. Preston had to do the decorating himself and he was no good at it. And just when he thought he'd got things straight it would require some major repair that didn't make it look any better but stopped it from actually falling down. Yet it always seemed to be on the verge of collapse.

The Fischers' house next door was in wonderful condition. The woodwork was freshly painted and all the mouldings were picked out in white. They had a gravel path and a gardener looked after the garden. Inside it looked like the Laura Ashley catalogue. The paint had been burned off the woodwork leaving it the colour of honey and each room was painted in different shades of yellow, green or red. There were potted plants everywhere. Not the spindly little spider plants or the torpid ferns that Preston and Polly struggled to keep half-dead, but flourishing palms and philodendrons and small trees. They had furniture from Heal's or genuine antiques. They had a wooden parrot in a cage. They had an old-fashioned street lamp in the back garden with a York-stone terrace and a white wrought-iron table at which they sometimes ate alone, on a summer evening. The Fischers didn't have any children but they had a huge Victorian rocking-horse in the front room, in the window. Preston suspected that they used it for sexual practices. He imagined Sarah Fischer riding it in the nude while Mark Fischer filmed her with their video camera.

Polly said Preston was obsessed with the Fischers. She said he was always looking up to people he thought were better off than him, instead of looking down and thinking how lucky he was. But she was wrong. Preston always looked down and was terrified of falling.

He opened the gate and fiddled with the hinge to try and make it hang right. But the woodwork was rotten. They needed a new gate. Polly said they needed a second mortgage. Or, at least, that was what she used to say before The Situation. But Preston was afraid of a second mortgage because it would make him feel more trapped than he was already.

Preston wanted to be in a monastery but he was afraid a tree would fall on it and crush him under the walls.

On the reverse side of Preston's image of the Fischers was his image of a man called Mr Studge. Mr Studge was the man Preston feared he might become if he sought security at all costs. Mr S. Studge. No one knew what the S stood for but it might be Stanley. Mr Studge was a combination of all the people Preston had ever known who were victims, starting with his dad. Mr Studge was a teacher, probably, who'd once had a wife and two children but she'd run off with another man because Mr Studge was so boring and secure. Mr Studge had never seen or heard of any of them again. The other man was probably a lion-tamer, Preston thought, or a man who boxed kangaroos.

Mr Studge continued to live alone in the house where he'd lived with his wife and two children. It still had the swing and the slide in the garden but he'd put the toys away in the attic. Every afternoon, about five o'clock, he used to come back from school with his brief-case and a little string bag containing the shopping for his evening meal. Whenever there was a circus in the area Mr Studge used to go to it in the hope of seeing his wife and children in the audience or doing an act on the trapeze. He imagined being in the front row when one or both of the children fell and rushing into the centre of the ring and catching them. And then his wife would come swinging down from the high wires and see him standing there with the children safe in his arms and they would be together again. But it never happened.

Preston was scared stiff of being Mr Studge.

He looked up and saw the children waving at him through the window.

'What are you doing in there?' Polly demanded. 'I want to give the twins their bath.'

Preston was in the bathroom with the door locked and what he was doing was looking at his penis.

The warts had started to hit back. They were red and angry and at least twice as big as they'd been before the treatment. And they hurt. He put some Vaseline on, and as an afterthought, a sprinkling of talcum-powder. It did little to improve their appearance. He put his trousers back on and opened the door.

'Thank you,' said Polly, darting suspicious glances at him and the room. 'You've gone very modest all of a sudden.'

'I wanted to be alone,' Preston said. 'To think.'

'Good God, after all these years.' She started to run the bath. 'Well, if you've caught some dreadful disease from Your Friend don't let me catch you using the towels.'

'I haven't caught any dreadful disease,' said Preston, indignantly.

He hovered in the doorway watching her, thinking what a nice bottom she had. It seemed to him that Polly had put on a bit of weight lately and it suited her. He considered the possibilities of a reconciliation. From his point of view there was a lot to be said for it, what with the children, and Carla, and the warts.

She stood up and turned to face him, pushing the hair out of her eyes. Preston smiled at her.

'If you've got nothing better to do,' she said, 'go and put the kids' toys away. Or can't you do that and think at the same time?'

Obviously there was a fair bit of groundwork to be done first.

'I've got to go up to Liverpool tomorrow,' he said. 'To do a recce for a shoot on Monday. I wondered if you fancied coming up with me for the weekend.'

She stared at him, saying nothing.

'I mean, I'd feel terrible going up there without taking Anna and Daniel,' he said. 'Mum and Auntie Ethel would never forgive me.'

'Well, take Anna and Daniel,' she said.

'They'd like to see you, too.'

'Preston, don't play these games with me,' said Polly.

Preston went for it.

'Look, I'm really sorry about last night,' he said. 'Please come up North. It's ages since we've seen them. Come on. You hurt me, too, you know. More than I hurt you. My big toe's gone black.'

'I'm glad.'

'We could drive up in the car in the morning, and you could take them back on Monday if you liked.'

'I've got the clinic in the morning and then I said I'd have lunch with Miranda.'

Oh yes? He wondered if that meant trouble.

'Well, we could drive up after lunch. I've got some phone calls to make in the morning and one of the tyres needs seeing to on the car. I could take it in.'

She looked at him again and he tried to read the expression in her eyes but it was like trying to read Cobber's.

She looked away and sighed as if she'd been suddenly deflated.

'Oh all right,' she said. 'Now go and get the kids. And tidy up after them,' she yelled as he fled down the stairs, before she changed her mind.

14
LUNCH WITH AN OLD FRIEND

'The trouble is I've got used to being alienated,' said Polly. 'I rather like it.'

'Oh Polly, you can't *like* it.' Miranda seemed quite cross. She put down her fork and stared across the table at Polly with an expression of anguished concern. It was an expression Polly had come to associate with Miranda since their days in the first form together.

'I'm sorry, but I do,' said Polly. 'I don't have to worry about his moods any more. I don't have to tolerate his obsessions, or pander to his fantasies. I don't feel obliged to make it *work* any more. It's very relaxing. I feel very liberated.'

The waiter came and poured more wine.

'Enjoy, ladies,' he said, beaming, 'enjoy.'

Polly beamed back at him until he went away.

'But it can't go on like this, surely?' said Miranda, still anguished, still concerned.

'That's just the point. I'm not sure I can cope if it doesn't.'

'You mean if you don't get divorced?'

'I mean if he wants to get back to normal.'

Miranda shook her head. They ate some more food and drank some more wine.

'If you really feel like that,' said Miranda after a while, 'you should let him know.' She used her firm voice, her head-girl's voice. 'You can't live like this indefinitely. Apart from anything else, it's not fair to him.'

'Hmmm,' said Polly.

Meaning Hmmph.

Thinking, he's got that bloody woman, total freedom to do what he likes outside the home, living space in it. He has an equal role in bringing up the twins. What's this not fair crap? She stabbed a prawn with her fork and raised it to her mouth.

'And another thing,' said Miranda, 'I don't think you should oblige him to come along to NCT classes. He's obviously uncomfortable.'

'Miranda.' This time Polly put her fork down. '*You* were the one who said you needed someone there. You said it was like going to dancing classes without a partner and finding everyone else had taken theirs with them.'

'I wasn't being serious,' Miranda protested. 'I mean, I didn't seriously *mean* you to send Preston along. He's so embarrassed.'

'He's always embarrassed,' said Polly heartlessly. 'Being embarrassed is a condition of being Preston.'

She ate the prawn.

'You want to try living with him,' she said, with the air of one who has and feels it deserves more recognition.

'I'm sure he's not that bad,' said Miranda.

Miranda always had a good word to say for everybody. If she'd been asked what she felt about Hitler she'd have said, Well, he was kind to Alsatians, wasn't he? But Polly sometimes wondered if Miranda didn't rather fancy Preston. She was always going on about what a good father he was and how he always seemed sensitive to Polly's needs.

'He always seems so sensitive to your needs,' said Miranda.

'If he was sensitive to my needs, Miranda,' said Polly, 'he'd dig a large hole in the garden and hop in it and let me push the earth on top and jump up and down on it.'

'You don't mean that, Polly,' Miranda said. Polly didn't mean it. Like Hitler, Polly believed in being kind to Alsatians, but there were limits to her tolerance.

Polly looked at Miranda thoughtfully over her glass of verdicchio. Polly was very fond of Miranda. She had known her a long time, longer than any of her other friends, but sometimes she wondered what was going on behind that frown of compassionate concern. Despite a certain vagueness of manner, Miranda always seemed to know precisely what she wanted and Polly, who didn't, found this mildly irritating.

Miranda was the most uncompetitive person Polly had ever met. For seven years they had shared classrooms, food-parcels, secrets and, occasionally, when the nuns weren't watching, beds. In all that time Miranda had never once expressed the desire to win at anything and yet, seemingly without effort, always succeeded in coming top of the class, or at worst, in the top three. More critical admirers than Polly said that Miranda could be a determined little madam when she put her mind to it.

It was very hard to imagine Miranda seriously putting her mind to Preston, but you never knew. Perhaps it had meant something to her, what had happened.

Polly caught herself up in alarm. She mustn't start thinking like this. This was Preston's doing. She was getting as bad as he was.

'I wish this hadn't happened so soon after ... What Happened,' said Miranda.

'There is absolutely no connection,' Polly snapped.

That was another thing about Miranda. She had a disconcerting habit of picking up the trail of your thoughts and ambushing you with the one you were most anxious to keep to yourself.

'You're getting as bad as he is,' she said.

'So Preston thinks there is?'

Polly could have bitten her tongue off.

'Polly?'

'It's just an excuse he uses,' Polly explained, wearily, 'when he can't think of anything better.'

'Polly, I wish you'd told me.'

'Miranda, believe me, there is nothing to tell you.'

'Did you enjoy, ladies, can I taka your plates?'

Polly averted her gaze from plates, waiter, Miranda and all and looked out of the window. It was raining. A gusty March rain, more Winter than Spring with not the slightest promise of Summer. The restaurant was near Miranda's office in Bloomsbury and through the streaming windows assorted office workers swam, heads down, struggling to keep their umbrellas afloat. Occasionally they came in bringing the rain with them and stood near the door dripping apologetically, waiting for a waiter to find them a table. Polly felt a curious, half-forgotten kinship with these sad, civilised, ordered people. Once, after secretarial college and before the Beeb, she had worked as a temp in an office nearby, in one of the side-streets near the Museum, and though she had hated it then she remembered it with nostalgia now.

Polly was married with two young children, she lived in a house in Chiswick, she had a degree from the Open University, she was a trained social worker and she had a lunatic desire to be someone's secretary again, to return from a sixty-minute lunch break to a warm office, smelling of damp overcoats and waterproofs hung over radiators to dry, with nothing to do but type a few letters and make a few phone calls. 'Hello, this is Mr Smith's secretary, could you put me through to Mr Jones. Hello, Mr Jones, Mr Smith for you. Mr Smith, Mr Jones on the line.' And then Polly would put the kettle on and make some tea with no more effort to be made than the effort of smiling brightly when he looked up from his desk and said as he unfailingly did, 'Ah tea, marvellous.'

But all that was behind her now. Liverpool, she thought, cor blimey, what 'av you come to, Poll my love, an' on a day like this, an' all?

'Look, Miranda,' she said, when the waiter had gone taking his plates and his beaming face with him, 'Preston isn't like you and me. He's like a child. He takes no responsibility for his own actions. It's always someone else's fault. The thing to do is not to start believing it.'

'But you were getting on all right before.'

'No, we weren't, we were getting on each other's nerves. You know what we were like on holiday.'

'But you were still a couple.'

'We're still a couple now, we just don't sleep together.'

The waiter came back with the main course and Polly observed respectful silence while dishes were served, wine glasses topped, pepper ground. It was an inexpensive little restaurant but the service was amiably brisk and the tablecloths clean. Miranda said it was fresh pasta, too, but Polly wasn't too bothered about that. She preferred the ritual of eating to the food itself. Polly liked ritual. She liked order. She imposed it, fairly determinedly, wherever she went. An unexpected journey to Liverpool in what was practically mid-winter smacked of disruption to Polly. Brought up in Fareham and Gosport and Lyndhurst, Polly felt bemused and occasionally harassed by the North of England and six years of living with Preston had not improved her understanding of it, or her tolerance. She sympathised with the plight of the people who lived there and she did not think they were to blame for the mess it was in, but it was still a mess and beyond Polly's powers to set to order. Besides, it was cold and they didn't seem to have learned about draught excluders.

And yet she was quite fond of Preston's mother and his Auntie Ethel who, though inclined to dottiness at times, had basic down-to-earth values not unlike Polly's own. They, too, liked order. Eighteen solid years of Preston must have driven them round the bend. But it wasn't just because of them that Polly had agreed to the trek northward. She wasn't quite sure what else it was, but she was afraid it might have been partly because, despite what she had said to Miranda, she knew The Situation couldn't go on for ever. It was too disordered. If she had rejected Preston's invitation it would have been too much like shutting the door on a mess instead of getting stuck in and tidying things up a bit.

Except that it was a bit like tidying up the North of England. You didn't know where to start and it might not be worth the bother.

'Don't you find that's a bit difficult?' said Miranda suddenly, as if she'd been thinking about something for a while and let it out in a rush.

'What?'

'Not sleeping together.'

'Not at all. It's nice having the room to myself and if I get too cold I have a hot water-bottle. It takes up far less room.'

'I didn't mean that. I meant . . . sex.'

'Oh.'

Polly sipped her wine and wondered what to say.

'Don't you miss it?'

'Not physically, exactly. I mean, you can always do it yourself. But I miss a cuddle sometimes. I suppose it's the emotional security. But then I've got the twins.'

Other friends of Polly's, more direct and less inhibited than Miranda in matters sexual, would have said, But what about *fucking*, but Miranda had always been a bit delicate about things like that and she'd only push it so far. In fact Polly did miss *fucking* occasionally but she felt it was something she could live with.

It was funny about Miranda and sex. For someone so together in other ways she was a mess so far as sex was concerned. She had difficulty talking about it and, to Polly's certain knowledge, she didn't do it much. She was a virgin until she was twenty-seven and then she'd had that strange relationship with an out-of-work television presenter from Tooting who did occasional voice-overs for Carling Black Label. After that it sort of stopped and Polly's greater experience in this field had given her an authority over Miranda which she felt was unmerited, given the control Miranda seemed to exert over almost every other aspect of her life. She owned her own house, she had a job which, while not paying very much, did seem to give her considerable satisfaction, and she always seemed to do very much as she liked. Yet because she didn't have A Relationship she deferred to Polly's judgment in most matters, not just the sexual. Which was ironic considering the problems Polly's Relationships had given Polly.

She had the impression Miranda was struggling to get something else out. Finally, after a larger than usual gulp of wine, she said, 'Polly, has Preston ever talked to you about What Happened?'

'No,' said Polly, neutrally, 'he hasn't.' She knew it embarrassed Miranda and was prepared to tread carefully.

'Doesn't that surprise you?'

'Not particularly. I suppose he thought I'd have been able to figure it out for myself without stretching the imagination too much.'

Miranda blushed.

'Well that's just the point,' she said. 'You might get the wrong impression.'

Polly's good intentions evaporated. Miranda was impossible sometimes. She still looked like the *earnest* sixth-former, with her *earnest* frown and her *earnest* expression, calling them all to order: '*But surely it's a-a-a sort of betrayal to have, gulp, sex before marriage, isn't it? Sister Amelia says . . .* ' and the rest drowned in hoots of sophisticated mirth, as if there wasn't an intact hymen among them. Polly had always thrown a protective veil around Miranda but she had her limits.

'I don't see how I could, in the circumstances, but if there's anything you want to tell me about it, dear, don't think you have to spare my feelings.'

'I was thinking more of his. Oh, all right, Polly Fairfax, I don't know what you're laughing at.'

'I'm sorry,' said Polly. 'Have you decided what to call it yet?'

It was meant to be a change of subject.

'No.'

'Miranda, I'm sorry, but you do ask for it sometimes.'

They forked pasta and salad for a while in silence.

'If it's a girl, Hannah. I don't know if it's a boy.'

'How about Preston?' Polly suggested, keeping her face straight.

'Permit?' said the waiter, gliding up to Miranda's shoulder and reaching for the wine. He emptied the rest of the bottle into their glasses.

'Have you heard why he's called Preston?' said Polly, quickly, in case she'd gone too far. 'It's a typical Preston story. His mum and dad went on honeymoon to Blackpool where Preston was conceived in a boarding-house run by a Mrs Munster – honestly, I'm not kidding – so Mum thought it would be nice to commemorate this in the choice of name but Dad said, We can't call him Blackpool, love, t'other kids'd only laugh at him. So they called him Preston, which was where they changed trains.'

'Poor Preston,' said Miranda.

'Poor Preston,' Polly echoed, raising her glass. 'And poor Polly, now he's dragging me up there.'

'I thought it was Liverpool.'

'Liverpool, Blackpool, Preston, it's all the same,' said Polly, looking at the rain. 'It's all The North.'

'You know what irritates me most about Preston,' she said, after a slow train of thought. 'It's his politeness. His sense of obligation.'

'You mean going to see his mother?' said Miranda. 'I think that's rather nice.'

'Not just that,' said Polly, irritated, 'everything.' Because she was irritated she felt an irresistible sense of mischief.

'Like the way he makes love,' she said. 'When he's lying on top he always leans on his elbows – to take the weight.'

Miranda blushed.

'And he doesn't like to come first. He likes you to come first. And when he does come he always says, Was that all right? I mean,' she said, 'it's very Off-Putting.'

Now, if ever, was the time for Miranda to come clean about What Happened, but Miranda, like the tar baby, was saying nothing. And Polly, like Brer Rabbit, felt a compelling but quite unforgivable desire to slap her across the face.

'Still, I suppose it's better than nothing,' she said, with a sigh, instead, 'though sometimes I do wonder. What do you think?'

15 GO NORTH
Do Not Pass Go

It stopped raining just as they hit the M62 and Preston said, as he usually did about then, 'There's Burtonwood, I always think it looks so sinister, don't you? I wonder what goes on there.'

Burtonwood had been a huge US air-base during the Second World War and its network of runways straddled the motorway for two or three miles. You could still see the original control-tower, bristling weeds instead of antennae, and dwarfed by massive grey-and-black hangars like an inner-city church among the high-rise blocks. Preston claimed no one knew what was kept inside the hangars. He said it could be supplies for US reinforcements in the event of another European war, or it could be poison-gas shells.

'Or maybe it's condoms,' he said. 'Millions and millions of condoms that were meant for the US troops in Europe, only due to a bureaucratic cock-up they forgot to issue them and no one ever wanted to admit it. So they just stayed there, perishing.'

'Until the next time,' Polly said, but she wasn't really thinking about it. She was thinking about what Miranda had said about not wanting her to get the wrong impression. What did she mean exactly, she wondered, but it was too late to ask her now and she wasn't going to ask Preston in case he thought she cared.

Preston was thinking about his roots. It had always seemed a bit of a wasteland, this southern approach to Merseyside, as flat as the Fens and as bleak. The silent air-base, the disused colliery at Cronton, the cold, dank fields where nothing seemed to grow except potatoes and the occasional, sickly tree. When Preston was at university he'd come hitching back here once with a girl-friend and, wanting to impress, taken her on a huge diversion into Wales so they could come into Liverpool the interesting way through the Wirral and across the Mersey by ferry to see the Liver birds and the docks and the ships on the river, but there weren't any ships on the river any more and even the Liver birds had to be tied down to stop them flying off to find work.

They came off the motorway at the Rocket where Stephenson's steam-engine had had its first trial run and run over the President of the Board of Trade, killing him instantly. It always seemed to

Preston a typical Liverpool joke, that. There used to be a pub there, named after the engine, not the politician, where Preston had gone with his mates for his first illicit pints when he was only fifteen. They'd knocked it down to make way for the motorway and then built another one, somewhere under the intersection. It had the same name but it wasn't the same pub.

Preston navigated unerringly to Old Swan where his mum still lived with his Auntie Ethel in the same pre-war council house where, it was said, Preston had been born and his dad had died (though, in fact, both acts had been perpetrated in Broadgreen Hospital down the road), and while Polly woke the twins Preston parked his car and got out and stretched and looked around to make sure nothing had changed.

This was the street he'd grown up in, the street where he'd run wild and joined the Derek Sumter gang and knocked on doors and run away and put fireworks through letter-boxes on Mischief Night, which the rest of the country called Hallowe'en. This was the street where he'd played Kick the Can and Reallio and Biggles, and Wars of the Roses and Robin Hood and Pony Express and Custer's Last Stand and once, due to an aberration and while most of Sumter's Riders were on holiday, with Mavis Arkwright's unbreakable dolls. This was where Sharon Foulds had lifted her skirts for him to see her knickers and been told off by his gran for being a saucy little hussy just like her mum, where, at the age of two and a bit, he'd been given a Coronation mug at a street party to celebrate the Coronation of Elizabeth the Second and seen television for the first time but not remembered it. This was the street where Audrey Blackett kept falling over and being rushed to hospital for a blood transfusion because, according to Alan Stokes, she was a her-maphrodite and where the bin lorry had nearly fallen on top of her brother Jimmy who was accident-prone. This was the street where Preston had come galloping home from the Saturday-morning matinée pretending to be Jesse James and the same Jimmy Blackett had come galloping after him pretending to be a posse and executed a magnificent leap from saddle to saddle just as Preston had put in a burst of speed causing him to miss and impale his cheek on a nail sticking out of the fence of Mrs Malloy's at Number Twenty-Six. Preston could still remember the blood, much darker and redder than when it came out of your knee or your hand, more like the blood that came out when you nicked a wart, and the scream when they pulled him off.

This was the street where Mrs Gladrags had lived. Preston could see her house from where he stood, except that it wasn't her house any more, she'd moved a long time ago and he didn't know where.

'I thought you'd got lost,' said Preston's mum, coming to the gate. 'How's my little cuddles?'

'We were late starting,' said Preston. He presumed she didn't mean him.

She put her arms out for the twins who were still bemused from sleep and clung to their mum in fear and trepidation.

'What's all this, then? Aren't you going to give your nan a hug and a kiss?'

'They've only just woken up,' said Polly. 'They're a bit grumpy.'

Preston never kissed his mum. It was considered soppy when he was a kid and he hadn't changed, even if she had.

He dragged the bags out of the back and the usual travelling circus that accompanied the twins on their nationwide tours and they all went into the house.

'Is that them?' Preston's Auntie Ethel came out of the kitchen, wiping her hands on a tea-towel and looking pleased and anxious at the same time. 'We thought you'd got lost.'

'They were late starting,' said Preston's mum.

'What's all this?' said his Auntie Ethel, when she saw the twins. 'There's a fine pair of faces.'

'They've just woken up,' said Preston's mum. 'Still a bit grumpy.'

This was the bush telegraph of Preston's youth, except that it would have been repeated twice more, then, for the benefit of his gran, who'd been a bit deaf at times. It could be quite relaxing once you got used to it.

'A letter came for you,' said his mum, 'on a motor bike.'

'Ah, good, that'll be the *Echo*.'

'They wanted paying,' said his mum. 'Four pounds.'

Shock, horror.

'I'm sorry, I should have warned you.' Preston dug in his pocket and flushed out a five-pound note.

'It's on the mantelpiece in the living-room.'

Preston tore the envelope open while the twins were wooed with biscuits, Polly notwithstanding.

'We've got several cuttings on a Miss Bernadette McCarthy,' the librarian had told Preston on the phone, 'but the last one's dated four years before you said.'

Preston tipped them out. The first one he saw was across two columns with a picture showing a tall black woman lifting a pair of weights beneath a headline that read, 'Brawn Drain Bernie Goes West.'

'It's steak and kidney pie,' Preston heard his mum explain to Polly. 'Do you like steak and kidney pie, Daniel, grow up a big boy like your daddy?'

'I think it's a bit late for them to have steak and kidney pie,' said Polly, 'perhaps a little scrambled egg?'

'I've got a surprise for you two,' his mum continued in the same daffy tones. 'Shall I fetch it for you? Do I get a kiss first?'

The twins, ever mercenary in such matters, dispensed kisses with abandon.

Six-footer Bernie, Preston read, was quitting the British athletics scene for the more lucrative shores of America. The promising 21-year-old Liverpool weight-lifter was leaving her home to take up a teaching grant at a Washington university. Details of events won. Quote from Bernie: 'I'll be sorry to leave in some ways but there's really no future for me in Liverpool. If I want to succeed in competitive sport I've got to go to America.' Quote from coach: 'It's a terrible loss et cetera et cetera but we can't compete with the kinds of grants and facilities et cetera ... wish her luck in her chosen ...' Bernie, who worked as a physiotherapist in Alder Hey Hospital ... And – wonderful – an address: Bernie, of Granby Road, Toxteth ...

Granby Road, why did that mean something? Preston couldn't think, but there was a faint tinkling of alarm-bells. The other cuttings were of less substance and seemed to be concerned solely with athletic achievements. Preston put them away to read later as his mother reappeared, bearing gifts. A doll for Anna, blonde and wearing a pink dress, and for Daniel a large monkey with a string that you pulled to make it speak. Preston avoided Polly's eye.

Anna sulked.

'Don' wanna doll,' she wailed, warming the cockles of her mother's heart. 'Wanna monkey what speaks.'

'Listen to this, Anna,' said his mum. 'If you turn her on her back like this she makes a noise.'

'Waaaa,' said the doll.

Daniel pulled the string in the side of the monkey. 'I am a very funny monkey,' said the monkey.

'Waaa,' said Anna, 'I wan' the monkey. I don' wan' a doll.'

Preston reflected that if she'd played her cards right she'd have got the bloody monkey. He'd noticed his son casting lascivious glances at the doll but now he knew how badly Anna wanted the monkey there was no chance. He pulled the string again. 'I liiiiiike banana-splits,' said the monkey. It spoke with a curious accent, almost a parody of Maurice Chevalier. Presumably that was how the manufacturers thought monkeys spoke, something to do with the protruding bottom lip. Daniel, beaming, pulled the string again. 'Oooh, oooh, oooh, oooh, you wanna maka monkey outa me?' demanded the monkey. Daniel corpsed. Anna threw the doll at him.

'All right?' Preston asked Polly, on the landing, when they'd put the twins to bed and were about to go downstairs for their steak and kidney pie.

'Yeah, I'm all right,' said Polly, though she didn't sound it.

'They're a bit over-excited,' said Preston.

'At least they're in bed now,' said Polly.

'I meant Mum and Auntie Ethel.'

'Oh.' She considered. 'Well, they're inclined to be a bit silly at times,' she said, tactfully, 'especially with the kids.'

'Let's go and eat,' said Preston.

Normally the evening meal would be consumed in the kitchen or on the lap in front of the television. It would be called Tea, no matter how substantial, and served no later than six o'clock. It was now after eight and the green baize had been taken off the table in the living-room and a white table-cloth substituted. This would be for Polly. Both sisters were slightly nervous of Polly. They thought she was posh. In her company they spoke in an exaggerated version of their own individually tailored and refined Scouse. They lengthened their *a*'s but dispensed with the letter *u* entirely, favouring the more manageable *e*, as in *shegger* for sugar and *better* for butter. They were painfully polite to each other, they switched off the television and had Conversation, they even spoke, tentatively, of Opening Up The Lounge.

The Lounge was the other downstairs room, though no one,

in Preston's memory, had ever lounged there. Preston's gran had preserved it for Occasions – the Occasion of Preston's christening, which he couldn't remember, and his father's funeral, which he could, and his First Communion, which he tried to forget – and the tradition was maintained by his mum and his Auntie Ethel, each blaming the other for being 'daft about it'.

'I'd love to Open Up The Lounge, if only your mother/Auntie Ethel would let me,' was an expression Preston could count on hearing at least twice whenever he came home. The idea vaguely alarmed him, like letting some mad old lady join in a family gathering after being locked up in the attic for half a century. The Lounge was a curious mixture of pre-war kitsch and post-war austerity, a discordance of colours and styles which had faded and settled over the years into a kind of reluctant tolerance, if not harmony. The walls were papered with a design that incorporated a flowering jungle-creeper of a similar pinkish hue but totally dissimilar nature to the one which entwined itself about the carpet. The creeper on the wall was thin and limpid, shrinking into its beigey background as if it didn't want to be noticed. The one on the carpet was a ravenous carnivore of a plant whose writhing stamens or stigmas had given Preston occasional nightmares as a child. In his youthful roman-ticisms he saw them as voracious serpents from the pit of hell, hissing in apoplectic fury at the clinging wraiths on the walls. But time and impotence had tamed them. The wraiths still clung, but the serpents had given up the ghost.

It was impossible to be romantic about the three-piece suite. This was post-war influence, straight, stiff, restrained and kitted in a respectable demob suit of battleship grey with an armour-plating of starched white anti-macassars to guard against the greasy locks that never came. There was a piano from the same era, upright but not grand, never played, but utilised as a stand for a collection of Capodimonte ornaments, each with its own little lace doily. There was a glass-cabinet, rarely opened, known affectionately as The Tallboy and filled with family mementoes including the decorations from Preston's mum's wedding cake and the silver spoon he had been given on his christening. And in centre stage there was an overstuffed mock-leather footstool, referred to, for reasons obscure to Preston, as the pouf.

Preston entered the room at least once during his infrequent visits home to make sure it hadn't changed. There was a cool green light from the curtains which were always half drawn but he hardly ever sat in the chairs or rested his feet on the pouf. He liked the room as a set but it was not that relaxing to stay in, unless, he supposed, you were dead. That was the thing about The Lounge. It was not a room for sitting in, more a room to be laid out in.

Preston preferred the living-room, which was the room for living in. Where he had played with his toys and been bathed as a very small child in a galvanised-iron tub by the fire and had goose-liver oil rubbed into his chest, after first warming in a saucer, as protection against A Chill.

But chills apart, there was a homely warmth about the living-room. This was where the board-games and the sewing-machine were set up on the green baize cloth and where the ironing-board would be established at least three nights a week for the endless piles of ironing, where his gran had reigned supreme and his dad had abdicated his hold on the world, where the TV and the budgie lived, and where his mum and his Auntie Ethel sat and sewed or knitted clothes for the twins and discussed the way of the world and tutted and nodded and frequently squabbled and less frequently ate.

'I hope you've got a good appetite,' said Auntie Ethel, bringing in The Pie.

'Gosh,' said Preston.

'Auntie Ethel, I'm awfully sorry, but I've stopped eating meat,' said Polly. 'Would it be awful of me to just have the vegetables?'

Aaagh, thought Preston.

'Ah,' said his Auntie Ethel.

'Preston, you might have told us,' said his mum, 'and we'd have cooked something else.'

'Sorry,' said Preston who hadn't known, or noticed. 'Forgot.'

'He never thinks,' said his mum to the world in general.

Auntie Ethel said nothing.

'I'm really sorry,' said Polly. 'Tell you what, give me a small piece.'

'Not if you don't want it,' said Auntie Ethel, a little too briskly. 'We wouldn't want to force you. Preston'll just have to eat more that's all.

'I hope,' she said, after the uncomfortable silence which followed this announcement, 'there's nothing wrong with *his* appetite.'

'You're still feeding the twins properly, aren't you, Polly?' said his mother anxiously.

Aaagh, Aaagh, Aaagh, thought Preston.

Polly was right. Mum and Auntie Ethel were inclined to be a bit silly at times. They'd always had that reputation in the street.

His gran said they were soft in the head, but she probably exaggerated. She often exaggerated when she was exasperated with people.

Preston could remember a picture he had once seen of his mum and his auntie, as teenage girls, dressed up in top hats and tights and tails, tap-dancing on a stage. It was a performance they were giving for some amateur do. The Sibell Sisters. Sibell was their maiden name.

He had a vague memory of watching them practise on the living-room floor with the carpet rolled up, arm in arm, kicking out with their short fat legs in the direction of the budgie's cage. But this might have been his imagination.

The point was, Preston felt, that this was their natural state, suppressed by his gran in the interests of respectability and domestic efficiency. And a bit of peace and quiet. Deprived of her moral rectitude, they would start to slide. One day he'd come home and they'd be at it again. Carpet rolled up, all the gear on, canes and all, practising for a Saturday night do for the over-sixties club.

They'd never really grown up, that was the trouble. Or rather, they'd been peculiarly selective about the growing-up process. They'd left a lot of things out because they were unpleasant, or frightening, or a bit too much to have to think about.

Under his gran's iron tutelage they had learned how to wash and press the clothes, hang them on the line, do the normal household chores, even a bit of cooking. Even how to bring up a child, after a fashion. But she'd never been very confident about them and nor was Preston. He didn't think it was their natural forte.

Their natural forte was, as his gran would have put it, to play silly beggars.

They'd got a bit better since she'd died. They'd become a bit more confident. They could even be quite shrewd at times, but they were very erratic. One minute they'd say something you thought was quite sensible and the next they'd be off with some loony theory about

The Causes of Cancer or Why It Isn't Safe To Walk The Streets These Days. At least he hoped it was loony.

On whole areas of knowledge, all the difficult areas: sex, politics, drugs and rock and roll, they were hopelessly ill-informed. They didn't want to know. They wanted to Play Safe.

'Oh, people don't want to know about things like that,' his mother would say, switching over from the news.

They didn't like any Unpleasantness.

They were very delicate about Language. They had their own special code for bodily functions. Thus 'weeing' was known as 'Hurrying Up', as in, 'Preston, do you want to hurry up?'

Anything more substantial was known as 'Doing a Big One'.

This was a considerable burden for Preston to carry through life.

They had a thing about Manners. Preston was taught to raise his hat to people in the street and put his hand over his mouth when he coughed and say, 'Excuse me.' He had to say 'Excuse me' if he made any kind of rude noise at all. Once, during Mass one Sunday, after a breakfast of baked beans on toast cooked by his mum, who should have known better, he'd had whole pews rolling in the aisles.

They were hopeless with drink. It made Auntie Ethel cry and his mum giggly. 'They'd get drunk on a packet of sherbet,' said his gran, who could knock back the stout when she put her mind to it.

Fortunately they didn't touch it much, except at parties, which they didn't go to often.

Another memory. Of Auntie Ethel standing in the middle of the living-room one evening wearing a ball-gown studded with hundreds of sequins he had seen her sewing on herself, wailing helplessly and hopelessly, her face a pathetic crumple of grief, and his mum trying to calm her down while his gran looked at her with her arms folded shaking her head and tutting. With Preston on the floor pushing some toy round in circles, sneaking looks but not wanting to get involved, not knowing how to handle it, this adult pain.

He never knew what it was about. He had grown up thinking it was because his gran wouldn't let her go to the ball, like Cinderella's wicked stepmother whom she resembled faintly, but later he'd decided it was probably some man. Either he'd stood her up or been killed in Korea and his Auntie Ethel was being hysterical about it.

His Auntie Ethel could be hysterical at the drop of a pin, his gran said. She meant at the drop of a hat. Gran was always getting her metaphors muddled but you always knew what she meant.

It was because she'd Never Married, she said. But other times she said, Our Ethel was always a bit like that.

Preston's abiding image of his Auntie Ethel was of her sewing sequins on to party frocks or standing in them in the middle of the room wailing while his mum ran round trying to do something about it.

His mum was hysterical in a different way.

His mum couldn't stop giggling.

The only time she'd stop giggling was when Auntie Ethel was wailing.

His mum was always coming home from the department store where she worked and telling them all some story which Preston could never see the point of but which always ended with her in fits of giggles.

'And then I got the giggles,' she'd say, giggling.

Then she'd start getting him ready for bed and she'd do something silly like putting both feet in the same leg of his pyjamas and that would set her off again. Preston used to watch her, smiling patiently, but really quite puzzled.

Giggling Sheila, his gran used to call her.

Grow up, Nelly, she'd say.

Her name wasn't Sheila or Nelly, it was Elizabeth, but no one ever called her that. It was usually Nell.

'Our Nell married too young,' he heard his gran telling Mrs Blackett, their next-door neighbour, once, 'that's her trouble.'

Preston's gran related most troubles to marriage. Or men.

'One way or another,' she'd say, 'men've made a right mess of our Nell and our Ethel.'

And she'd look at Preston sometimes when she said it, mean-ingfully.

No wonder he'd grown up feeling guilty.

And repressed.

It was his gran who was to blame. She was probably to blame for his mum and his Auntie Ethel and all their problems, too. She was too domineering, that was his gran's trouble.

Preston's gran, who was also called Nell, was a formidable force in the neighbourhood of Old Swan. Preston could remember her slow, stately progress through the shopping-centre with himself in tow, raising his hat to anyone who as much as glanced in his direction. Cronies would come rushing up with the latest scandal which his gran had either heard already or invented. But she'd frown and tut and shake her head and deliver judgment, which was expected of her. Shopkeepers would give her their blarney and be put in their place and be satisfied because that was expected of her, too. Lives would be ordered. Licence condemned. Roguery admonished. Honour satisfied.

And if shopping was the court on tour, the garden gate was her regular Star Chamber. Here she held her audiences and dispensed her rough justice. It was at the gate, of a summer's evening, that Preston remembered her best. Arms folded across her apron, chin wagging, or mouth compressed in a line of silent disapprobation.

Her influence and prestige were a grave disadvantage to Preston. If he was with a crowd of other kids up to mischief of some sort or another, you could be sure someone would be yelling down the street after him, 'I saw you, Preston Moody. I'll be on to your gran about you.' As if the rest of them were invisible or something. Once, one Saturday, he'd been down the railway-cutting all day making a den with the Derek Sumter gang and three women had been on to his gran about him before he got home for tea, and one of them was the wife of one of the train drivers who'd come all the way from Knotty Ash to tell her.

His gran was always the one who sorted him out when he was up to no good, the only one he feared. She was the matriach. She was 'She'. 'She's always getting at me,' he'd complain tearfully to his mum or his Auntie Ethel. 'She's always saying I can't do this and I can't do that.' And his gran would stand there and say, 'Who's she, the cat's mother?'

She was a stout, strapping woman with arms made strong from the beating of carpets and the stirring of scouse and no one dared cross her. 'I'll take the poker to you if I have any more trouble,' was her favourite threat, but she never raised a finger to him, not as far as he could remember.

He sometimes wondered what she was like with his grandad, who'd died during the war, before Preston was born. He'd been killed while he was working down at the docks and Preston had assumed for a long while that it was a bomb that did it, but it wasn't, it was a crate dropped accidentally from a crane.

'Ah, he was always getting things dropped on his head,' his gran said, when he asked her about it. 'Always coming home wrapped up in a bandage.'

From then on Preston had always imagined his grandad scurrying about the docks in splints and bandages while crane drivers dropped crates on him. He asked his gran what was in the crate that finally killed him but she said she didn't know. Preston thought she was lying. It was inconceivable to him that she wouldn't have asked.

Death seemed to have it in for the men of Preston's family and Preston grew up in the belief that it was mostly their fault. They didn't take enough precautions, or they weren't sufficiently informed, like his dad.

Preston's dad, having joined the Navy in the last year of the war, had decided to stay on and make it his career. To further compound this foolishness he had volunteered, while attached to the Caribbean station as a leading-seaman, to serve in a tank-landing ship that was being used to monitor the effect of radiation in a nuclear war.

The ship had duly put to sea and been bombed with bags containing radioactive dust so that scientists could measure the effect it had on the steel plating. It didn't seem to occur to them, and it certainly didn't to Preston's dad, that it might have a rather more drastic effect on the men below decks.

There was never any suggestion that this was a possible cause of the leukaemia and certainly no suggestion that he might be compensated for it. Indeed, it was only when Preston was in his twenties that his mum had told him about the incident. She'd 'read something in the papers' she said, and wondered vaguely 'if it might have had something to do with it'.

So Preston became the only child of a three-parent family, all women. They comforted him, cosseted him, disciplined him and dressed him decently. They helped him with his homework, fought his battles, bought him books and taught him Manners. If his mum and his Auntie Ethel were inclined to be a bit silly at times, well, it didn't really matter while his gran was alive. His gran was never silly. As a collective parenthood their only serious defect, Preston considered at the time, was that they were no good at boxing or football, though his gran might have been if she'd put her mind to it, and it was no use going to them for any information about Sex. Not if it could be classed as Smut, which it usually was.

Which was why it was such a problem when Billy Quirk told him a lady's front was much better than the back because it had two tits and a willy.

Billy claimed to know this because he'd seen his mum lying in the bath. Totally Nude.

This was pretty sensational and Preston suspected it to be Totally Untrue, but it was a difficult lie to challenge. If Billy Quirk had said he'd seen Biggles in the nude, Preston could have asked him where the scars were and been pretty confident of catching him out, but so far as the female body was concerned, Preston was at a bit of a loss. Vaguely, almost instinctively, he knew Billy Quirk was wrong, and that ladies couldn't possibly have willies, but he didn't know why he thought that. It was a subject he hadn't actually considered before and when he did start to consider it he came to the conclusion that they had to have something to wee with, and what could it possibly be if it wasn't a willy – a big hole in their skins? The wee would just trickle down their legs.

As a normal healthy child of seven and a bit, Preston's knowledge of female anatomy was confined to what he'd seen of his gran and his mum and his Auntie Ethel, which was not a lot. None of them had so far felt inclined to invite him into the bathroom for a view. They had their baths behind locked doors and, for all Preston knew, wearing a bathing costume. It was impossible to imagine any of them ever Totally Nude. And what had evaded him in the flesh was not then readily available between the covers of a magazine. In those days children of seven and a bit did not browse through soft porn in the newsagents where they bought their packets of penny chews, liquorice allsorts and sherbet dips. They were the children of soldiers and sailors and airmen, of Wrens and Wracs and Waafs, and Preston's reading matter was confined to comics which showed full frontals of Spitfires and Hurricanes, Sabres and MiGs. He could tell a Sherman tank from a Churchill at a thousand paces. He could mentally strip a Bren gun and put it back together again in 35 seconds flat, but a woman's body, back or front, was a total mystery to him and if his gran and his mum and his Auntie Ethel had anything to do with it likely to remain so well into the foreseeable future.

'They've got hairs on as well,' Billy Quirk had said. 'All around their willies. Little curly ones.'

It was unthinkable, of course, that he could have come straight out with it and asked them. This was Smut, no question.

'Who told you that?' they'd say, and when he said, 'Billy Quirk,' they'd say: 'That Billy Quirk's a bit too advanced for his age,' and he'd be sent away with a flea in his ear, none the wiser. Or they'd stop him from playing out for a week like they did when his gran caught Sharon Foulds lifting her skirt to show him the colour of her knickers.

Sharon was a possibility, of course. Or any of the girls in the street, but it wasn't the sort of thing you could come out with and ask, not if you were brought up with manners like Preston, and ever since the Sharon Foulds incident they were a bit wary of Preston, or his gran which came to the same thing. The lads of the neighbourhood were out of the question for quite a different reason, but one which could also be blamed on his gran and her minions. In the misguided belief that something you paid for had to be better than something that was free, they had sent Preston to a small fee-paying private school, rather than the local state primary which accommodated the rest of the Derek Sumter gang. This meant that Preston had to be careful about getting things wrong, because they'd never let him forget it, and even more careful about getting them right. Superior knowledge in the Derek Sumter gang, unless you were Derek Sumter, could be a dangerous thing.

So Preston learned to live with the problem, while desperately scratching around for clues. He'd come close to cracking it once or twice, but never conclusively. There was the time when his class had been taken to the Walker Art Gallery in William Brown Street and there, on the stairs going in, he'd seen a huge portrait of a woman, tied to a rock, Totally Nude.

The Totally Nude Woman possessed two very substantial breasts, complete with nipples, but there was nothing remotely resembling a willy. Just a mass of tight curly hairs where, according to Billy Quirk, the willy should have been.

Preston had been staring at this, exulting quietly, when a familiar voice had said, 'They won't let 'em paint it on.'

Preston had turned to find Billy Quirk standing at his elbow, looking relaxed and confident.

'It's against the law,' he said. 'They'll allow tits but not willies. It's the same with men.'

This was infuriating but true. There were paintings of Totally Nude Men distributed generously throughout the gallery but none with willies. Leaves, yes, bits of old cloth, posies of flowers even, but not willies.

Preston couldn't recall the magic moment when he had resolved the matter to his complete satisfaction. It was possible that he never had. Perhaps, in abstract terms, Billy Quirk had been right. Perhaps Billy, gifted beyond belief, had seen something which evaded lesser men, something in the fundamental posturing of women which bespoke two tits and a willy.

Preston had grown up surrounded with women but he had very limited knowledge of them, Totally Nude or otherwise. He was attracted to them from time to time, and he liked them to be attracted to him, but his fear of them was stronger. It seemed to him now that while he had always found women's underwear a real turn on he had never been entirely sure about the women for whom it was designed. In the language of the Derek Sumter gang he had failed to gerragrip on the subject.

It would be interesting to go to bed with his wife again. He contemplated the prospect while in the bathroom examining his warts and wondering if they'd pass muster in a poor light. He hadn't actually discussed sleeping arrangements with Polly but he assumed an unspoken truce was in operation while they were up here. She couldn't very well expect him to sleep in a separate room. Apart from the effect this would have on his mum and Auntie Ethel there wasn't one. The twins were in the spare and there was only a double-bed in the room they were sleeping in. She could ask him to sleep on the floor, but this would be unreasonable. Of course, sleeping together was one thing, sex quite a different matter. He'd looked in Polly's washbag to see if she'd brought her cap but if she had it was somewhere else. Inside her? This seemed unlikely, but Preston had purchased a packet of Durex just in case. He took them out of his pocket and wrapped them carefully in a wad of tissues which he could keep under the pillow. It was an outside chance, but you never knew.

Before he went to join Polly he checked on the twins. They were sleeping top to tail in a single bed in the box-room. The covers had fallen on the floor and Preston rearranged them over the recumbent figures. Going out he trod on something that said Waaa. The doll. There was no sign of the monkey.

As he emerged from the room he just caught sight of Polly going into the bathroom. To put her cap in? But if she did he would have the moral dilemma of whether to tell her about his warts, whereas if he wore a Durex he wouldn't have to. Sex was never simple, even when you wanted it.

He walked into the bedroom and stopped dead. The monkey was in the bed. Dead centre, with its idiot smiling face just sticking out of the sheets. Preston stared at it, his mind working fast. Had Polly put it there? Or perhaps his mum as a joke? Or Daniel to keep it safe from Anna?

He was clutching at straws. It was Polly. It was an unspoken warning to him to keep his distance. He put the tissues in his hold-all and took out the book he had bought by Eva Eichler, the precursor to *Men – the Second Sex*. Then he took off his jeans and got into bed with the monkey. He could hear the sound of running water in the bathroom. He pulled the string in the ape's side.

'Oooh, oooh, oooh, oooh,' it said. 'You wanna maka monkey outa me?'

Preston opened his book. The precursor to *Men – the Second Sex* was about women and it was called *Coming First*. Preston began to read Chapter One.

'When a woman is taught self-defence,' he read, 'the first rule she must learn is to overcome her natural reluctance to hurt.'

16 GO TO TOXTETH
Throw Six to Escape

He knew why he'd heard of Granby Street now. Granby Street was the Front Line. The epicentre of the Toxteth riots. The moment he turned off Upper Parliament Street Preston was in bandit territory.

'You're never going to Toxteth,' said his Auntie Ethel, 'I don't know, some people need their heads seeing to.'

His Auntie Ethel tended to exaggerate the perils of living on Merseyside.

'Whatever you do,' she said, 'don't stop at the traffic-lights.'

'Pardon?' said Preston.

'They smash your windows with bricks and steal your handbag,' said Auntie Ethel. 'It happened to Mrs Butler at Number 28.'

'They' were the blacks. In Auntie Ethel's violent world of sex, drugs and civil disorder, the blacks were the Red Indians and certain parts of Liverpool the Wild West. But Preston didn't have a handbag and he was far too law abiding to jump the lights, even in Toxteth.

It wasn't the Wild West, but it reminded Preston of Belfast, except that there were no army patrols, yet. The streets were the same back-to-back terraces he'd seen in news reports of the Crumlin Road and the Falls, but instead of the Union Jacks and the Republican battle cries there was the red, orange and green of pan-Africa and the Rastas and the African National Congress. The Front Line, said the graffiti on the red-brick walls. Stay Cool in the Pool. Smack City. Preston parked the car outside a row of shops and decided to walk the rest of the way.

The shop windows were protected with steel mesh and outside the Halal butchers there was a huge scorch mark in the road. Preston wondered if it was the last car that had been parked there.

He'd checked the telephone book but there wasn't a McCarthy in Granby Street and he didn't fancy knocking on every door until he found one. So he crossed the barricades into one of the shops and asked the woman at the cash register.

'I wonder if you could help me, I'm looking for a family called the McCarthys. I believe they live in Granby Street.'

Silence. Not just from the woman but from the whole shop. It was a supermarket, run by Asians. Half a dozen shoppers browsing among the shelves and Preston the only white face in there, except that it was slowly turning red.

'Bernadette McCarthy, does the name mean anything to you? She was an athlete. A weight-lifter.'

'Can I help you?' A man came and stood next to the woman. Small, dapper, a little black moustache. Preston smiled hopefully and repeated his request but the man also shook his head.

'Who's askin'?' This was another woman, beads in her hair, wearing jeans and a white T-shirt with a flag the same colour as the street-signs.

'I'm trying to trace a woman who was a weight-lifter. Quite well known. There were stories about her in the *Echo*.'

'And what's it to you?'

'It's for a sports programme,' Preston lied, 'for the BBC.'

'What? You from the BBC?'

'Yes,' said Preston, still smiling.

The woman looked at him for a moment. Then she said, 'Fuck you,' and walked out of the shop.

Preston nodded as if in silent agreement.

The small man with the moustache said, 'You better leave this place.' He seemed anxious about it.

'Perhaps there's a newsagents,' Preston said, 'where I could ask. She's probably left the area but the family might still live here.'

No one answered.

'Please. Leave now,' said the shopkeeper.

This was silly and Preston scratched his chin, frankly embarrassed, trying to think of something to say to save face, but he couldn't and there was no other point in staying. He went outside and looked up and down the street as if it might provide a clue. There was no sign of the woman in the white T-shirt. His car was still there. Still intact.

'Number 42,' said a voice and another woman hurried past without looking at him, pulling a small trolley loaded with shopping. Preston opened his mouth to say thank you, but decided against it. This was the world of Auntie Ethel's nightmares. He walked up the street feeling like the sheriff in *High Noon*. There was no one in sight, not even a dog, and it had started to rain, a thin drizzle, but very wet.

Number 42 was just like the rest of the houses. Two floors, a bay-window with net curtains, red-brick walls. There was no bell, no knocker, and he had to rap with his knuckles on the wood. A dog started to bark and after a short while a claw appeared through the letter-box. Jesus, thought Preston.

He looked up and down the street but it was still empty. At the very far end was his car. He heard a voice, reassuringly human, shouting at the dog and then the door opened.

'Hello,' said Preston. 'I'm sorry to bother you . . . ' The dog sprang for his throat. A strong arm intervened. The door was closed. Preston listened to the sound of blows from within. The dog yelped and then was silent. The door opened again.

'Sorry about dat. Fuckin' dog's a fruitcake.'

This was an elderly man, though by no means feeble, with grey woolly hair cut close to his skull and the features of an amiable prize-fighter who'd lost a lot of fights but had no hard feelings.

'That's quite all right,' said Preston. 'I was looking for a Miss Bernadette McCarthy.'

'Why, what's she gone an' done?'

'Nothing,' said Preston, encouraged, 'not to my knowledge, at least. I'm from the BBC . . . '

'Fuck Nell and you're still livin'? Get in, quick.'

Preston got in, and the man looked down the street both ways and shut the door.

'They've gorra down on your lot. Don' ask me why. Whararyer, Sports? Might geraway wiv it, but I wouldn't put money on it.'

Preston wondered who 'They' were, but it was probably better not to ask. With luck he'd never need to know.

'I won't stay long,' he said, 'I just wondered where Bernie was living these days. She's not here is she?'

'Bleedin' right she's not. Yer better speak to 'er mam.'

'You're Mr McCarthy?'

It was a reasonable assumption. Though Liverpool to the core he was at least as black as the woman in the picture.

'Give over. 'E done a bunk years ago. Stick yer nose in dere yer'll see why.'

He opened a door and Preston walked into a rehearsal for the next Toxteth riots. He had been wondering what the noise was. Now he knew. The room was full of children, in many shapes and sizes and all shades of brown. At a quick guess, without conducting a roll-call, Preston would have said there were at least six of them and they were all shouting. In an armchair, in the far corner, with her feet up reading the paper was a very large woman.

''E's after your Bernadette,' said the man who wasn't Mr McCarthy. 'From the BBC.'

The woman put the paper down. She was white and all shades of grey.

'And what does 'e want with our Bernadette?'

'Mrs McCarthy?' said Preston. He had to shout a bit.

'Shut up you lot I won't tell you again,' said the woman.

There was a slight reduction in the noise level. A couple of the older boys looked at Preston curiously.

'What's it to you?' she said.

She could have been any age from forty to sixty, Preston judged. Her face was unlined but in the way that many fat faces are, hiding a multitude of sins, and her hair was tied in a scarf with a few greyish strands escaping. She didn't stand up but Preston saw that his first impression of her size was accurate. This was the mother of six-foot Bernie.

'I'm trying to contact Bernadette,' said Preston, 'for a sports programme.'

'For a what?'

''E's from the BBC,' the man repeated irritably, 'doncher ever listen. Fuck Nell.'

'Well you won't find 'er here,' said the woman. Her accent was less pronounced than the man's and Preston thought there might be a touch of Irish in it. There were Catholic prints on the walls, the kind his Auntie Ethel would have called common, and a photo of the current Pope on the television set.

'Have you any idea where I can find her?' said Preston, jollying her along.

He might as well have tried to throw her over his shoulder. 'She went to America,' she said, sly with suspicion.

'I heard she came back, though, with her employer.' He pretended he had to think of the name. 'A woman called Eva Eichler.'

She shrugged. If the name meant anything to her she hid it well.

'News ter me,' she said, 'but I'd be the las' ter know.'

'What sports programme d'yer work on?' This was from one of the lads, the eldest, a wiry-haired scally of ten or eleven. 'D'yer know Greavesy and the Saint?'

'Shut yer face, you, it's the engine-driver 'e's speakin' to, not the oily rag.'

Through the window behind her Preston saw four men crossing the street towards the house. They wore T-shirts worryingly similar to that worn by the woman in the shop.

'Fuck Nell.' The man who was not Mr McCarthy had seen them too. 'It's the 'eavy mob.'

'What's up?' She twisted round in the chair. Several of the kids ran to the window.

'Quick, out the back.' The man grabbed Preston's arm and hustled him through to the kitchen. ''Ow d'yer gerere?'

'By car,' said Preston, thoroughly alarmed, 'I left it up at the shops.'

The back door opened on to a small yard with a line of washing and the dog. It bared its teeth hopefully and snarled.

The heavy mob began to pound on the front.

'Kenny, where are yer?'

The oily rag materialised, loving every minute of it.

'Gowirim. Down dthe jigger. 'Is car's at dthe shops.'

He slammed the back-door shut behind them and the dog lunged a second time. The oily rag kicked it in the head and as it retreated followed up with a boot up the bum. Preston opened a rotting wooden door in the wall and looked up a dingy back-entry full of rubbish and more dogs, scavenging. The oily rag pushed him out and they ran.

When they reached the end of the entry Preston looked back and saw the first T-shirt come shooting out of the door.

He ran on, faster than he'd run in years, the oily rag a length ahead. Down another entry and into the street. The car was still there. Preston fumbled with his keys.

'Fuck Nell,' the oily rag said. 'Gerragriponit.'

The door opened. Preston fell into the driver's seat and tried with trembling fingers to fit the key into the ignition. He didn't dare look round. The kid was pounding on the window. Help me, God, Preston sobbed, Holy Mary, Full of Grace.

The key turned, the engine started. Preston leant over and opened the passenger-door and the kid dived into the car and put his arms over his head and they were halfway up Upper Parliament Street and still going strong before Preston started to wonder what he was doing abducting a ten year old.

He pulled up at the intersection with Smithdown Road where even Auntie Ethel might have lingered for a minute or two.

'Well thanks very much,' he said. 'But shouldn't you be getting back to your mum?'

'I thought you wanted to know about our Bernie,' he said.

Preston looked at him. 'You know where she is?'

'No,' he said, 'but my sister Terry will.'

'Your sister Terry?'

'Short for Teresa.'

'And where's she?' said Preston.

'Cost yer a tenner,' said the oily rag.

17 MEET TERRY
Go on a Bit

Ten minutes later, ten pounds the poorer, Preston drove through heavy rain towards the south of the city.

He drove very carefully, wondering if he was in a state of shock.

He asked himself a number of times what he was doing, but the possibilities were endless. Impersonating a BBC sports producer, distributing tenners to the deserving poor, having a nervous break-down, digging himself out of a mire, digging himself further into a mire, playing some grown-up, deadlier version of Right Roads and Wrong Roads ...

He thought he knew what he had in mind. A documentary for network features, an escape from *Shrews at Ten* and Carla and Mr Studge and the future prospects of Mr Studge, but he was beginning to have serious doubts about the route.

He was driving to Netherley, one of the vast council estates in the outer suburbs, built in the sixties for refugees from the inner-city clearances, now just another eighties' slum, all soaring concrete and breeze block. High-rise blocks, low-rise blocks, gaunt monoliths linked by overhead walkways and dark, dangerous underpasses. Preston knew it by repute. His mum called it Alcatraz and lately, it seemed, a more progressive council had come to the same conclusion and resolved upon whole-scale evacuation. Many of the blocks were empty and presented a broadside of black, broken windows behind a barricade of barbed-wire and corrugated-iron. Signs warned of security patrols and guard dogs. Others, with desperate optimism, advertised sites for light industry.

But not everyone had escaped.

He was driving to Netherley because this was where Bernadette's sister Terry lived. In Number 66 Dorchester Heights. According to their little brother, the oily rag, who had sold her for a tenner. A tenner for Terry. Terry for Teresa. Another good Catholic girl.

Dorchester Heights was one of the tower blocks. Half the windows were boarded up, but the rest kept their net curtains flying like dingy white flags waiting for the housing officer to present his terms. Preston took the lift up to the sixth floor and knocked on Number 66.

There was no answer. He knocked again, turning to look out over the balcony. He could see the outer ring-road of the estate marked by a line of tall street lights, oddly sinister, for all their familiarity, like floodlights guarding some dangerous frontier, and beyond, in another world, fields, pylons, a couple of farmhouses, barns. A door opened and he turned but it wasn't the one he was standing at.

'Who you after?'

A woman, from the next-door flat, neither young nor old, just tired, surrendered a long time ago and no one taking a blind bit of notice.

'Teresa,' he said.

'Oh aye,' she said. 'You a friend of hers?'

'The family,' he said.

'Oh aye?'

He watched her and wondered if being a friend of the family was worse than being a policeman or a snoop from Social Security.

'She's gone to the precinct,' she said.

'Ah?' he said. 'Well, I'll pop back later.'

Depressed by the estate he drove past the perimeter in search of a pub to pass the time until Teresa McCarthy came back from wherever the precinct was. He found a refurbished country-inn on the road to Widnes full of repro brass and harness where he bought himself a beer and a cheese sandwich and settled down in a corner with his copy of *Coming First*.

He was well into it now and he thought he knew what it was about. It was about Success. It was about how an intelligent female with her wits about her could overcome the crippling handicap of being a woman and achieve Fame and Recognition, along with a considerable amount of Material Comfort, Political Power and Sexual Pleasure, by arguing fair play for cripples while tripping up all competition with her crutches.

'Success for one individual woman,' wrote Eva Eichler, 'is one more battle won in the long struggle for sexual equality.'

'Don't be reluctant to learn from men,' wrote Eva Eichler, 'look who runs the world.'

'Women,' wrote Eva Eichler, 'if they are to compete with men, must learn to overcome their natural reluctance to draw blood. Lady Macbeth came to a bad end, but remember, the writer was a man.'

Preston bought himself another half from the bar and trudged miserably back to his corner.

'Don't worry,' said a man on the next table. 'It might never happen.'

Preston put a brave face on it, that is to say he smiled reassuringly, but he was thinking hard. But what if it does, he was thinking, but what if it already has?

Preston was the New Man, a born-again feminist. Preston believed in sexual equality. In theory. He was just a bit worried about how it worked in practice.

In practice, it seemed to Preston, sexual equality posed something of a threat to the working classes.

The problem, as he saw it, was that the working classes had just, for the first time in history, won limited access to the glittering prizes. Ironically, it was at that precise moment that someone had invented Feminism.

Preston wasn't saying this was a conspiracy. If anything he subscribed to the cock-up theory of history. But it seemed to him that an awful lot of middle-class feminists were after the same slice of the cake so recently carved up by honest aspiring working-class lads like himself. He didn't mind so much if they were prepared to fight fair. But they weren't. They used crutches, and if they didn't trip you up with them they put them between your legs and brought them up sharp.

It made it very difficult keeping to the code of conduct imposed on the New Man. It seemed to him that either feminists knuckled down and helped to make the cake a bit bigger or else you had to take their crutches away from them.

'I'm not a violent man,' said the man on the next table, to his companion, 'but I'd put a bullet between her eyes, no hesitation, after what she's done to the working classes.'

Exactly, thought Preston.

He finished his beer and took himself off in search of Teresa McCarthy.

The ideal size for a woman was, in Preston's opinion, five foot two and a half. He wasn't absolutely sure why this was but he had once known a woman of five foot two and a half and he had felt very secure with her. He could look over her head without standing on tiptoe and yet she was not so small as to increase the risk of trampling on her by mistake.

Preston didn't know why it was so important to look over a woman's head. Perhaps it went back to his early ball-room dancing days when it was a definite advantage, or perhaps it was something altogether more significant. He worried about it a lot without coming to any concrete conclusions, except that he liked a woman to be five foot two and a half.

Polly was five foot seven.

Carla was five foot six.

Teresa McCarthy was, at a rough estimate, six foot two.

'We've always been big girls in our family,' said Teresa, when he remarked on it, 'and the lads've bin titches. I think it's something to do with me mum.'

They were sitting down in her kitchen, which was better, from Preston's point of view, than standing up.

'Mind you, I'm only five foot eleven,' she said, 'but I s'pose I'd seem bigger to you.'

Preston felt like pointing out that a man of five foot eight and a half was not officially classed as a dwarf but decided to let it pass for the time being.

''Course our Bernie's six foot. She was always trying to go one better than me. Wouldn't be surprised if she had two kids by now.'

Teresa's daughter Justine sat in her high-chair across the kitchen-table. Preston had no problem with Justine's height, even standing up.

'Hello then,' he said. 'There's a big smile. Tchkk, tchkk.'

She was even easy to talk to.

'She's the main object I got this place, Justine, well, I wasn't going to bring a baby up at me mum's, well you've been there, you've seen it.'

'Mmmm,' said Preston.

'There was ten of us living in Granby Street an' only one with any clout and that was 'er. An' if there's a programme she wants the rest of us might as well sit on our fingers. She'd 'ave *Coronation Street* an' *Crossroads* morning, noon an' night. You'd go soft in the 'ead. I mean you've seen me mum, you know what she's like.'

'Mmmm,' said Preston.

Terry was a telly addict. That, Preston suspected, was the sole reason he was sitting here with his feet firmly planted under the table, dunking ginger-nuts in his tea and making gurgling noises from time to time at the baby. From the moment he'd announced he was from the BBC it had been plain sailing. He'd stuck to his story about trying to make a documentary about young athletes but she seemed more keen to talk about herself than Bernadette. Preston didn't mind. He was interested.

'Mind you,' she said, 'it's a terrible place for a kid, Netherley. Bleedin' awful for a grown-up, too.'

Terry looked as if she was making the best of it. The flat was cold and the furniture sparse but it was painted in bright, cheerful colours with plenty of posters on the walls. She'd done it up herself, she said, and Preston gathered there wasn't a man around. She was twenty-two, big-boned and gawky, but he thought she was beautiful. She had wide-open features and huge brown eyes and a grin that lit the room up, let alone her face. She had the wry, self-mocking humour of the typical scouse but she wasn't going to let anyone else put her down.

'Yer've got t'stand up for yerself or they'll walk all over yer,' she said, 'I learned that from our Bernie. She won't take nothink from no one.'

Preston took his cue.

'When d'you last hear from her?'

'Let's think, Justine would've bin about six months, so it must've bin a year ago.'

'And she was in England?'

'Well that's where she posted the letter from.'

'No address?'

'No, but that's typical of our Bernie. Didn't say much neither, just that she was doin' all right an' a postal order for five 'undred quid so I s'pose she mus' be.'

'She sent you five hundred quid?'

'Yeah.' She gave him the look he'd seen at the door, before he told her he was from the Beeb. 'Ey, you're not 'avin' me on are yer, an' yer from The Sosh all along.'

'Ah come on, Terry, I showed yer me security pass.'

Among compatriots, saving his Auntie Ethel, Preston tended to lapse into the vernacular after a while.

'Yeah,' she said, 'but they could 'ave them forged. I wouldn't put anythink past that lot.'

His laughter encouraged her to launch into a long diatribe against The Sosh and the housing office and every other authority she'd come up against including the courts who she accused of being biased towards men in their assessment of maintenance orders.

'I get twenty quid a week out of the bugger an' his bleedin' lawyer says 'e needs thirty for 'is bleedin' car.'

By 'The Bugger' Preston gathered she meant Justine's father.

'An' then they wonder why you go on the game,' she said.

Preston made a gurgling noise at Justine to cover his confusion. But Justine was well into a plate of rice pudding and not to be distracted. Terry launched into a long summary of her various encounters with Authority. She'd recently been put on probation, she confessed cheerfully, for CPL.

Preston wondered if this was a drug.

'Common Prostitute Loiterin',' she explained. 'Bleedin' nerve, I said to them, there's nothink common about me, kid. Then they switched off me electric.'

'I'm sorry?' said Preston, confused. 'For CPL?'

'For not payin' the arrears.'

'Ah.'

They in Terry's book meant anyone in authority – from the Electricity Board to the Government.

'I re-connected soon as they was out the door. I wasn't goin' to freeze for them bastards. An' they done me for that, too.' Justice, Terry implied, had it in for her personally and with malice afore-thought. But the ferocious scowl turned into a swift grin.

'When they came round the bloke said I'd joined the wrong wires together. 'E said, You could have taken this place off the map.

'They took me screwdriver away.'

Preston rehearsed a conversation he would have with Polly or Carla one of these days, when he was feeling brave, when he would tell them about Teresa and how she was what Real Feminism should be about, not just jobs for the girls. Teresa and Women Like Her have basic needs and problems which All True Feminists should tackle as a priority, he would say. The struggle for the rights of Teresa and Women Like Her was one which Preston, as a New Man, could enter into without reservation. He didn't feel threatened by Teresa. He didn't think she'd be after him with her crutches. Teresa was a breath of fresh air after *Coming First*. It was just a pity she wasn't five foot two and a half.

'I was in dead stuck till our Bernie come up with that money I don't mind tellin' you. She said I'd got to spend it on me and Justine. She said I wasn't to go spendin' it on no blokes. Typical Bernie, that.'

'So she knew you'd had Justine?'

'Must've. She knew I was pregnant, anyway, cos she was up 'ere just before she was born.'

'What, in the Pool?'

'Yeah she came to see us all. Well, the kids anyway, she never had no time for me mum.'

'And how old's Justine?'

'Sixteen months.'

'Was she with anybody?'

'How d'you mean?'

'I mean, she'd just got back from the States, right? Was she with anyone?'

'A bloke, you mean? Our Bernie?' Teresa seemed to consider this amusing but unlikely.

'Well, I was thinking of a woman, actually.'

'Well if she was she din't bring 'er round Granby Street. She was stayin' at the Adelphi. Looked dead flash an' all.'

'You mean the way she was dressed?'

'Yeah, you know she's always dressed a bit down, our Bernie. Boiler suits an' that, when she could find anything to fit 'er, but she was wearin' some dead smart gear this time. Still a boiler suit but it was a smart boiler suit.'

'Was she still into weight-lifting and all that?'

'Naw. Not competitive any road. Tell the truth I don't think she was ever that interested. It was just an escape for 'er, like, a way of gettin' outer the Pool.'

'What was she doing then, did she say?'

'Yeah.' She looked at him as if she was a bit puzzled, either that or weighing him up. 'Said she was somebody's minder.'

'Somebody's *minder*?'

'Yeah. I thought she was havin' me on to tell the truth but you never know with 'er. She's a big girl, our Bernie, an' she's been doin' karate since she was seven years old.'

'Did she ever mention someone called Eva Eichler?'

'No. Who's she when she's about? A Germin?'

'Someone she worked for. She'd have been working for her when she came over that time.'

'Well maybe it was 'er she was mindin'. She must've paid well. Ey, you, up the dancers.'

This last remark was addressed at Justine who had tired of smearing rice pudding and raisins over her high-chair and was emitting a high-pitched wailing noise.

With ruthless efficiency she was wiped clean and whisked away to her quarters. The wailing continued but behind closed doors.

'God 'elp us if she takes after 'er dad,' said Terry when she came back.

Preston inclined his head in polite interrogation.

'Bleedin' noise,' she said. ''E's a singer. Least 'e bloody thinks 'e is. I found this, by the way, didn't think I'd kept it.'

It was the letter from Bernadette.

Terry was right. She didn't say much. *Hope you're all right and the babe. I've come into some money so I'm sending you a few quid. Don't spend it on blokes.* Written in a bold, sprawling hand and filling one side of a sheet of notepaper. No address.

Preston looked at the envelope. It was postmarked Felixstowe and dated a month after Eva Eichler's midnight swim.

'Now she's gone down, fancy another cup of tea,' said Terry, 'or would you rather have a fuck. Special rate for shortarses.'

18 DINNER WITH THE WIFE
Throw Again

'Where d'you think you've been?' said Polly, or his grandmother reincarnate.

'Sorry,' said Preston. 'Took longer than I thought.'

'You drag me up here and then leave me three hours with your Auntie Ethel. This is grounds for divorce, Preston.'

'Ho, ho,' said Preston, 'I thought you liked my Auntie Ethel.'

'In small doses. Three hours is not a small dose. Three hours could kill.'

This exchange was conducted in the usual low level hiss that passed for conversation between them during their infrequent visits to Preston's family home. They could hear the subject of the discussion clattering pans in the kitchen and humming a hit tune of her youth. His mum had taken the twins to the park.

'I've had Auntie Ethel's views on child rearing, the breakdown of law and order and why you turned out the way you did,' said Polly. 'And frankly, I can't take any more.'

'You should have gone with my mum,' said Preston, but his mind was on other things. Within minutes of leaving Netherley he had experienced a sharp burning sensation in his penis and he was anxious to inspect it in the privacy of the bathroom. It was possibly a psychosomatic response to his polite rejection of Teresa McCarthy's generous if unexpected offer. On the other hand it might be the stuff Dr Blackwell had put on his warts, burning its way through. He was going to die in unspeakable agony over several days with a neat hole bored in his willy. This was what Dr Blackwell meant by 'unfortunate accidents'.

'There isn't a lot of difference, Preston, or haven't you noticed? Still, I suppose I could have thrown myself in the lake. I did consider putting my head in the oven, but your Auntie Ethel was baking cakes in it.'

'Excuse me,' said Preston. 'Got to hurry up.'

Safe in the bathroom, with the door locked, he pulled down his pants and inspected the war zone. It was not pretty but there was nothing he could describe as an unfortunate accident. He decided that the burning sensation was a localised protest to the current state of play *vis-à-vis* imperialist aggression. There was a part of Preston that appreciated the irony of his situation, involved with three women and technically celibate, but this part did not include his penis. It was probably trying to tell him it was still there.

Preston sat down on the lavatory to consider the problem. He was in no doubt that he had done the right thing in spurning Ms McCarthy but it brought home the need to put his house in order.

The obvious route to sexual fulfilment was reconciliation with Polly who, whatever her faults, had no apparent objection to penis penetration, and he had already taken the first tentative steps in this direction. Both his conscience and his desire for a quiet life prompted such a course.

On the other hand he didn't like her very much.

This was not a recent discovery. It was a knowledge accumulated over several years of marriage, but he had never really considered it to be relevant. Polly was just Polly. His wife. Liking her didn't enter into it. And yet, perhaps it should. Perhaps this was the fundamental cause of the friction between them.

Why didn't he like Polly, he wondered. Because she was so bossy? Yes. Because she treated him like a prat? Yes. Because she was a woman? That, too.

But did it matter? Could he expect any better? After all, he'd be up against the last problem whatever he did, unless he developed a sudden taste for male intercourse, which seemed unlikely at his time of life and not without attendant risk.

The advantage of Polly as a woman was that he knew where he was with her, that she was the mother of his children and that if they had a reconciliation they could get a second mortgage and do up the house. Also have a fuck from time to time.

Moreover, he conceded with a small sigh, it was The Right Thing To Do.

Sitting in the bathroom of his family home, where he had been weaned off his potty, scrubbed clean of germs and neighbourhood squalor, a place redolent with the influence of his mum and his Auntie Ethel and his long-dead gran, Preston could not resist the pull towards Conformity and Righteousness. Liking did not come into it, much less Love. He pulled up his trousers and reported for duty.

'Fancy eating out tonight?' he suggested to Polly. 'Just the two of us?'

Polly put her book down and regarded him with frank suspicion. 'What for?' she said.

Preston sighed. Because it would be nice, because we have known each other, man and wife, for six years, because we must learn to talk to each other again, perhaps even to like each other a little, perhaps even to love. 'Because the alternative is my mum and Auntie Ethel all evening,' he said.

'I'll have to think about it,' she said.

This was not the right answer.

He went off in a huff and joined his auntie in the kitchen.

'I don't know where your mum's got to,' she said. 'She must've got lost.'

'I expect they stopped at the lights,' Preston said, 'and the whole bus got wiped out by a panga gang.'

'It's not something to joke about, Preston,' said his aunt, severely. 'They set fire to a bus during the riots.'

Preston sat at the kitchen table and watched, morosely, as she removed trays of cakes and scones from the oven.

'They've turned out all right,' she remarked with satisfaction.

This reminded Preston of something. He went back into the living-room, shutting the door carefully.

'What d'you mean, *Why I turned out the way I did*?'

Polly put her book down with a sigh. 'Pardon?'

'You said Auntie Ethel was going on about why I'd turned out the way I have. What did she mean exactly?'

'Well, I suppose to paraphrase a three-hour lecture, she thinks you don't think enough.'

'Oh, she does, does she?'

'Mmmm. She doesn't think you think things through.'

'I see.'

'She thinks you just leap into things. You don't weigh up the consequences of your actions.'

'My Auntie Ethel said this?'

'Well ... more or less.'

'I suppose this is because I went to Toxteth this afternoon.'

Polly shrugged.

'Well it can't be anything else can it? I mean, here I am, happily married – so far as she knows – with two kids and a safe, steady job with the BBC. I mean, I would hardly call this reckless behaviour, would you?'

'Perhaps she thinks you could have done better,' said Polly, with a small bitter smile.

'I see. Well, leaving that aside for the moment, why does she think I'm the way she thinks I am?'

'She thinks you might have relied on other people to do your thinking for you when you were little.'

'Like her, for instance?' Preston's lip curled.

'Your gran mostly.'

'I see.' Preston brooded.

'She also thinks it's something they put in National Health orange-juice.'

Preston was relieved. This was more like his Auntie Ethel.

'And do you agree with this analysis?'

'You mean about the orange juice?'

'You know what I mean.'

Polly considered.

'Not really. I think you think too much, as a matter of fact. I think you think too much about what you ought to do instead of just getting on with things. But I do agree it's probably their fault. Them and the Catholic Church.'

'This is very interesting. Can you think of any specific examples?'

'Not offhand. I expect I could if I put my mind to it. By the way, I think it would be a good idea to eat out tonight. So long as your mum and your Auntie Ethel don't mind.'

They ate in the Adelphi. The Adelphi was the posh hotel of Preston's youth, the place where all the nobs stayed before they caught a liner across the Atlantic. The liners had stopped sailing and the nobs didn't come here any more but the Adelphi retained its oceanic grandeur, all mirrors and marble and potted palms. However, in pursuit of a more downmarket clientele the management had slashed the prices in the restaurant and introduced a Saturday-night disco. Preston was reminded of the ostensible purpose of his trip north.

'I must look in on this club where we're filming on Monday,' he told Polly, 'I'll have to see what kind of lights we'll need. D'you mind if we drop in on the way home?'

'Not at all,' said Polly, 'I haven't been to a club since we were married.'

Preston let that go and perused the menu. His penis had stopped burning and he was hungry. Relief always gave Preston an appetite, but then so did worry. He couldn't imagine why he wasn't enormously fat. He thought it might be because he had AIDS.

The waitress came and while Polly made up her mind he ordered duck terrine for starters and a ragout of venison and hare for his main course. Polly selected celery soup and an omelette with green salad. Preston remembered, too late, that she'd gone vegetarian. He watched her face anxiously, wondering if his choice had disgusted her. He determined not to look as if he was enjoying it.

This was the first time they had eaten out together, just the two of them, since he had told her about Carla. Preston had told Polly about Carla because he felt he ought to, and because he knew Polly suspected something. She had found two cinema tickets in the pocket of a pair of trousers she was putting through the wash. This had been careless, so careless that Preston had told himself that he must have wanted to be caught. He could have lied, but telling the truth made him feel a lot better. He had told Polly that he did not love Carla but that he was fascinated by her. Polly had been tight-lipped about this but not openly violent or upset. Later he had thanked her for being so understanding. He had told her that she had lifted a great weight from his mind. Inexplicably she had punched him in the mouth.

Preston decided to handle the evening with kid-gloves. He drank only his fair share of the wine and tried not to talk too much. Most of all he tried not to talk about politics. Polly thought Preston's views on politics were crass. He considered talking about religion but Polly thought his views on religion were crass, too. She had forbidden him to talk to the children about them. She said they'd have nightmares. Once, struck by guilt at not having had his children christened and alarmed by a programme on cot death, Preston had crept into their room at night with a bowl of water and attempted to baptise them secretly. Aroused by screams, Polly had come rushing into the room and obliged Preston to explain. She had accused him of creeping about the house like Dracula.

For obvious reasons sex was out of the question so there wasn't much left to sustain a conversation. He had a bash at food. He said he was thinking of giving up meat himself. He said that when he thought about the poor hares and the poor deer running wild and free in the forest it practically stuck in his throat. He said his favourite film as a child was *Bambi*.

'I'm not not eating meat for any moral reason,' Polly pointed out. 'I just think it's healthier not to. If you want to kill yourself with cholesterol, go ahead. It's nothing to do with me.'

Thus encouraged, Preston continued to eat in silence for a while. He became aware of the couples on the adjoining tables. He wondered if they were having as good a time as he was. They looked relatively content but Preston had an ambivalent attitude to other people's peace of mind. On the one hand he thought everyone was happier than he was, he envied the solid front and the secure presence, on the other he suspected that deep down everyone was racked by emotional anguish and tortured by personal problems that put his own in the shade. Take the couple nearest, he thought. The man was much older than the woman but they looked curiously suited. The man had probably left his wife and children for her. He was devastated by his decision but knew it was the right one for him. He loved the younger woman very much. She was good for him. You could tell by the way he looked at her. She had taught him to live for himself and the day, to forget his self-destructive obsession with growing old and dying. But the woman did not return his affectionate glances. She even looked a little bored. She had fallen in love with someone else. A young medical student. Preston hated doctors. Later, over pudding, she would tell him of this and the man would go away, alone, and consider suicide. He would walk along the Pier Head and stare into the dark water but he would not have the courage to jump. Unable to return to wife or mistress he would spend the remainder of the weekend in a lonely hotel. On Monday morning, on the way into work, severe stomach cramps would give him the first intimation of the serious illness that would kill him.

He watched the waitress take their order and the man lean over to his companion and say, clearly enough for Preston to hear, 'And I wouldn't mind her for dessert, neither.'

His companion sighed. 'Oh Dad,' she said, in tones of infinite weariness.

'Preston, is anything the matter?' Polly asked him. 'I mean, is there something you want to tell me?'

Preston looked at her, startled.

'Is that the purpose of the meal?' Her manner was gentle and only faintly mocking. 'Do you want a divorce, Preston, is that what you're trying to tell me?'

The hare came alive in Preston's stomach. The deer kicked him in the groin.

'Don't worry,' she said. 'If that's what you want I won't make a lot of trouble about it.'

Preston shook his head violently from side to side, trying to find the words.

'My God, I don't want a divorce,' he said. 'Do you?' The words came out in a rush and rather louder than he intended. The man and his daughter stiffened slightly and the daughter began to smile. Polly was turning the salad over with her fork and staring fixedly at it as if it was going to come up with the answer.

'I don't really know,' she said. 'I don't think I want to decide. I'd rather you did.'

Preston kept his voice low but he felt as if people were straining to listen. 'I'd like us to get back together again,' he said. 'I mean, live properly, as a couple.'

This was terrible. This was what happened on other tables, not his.

Polly looked at him, warily. 'Are you sure about that?'

'Of course I'm sure,' Preston said, wondering what he'd say if she asked why. But she didn't.

'I'll have to think about it,' she said. 'And I'd expect certain assurances.'

Preston nodded. 'I know,' he said, 'I know. And there is a bit of a problem with Carla.'

'Ah,' said Polly, 'she's pregnant.'

Preston heard a distinct splutter from the next table.

'Do you think you could keep your voice down?' he said. 'Of course she's not pregnant. I was thinking of the show.'

'Oh yes. The show. It must go on.'

The waitress came to clear away their plates and Preston squirmed, saying nothing.

'D'you know what you want for dessert?' asked the waitress.

'Just coffee, please,' said Polly.

'Coffee,' said Preston, regretfully, thinking it might detract from his sincerity if he ordered Black Forest gâteau with cream as he had intended.

'I can't break things off halfway through the series,' he said, 'it's only got a few more weeks to run.'

'Perhaps that's all we've got,' said Polly.

Preston felt a small whimpering noise start at the back of his throat. Polly put her chin in her hand and stared at him moodily. It was difficult to read her expression but he thought it was more resigned than anything.

'I think you're saying this because you think you ought to,' she said.

'That's because you've had three hours of my Auntie Ethel. No, honestly, I mean it. *It's what I want.*'

'That's what I want,' they were singing in the club. 'The best things in life are free ... ' Early Beatles. The city clinging to its past when there were ships in the river and jobs in the factories and Merseybeat ruled the world and everyone was famous.

'Yesterday, all my troubles seemed so far away ... '

Perhaps they knew something we didn't, Preston reflected, perhaps that's why they grabbed the money and ran, got out quick before the roof caved in. But who could blame them? Certainly not Preston, who had got out too.

The band was all-male and hopeless and popular. They belted out the music and the room shook and they all danced and no one cared if it wasn't the real thing. It was Saturday night and the whole world was tarted up to the nines and the bevvy flowing free.

'The lads are having a bit of a blow, now,' said the compère, a man called Andy, who modelled himself on Tom Jones, all curls and medallions, 'but they'll be back later on in the evening.' Applause, cheers. 'And in the meantime we have great pleasure in presenting Live Cabaret with ... the Great Kazooooooo ... ' Boos. Puking noises ... 'And those lovely ladies, the Gang Bang. I mean, the Gang Band.' Louder boos, cries of Gerremoff.

Preston watched from the wings with Polly while the Great Kazoo went through his act.

The Great Kazoo was a youth of about nineteen with spots and a mohican haircut. He was dressed in leathers and studs. His act consisted of a series of filthy jokes delivered in a monotone, and a song which was difficult to differentiate from the jokes but which ended with him breaking a wine bottle over his head. This was described by the compère and the Great Kazoo as alternative comedy.

Tonight the Great Kazoo was having trouble with the wine bottle. It wouldn't break. He kept belting himself over the head with it to the obvious delight of the audience. After a while he began to draw blood.

'I'll give him another minute, then drag 'im off,' the compère muttered to Preston, but he didn't seem too keen.

Finally the bottle smashed and the Great Kazoo staggered off to rapturous applause.

'Why do you do it?' Preston asked him, genuinely impressed.

'I've always wanted to be in show business,' the Great Kazoo informed him seriously.

'But doesn't it hurt?'

'Don't be a cunt,' said the Great Kazoo. 'Of course it hurts.'

'And now, folks, a real treat for youse ... the Gang Band.'

The Gang Band was the all-women band that had given Preston his excuse to come North. There were five of them. Their clothing was torn and tattered. Their faces daubed with stage-blood and runny mascara. This was to indicate that they were rape victims.

'All women are victims of rape,' the lead singer, Mags, had explained to Preston earlier, 'even if it hasn't happened to them physically.'

They, too, described their act as alternative comedy.

'I suppose you think we're going to do a strip,' yelled Mags at the audience. 'Well you can fuck off.'

This was the wittiest part of the act, but Polly said the music was good.

'Better than the blokes anyway,' she said.

'What about the Great Kazoo?' asked Preston.

'We try to make the audience *feel*,' Mags explained to him when she came off stage and he bought her a pint, 'we try to make them bleed. We're not just in it for laughs.'

'That's probably just as well,' said Preston, trying to make a joke out of it, but Mags didn't laugh.

'What we're saying is that all women are essentially regarded as sex objects, whether they're nuclear scientists, nurses, doctors, politicians or musicians like ourselves.'

Without the make-up Mags looked about nineteen, though Preston knew from the researcher that she was three years older than that. Almost in defiance of her scowling, tomboy features her body burst out in plump abandon. She was wearing a thin cotton vest, torn under one sleeve, a leather mini-skirt and a pair of stockings round her ankles. She was almost certainly five foot two and a half.

'Yes, yes, I can see that,' said Preston, the New Man, carefully looking at nothing but her eyes. 'And I think you're right up to a point, but sex objects aren't necessarily rape victims, are they?'

'Oh come on,' said Mags. 'And I suppose you think Page Three girls are just a bit of harmless fun.'

Preston could see that she and Carla were going to get along like a house on fire.

'I really will try harder,' he said to Polly on the way home, nervously stopping whenever the lights were red. 'I really do want to make it work, you know.'

Thinking, I always do when I'm feeling insecure. That's why I got married in the first place. But what about tomorrow and the day after that? What about the day I wake up confident?

'I suppose we've got the children to think of,' said Polly.

She doesn't like me, either, Preston thought. She's only doing it for the children. It's ludicrous, we mean nothing to each other.

But it was cold outside.

'I know I'm a pain sometimes,' he said, 'but you haven't seen the best of me.'

'After six years,' she said. 'I can't wait.'

Later, as they were getting ready for bed, she said, 'It's going to be a long time before I can feel relaxed with you again.'

Meaning fucking, Preston thought, climbing into bed on his side of the monkey, but that was all right with him. Dr Blackwell had said it would be a long time before his warts disappeared, even if there weren't any unfortunate accidents, and although Durex was a possibility Preston felt he could afford to wait, at least as far as Polly was concerned. He kissed her politely on the cheek and switched off the light.

19 THE GANG BAND
If Male Go to Jail

The riot began, like most riots, with a small incident – one of the lights exploded and someone panicked – and even then it might have been contained if Carla hadn't thrown a tantrum and Mags thrown a pint of beer over her but then there was no stopping it until the police arrived, and Preston ever afterwards maintained he was right to keep the cameras turning, even if it did cost him a lens and one of the mikes. But by then no one was listening.

The day had begun peaceably enough with the arrival of the OB unit from Manchester. It was a mini-OB really, just two cameras, but the lighting was complicated and it took them all morning and most of the afternoon to rig.

'I don't want to over-light,' Preston explained, 'I want to keep the atmosphere as much as possible.'

'What atmosphere?' the senior cameraman asked him.

He had a point. The club was basically the ground floor of a disused warehouse with a bar, thirty or forty tables and a bit of a stage. If, by night, it had a certain seedy charm, by day, in the wan light that filtered through the high window-grilles, it was merely seedy. It looked like an aircraft-hangar that had been pressed into service for a knees-up.

'It'll liven up with a crowd in,' said Preston, unknowingly prophetic, 'and if we use a lot of gel ... '

They'd got most of the polecats up and were busy fitting the lights to them when the production team arrived. Preston pretended to be involved with the rigging but a covert glance at Carla advised him that she was in no mood to be trifled with. She sat alone at one of the formica-topped tables hunched in her leather jacket, smoking and turning the pages of a women's magazine with savage disinterest.

'Good journey? Everything all right?' Preston asked the PA when she came over.

'Not really,' she said. 'Ratings are down again and Wagstaff wants to see you. He wanted to see you Friday actually, but no one could get hold of you.'

She sounded miffed.

'You knew I was coming up here,' Preston pointed out.

'Yes, but a contact number would have helped. I had an earful from his secretary. She's put you down for three o'clock tomorrow.'

Maurice Wagstaff was the head of network features. He did not meet Preston often and this must be regarded as an ominous development.

'Any idea what it's about?'

'No, but there was a bit of a fuss about last week's show. I mean, you know.'

Preston knew.

'Oh, and you had a call from Suffolk Police. The person you wanted to speak to is on leave. He'll be back next week.'

Preston filled two cups of coffee from a flask in the kitchen and approached Carla with spurious enthusiasm.

'Welcome to Liverpool,' he said.

She looked at him.

'Met the band on Saturday,' he said. 'They're fine, you'll like them.'

'Why?' she said, coldly.

This could easily be a trick question. Preston thought about it carefully.

'The lead singer's very sharp,' he said. 'Got a lot of strong views.'

Carla said nothing. Preston sipped his coffee and tried to think of some way of making himself agreeable. He was even more nervous than usual with her. His decision on the domestic front meant that he and Carla were on borrowed time and he was worried about how she was going to take it when he finally plucked up the courage to tell her. As he knew he must, rather sooner than later.

The Carla Situation had brought him far too many problems, at work and at home, to be tolerable, while Carla herself, to be fully appreciated, required a degree of masochism he had not yet attained, for all his years of practice. And yet Preston experienced a curious sense of regret, of failure, really, when he contemplated the termination of what, for want of a better word, he must call Their Relationship.

Shortly before it had begun, Preston had seen an Agnès Varda film called *Vagabonde*. It was about a young woman who had become a tramp in the South of France. She mooched about the Midi in mid-winter, indiscriminately cadging lifts, beds, food and fags from a largely uncaring public until finally dying of exposure in a ditch.

The film was as much about the people she encountered as the woman herself. It examined their attitudes to her. Some exploited her, others were exploited, some were fascinated by the sense of freedom she seemed to convey, others repulsed by what they saw as her degradation, her self-destructive rejection of society.

Preston, with his romantic inclinations, felt there was something of the *vagabonde* in Carla. The clothes she wore, the way she slouched about, her tough, prickly shell, all bespoke the estrangement of the tramp. She was an outsider. She might have come inside for a while, she might want fame and recognition as a tramp wants a warm bed from time to time and a free meal, but she kept that brittle delitescence that so intrigued Preston and had been the basic attraction for him.

He felt that in his failure to come closer to her, to sustain the relationship and make something of it, he had failed to live up to his image of himself, or at least the image of the reckless buccaneer. Instead, he had been like the bourgeois provincials of Varda's film, inhibited by their own fears from reaching out and touching the anarchic outsider.

And that was another thing. He hadn't touched her, emotionally or physically.

Or perhaps what he meant was, he hadn't *fucked* her.

Stop it, he thought. This is not New Man thinking, this is an older, more primitive machismo, this is Neanderthal Man unleashed.

'Where're you staying tonight?' he asked her.

'The Adelphi,' she said. 'What about you?'

There was an edge to the question. She knew he had been staying with his mum for the weekend and she might have guessed Polly had been with him. But he had dropped Polly and the twins at Lime Street station on his way into town and they would be back in London by now. Polly had to do a shift at the Citizens Advice Bureau in the morning. All he had to do was phone his mum and say he wouldn't be back, he was working late and would book in at the Adelphi with the rest of them. Carla would probably expect it. There might even be a scene if he didn't.

Stop it. Remember the warts.

But he could wear a Durex. He'd bought a packet specially in case Polly had relented.

STOP IT. How could he even think like this?

'See how late we finish,' he said. He smiled. 'You might be tired.'

Aaaagh. You incredible prat, Preston, he told himself, walking back to the kitchen with the empty cups. *You might be tired*. God, you are so *embarrassing*. Alone, in the kitchen, he put his head in his hands and moaned, shuddering, then did a small dance raising one shoulder and making his hands into withered claws. The bells, the bells, he silently chanted, sanctuary, sanctuary.

'You all right, guv?' said one of the sparks, watching him from the door. 'Something they put in the coffee?'

By the time the band arrived for rehearsals the lights were rigged and the cameras in position and the crew putting their orders in for drinks with the PA. Preston should have been pleased they were on schedule but he was worried that his little display in the kitchen might have got around. Initially, the crew had treated him with the courteous tolerance they extended to most directors they had not worked with before. An attitude of: this man might be a total incompetent but we might as well give him the benefit of the doubt and he probably won't fuck it up completely. Now, there was a more uncertain mood as if they thought anything could happen.

And when they saw the band and the band took their coats off they obviously thought it had. No one actually whistled, no one shouted, but there was a tremor like the first rustle of leaves before a storm. Preston approached them diffidently, holding his breath. Mags was wearing the leather skirt again, over torn fish-net stockings this time, and a bright-red frilly blouse which had been ripped at one shoulder and down the front. It covered her breasts, but only just. After the one glance which took this in Preston sought eye contact and held on to it desperately as a drowning man, he was reliably informed, holds on to a straw. But he was still drowning. He explained how he wanted them to set up and Mags shook her head, frowning, and said that wouldn't do at all.

'But I've lit for these positions,' he pointed out.

'That's your problem,' said Mags.

Preston thought about this while five faces viewed him with unmitigated hostility, as if he personally was responsible for most of the crimes against women this century.

'Well, actually it's our problem,' he said, 'because it's too late to re-light now, we've got the audience arriving in half an hour.'

Mags clamped her jaw shut and turned to face the wall. Preston sought other eyes but found no relief.

'It's the way you were set up on Saturday,' he said.

'We've changed since then,' the sax player explained with weary patience.

'But why? It was very good.'

'Gee thanks,' said Mags, still with her back to him.

Preston put it down to pre-match nerves.

'Look,' he said. 'Provided the drums stay in this area, and the keyboard's over there, we can cope – whatever you do.'

He was wrong about that as it transpired, but Mags adopted it as a face-saving formula and they set up more or less as he wanted. Then one of the researchers came up to him with another problem.

'Half the audience is outside already,' she said, 'screaming to be let in.'

Preston called the floor-manager over from the bar.

'D'you think we could start letting them in,' he said. 'They can get drinks and watch the rehearsal.'

'OK by me,' she said. 'No problem.'

The floor-manager was a woman called Naola who had lived until quite recently in South Africa and still had the accent. Preston thought this might be a problem if there was a contingent from Toxteth in the audience. He didn't know her politics but she was clutching a pint carton of fruit juice labelled Um Bongo, Um Bongo, they drink it in the Congo.

'Right leds,' she yelled. 'Let's heve you on the dence floor.'

Resignedly, like troops moving up to the front, 'the leds' took up their positions and the audience began to burst through the doors.

Preston took Mags off to meet Carla, who was still sitting at her table as if it had nothing to do with her.

'We thought, you know, after a few numbers to loosen up we'd do the interview at one of the tables,' he explained, 'with the audience all round.'

'Whatever you like,' said Carla.

This was out of character but gratifying.

'Just a minute,' said Mags. 'We've been discussing this and we'll only agree to be interviewed as a collective.'

'I'm sorry?' said Carla.

The plan had been for Carla to interview Mags and the drummer, whose name was Ginny and who was the next most articulate, according to the researcher.

'That's all right,' said Preston, hastily. 'It might be better that way – if that's OK with you, Carla.'

But he'd been lulled into a false sense of security.

'No, it's not all right with me,' said Carla. 'You can't seriously expect me to interview five people on the same subject.'

'It's five or none,' said Mags.

Contrary to Preston's expectations Carla and Mags were not getting on like a house on fire. In fact, there was a definite chill in the air. This was interesting, but something he would have to think about later.

'Look,' he said, 'say we agree there'll be two main talkers but the rest can chip in from time to time. I mean,' he appealed to Carla, 'it'll make it quite lively which was why we wanted to get out of the studio in the first place.'

'Why can't there be five main speakers?' demanded Mags.

Oh God, thought Preston.

'Because we haven't got enough mikes,' he lied. 'I'll have to fishpole you.'

This was a professional foul and he blushed for shame but Mags let him get away with it. Preston wished he did not feel so sexually disturbed by her, but doubtless this was the object of the exercise. He wondered if her appearance was the reason for Carla's apparent dislike. Carla dressed flamboyantly sometimes, but always modestly. The only flesh she ever exposed in public, besides her face, was the thin strip between her ankle socks and the bottom of her trousers.

The problem between her and Carla, Preston decided, was that they were both ruffians, and recognised each other as such, but Mags was an altogether more nubile, erotic ruffian and at least three years younger.

But perhaps it wasn't as simple, or as superficial, as that. Perhaps it was more about insiders and outsiders. For all her 'outsider' image, Carla was the Establishment so far as Mags was concerned. Carla was the tramp who'd found a place in the warm, and Mags was still out in the cold, trudging the streets and rattling on the latch.

'Will you people git your drinks and sit et the tables,' the floor-manager yelled, 'I don't want no people stending et the bar.'

'And another thing,' said Mags, 'no one said anything about working with a Fascist.'

Preston knew the number he wanted to record. It was called 'Reclaim the Night' and he'd heard it on Saturday:

Man is paddin' 'long the sidewalk now,
Man is cruisin' 'long the curb.
Doncha look back ah, doncha look back
Doncha look back ah, doncha look back.
Got a hammer in his hand ah,
Got a knife in his fist ...
Doncha look back ah, doncha look back.
Gotta Reclaim the Night ...
Gotta Reclaim the Night ...

And so on. It was a problem shooting with only two cameras but he was recording on two machines and editing later. He could keep one camera on a wide for safety and the other on Mags, then run through the same number twice more picking up close-ups of the rest of the band. He could get some shots of the audience while the band were running through their warm-up.

'All right,' he said. 'Let's have a rehearsal. Ready on the floor.'

'Quiet on the floor,' yelled the floor-manager.

'In ten.'

The PA began to count.

'I said quiet on the floor,' Naola yelled louder.

Preston set up his shots, thinking about sex-objects and rapists. Preston couldn't imagine ever raping anyone. It had never figured in his fantasies, awake or dreaming. He was opposed to capital punishment for murder but he thought all rapists should be castrated. Him and his Auntie Ethel. Preston could never imagine violating someone, or being turned on by someone else's pain, but looking at Mags, writhing around the stage, he had a definite desire to tear the rest of her clothes off. She had to be willing, she had to ask him to do it, but he could imagine in the right circumstances it could be a lot of fun for both of them.

But was this the right kind of thinking? Or Neanderthal Man making a pig of itself again.

Preston's sex education had been woefully inadequate but, except in the purely biological sense, there had been no essential difference between him and his friends at the Quarry Bank High School for Boys. They had all operated in a grey area of mystery, superstition and suspense, enlivened by the occasional illicit trespass. A 'dirty' film, a 'girlie' magazine, a peek up the skirts of the unknown. Preston remembered the excitement when one of the *cognoscenti*, all bumfluff and swagger, had produced a photograph of a woman who lived on his estate – obviously the local Mrs Gladrags – Totally Nude. It was the first time Preston had ever seen pubic hair on a woman and it was a surprise to him, but apart from this interesting physical detail what really moved him was the fact that this was someone real, someone you might bump into in the street, someone a fellow fourteen year old knew to pass the time of day with. Someone who had knowingly exposed herself for a dirty picture, knowing that school-boys would lust over it. That was the thing. It was naughty. And this became the key element of Preston's desire, it conditioned his sexual reflexes ever after. The idea of Frau Fischer, a woman he knew, a woman he encountered socially every other day, clothed and respectable, parading around in the nude, or rollicking, naked, on a rocking-horse, was extremely stimulating to Preston. It excited him. It turned him on. But did it make him a potential rapist?

Mags and the Gang Band would doubtless say it did and Preston, the New Man, didn't know. He didn't know what was acceptable lust and what wasn't. He didn't know if any lust was acceptable. He had been told penis penetration was an act of imperialist aggression, just as he had been told, as a young Catholic boy, that masturbation, or as Mother Bernard put it, Being Tempted In The Night, was also wrong, but the combination of the music and Mags was making him realise what he was missing. It was all very well being the New Man, it was all right giving a woman a lot of pleasure, but now and again, not necessarily every time, Preston wanted to give a woman a lot of pleasure by fucking her. He missed the thrust of it all, the basic in-and-out, the letting go. Too much Carla was like nouvelle cuisine, he decided, from time to time you fancied getting stuck into the kind of food mother used to cook.

He was startled out of this unproductive train of thought by the words, 'Eva Eichler'.

They were being screamed at him by Mags.

Who killed Eva Eichler? she chanted,
Who dumped her in the sea?
Did they rape her before they slew her,
'Cos she dared to be free,
'Cos she dared to be free,
'Cos she defied their mastery.

The cameraman began to pull out.

'No,' said Preston. 'Keep her in close-up.'

He stared at Mags's face multiplied by three monitors, the mascara weeping down her cheeks, the lipstick slashed across her mouth. She was looking straight into the lens, straight into his eyes, and she was yelling the words into the mike and they were ringing through his head.

Men, wrote Eva Eichler,
Are continually at war,
They fight for satisfaction,
And more and more and more.

She didn't have much of a voice, except that it was loud and harsh, and the lyrics were terrible, but Preston was transfixed, sitting rigid in his seat staring at that ghoulish face.

She wrote about their fears
And male inadequacy,
So they slew her woman's body
And dumped it in the sea.

Was this poetic licence, or did she know something he didn't?

Who killed Eva Eichler?
Does he bear a name,
Or was it you who slew her
'Cos she dared expose your shame,
'Cos she dared expose your shame,
'Cos she said you were to blame.

He grabbed her after the rehearsal, glaring at her like the Ancient Mariner.

'The Eva Eichler song, did you write it yourself?'

She looked startled. 'Yeah, more or less. Took it from a poem.'

'But her body wasn't dumped in the sea, was it? I mean, there was no evidence of that.'

'Evidence,' said Mags, scathingly. 'You mean as in police evidence?'

'I mean, I didn't see anything in the press . . . '

He flinched from the scorn in her eyes. 'No, well you wouldn't, would you?'

Naola was hovering.

'The clientil is gitting viry ristliss,' she said.

Intimations of this had seeped through to Preston's tiny control-room while they were recording 'Reclaim the Night'. Occasional catcalls, a background buzz between takes, like an aggrieved swarm.

'And it's net jest the audience,' said Naola. 'We hev a small problim with the presinter.'

A glance at the 'presinter' assured Preston that Carla was in no small sulk.

'All right, we'll do the interview now,' he said.

He had planned to have a small break for the crew.

'Quiet on the floor, please.'

But the floor was not quiet, and Preston had a feeling it was shifting under his feet.

'But what I don't understand,' said Carla, with the familiar edge to her voice, 'is how you can protest that women are treated as sex objects and still dress like that.'

'If we are sex objects dressed like this,' said Mags, 'then all we are saying is some men have problems. Maybe some women, too.'

Apart from the use of the collective pronoun there was no apparent sign of the collective interview. The rest were there but Mags was doing most of the talking and for once Carla seemed to be on the defensive.

'Close on Mags,' said Preston in the truck.

'If you're saying we bring out the animal in men, then that's one of the points we're trying to make. I don't think that's our fault, I think that the problem's with men, except that it makes a pretty serious problem for women, too.'

'But Maggie, you really can't have it both ways. You can't criticise women for using make-up, because it turns men on, and then say if men are attracted to you, dressed like that, they're animals.'

'Look, we do not dress to attract men, how many times do we have to tell you – to me this is repulsive.'

'Bullshit,' yelled someone from the audience. A male voice.

'Animal,' yelled someone else. A female.

'Two pull out to a wide. One give me the audience.'

'It's not lit,' said the cameraman over talk-back.

'Some of it is,' said Preston, 'give me that.'

'Don't you give me that shit, man,' someone was shouting, and then a lot of people were shouting at once. Dimly, on camera two just beyond the circle of light, Preston saw a woman on her feet haranguing another section of the audience but without a mike he couldn't make out what she was saying.

'Preston, they're fighting.' Naola's voice in his ear-piece, crisp with tension. Camera two swung in a wide pan and found it, dim but discernible, two men slugging it out and a woman laying into one of the men with her shoulder-bag.

Then the light went. Preston just heard the bang and saw the colour change on the monitor.

'Don't look up,' one of the cameramen shouted and someone screamed.

'Oh for Christ's sake.' Preston heard Carla's voice, over the edge now. 'If it's not bad enough having to interview morons . . .'

On camera one's monitor, in wide, Preston saw Mags throw the beer in a rainbow-arc across the lights.

Unrequested, the camera zoomed in on Carla's dripping face.

'Wow,' said Preston, impressed.

'Will you sittle down, you people,' Naola was yelling. 'Christ, what an audience.'

But whatever else it was, as an audience it was not slow to catch on.

'What's going on?' Preston demanded when he heard Naola's expletives on talk-back.

'Someone threw a beer at Naola,' a cameraman informed him on talk-back.

It was more or less open house after that.

'Hadn't we better cut?' Preston was asked.

'What's the point?' said Preston. 'We can't get the gear out.'

Shortly after that one of the cameras went over and the PA called the police. They arrived with impressive speed, but then, as Preston said later, it is Liverpool.

This was when he'd come back from hospital with one of the camera assistants who'd been hit by a piece of flying glass and the rest of them were sitting in the lounge of the Adelphi recuperating with large measures.

Except for Carla, who'd gone to bed.

Preston didn't think he'd join her. If there was going to be a post-mortem, he thought, he'd rather put it off until the morning.

He drove back to Old Swan, quite looking forward to a night with the monkey, but he'd forgotten, Daniel had taken it with him to London and Preston had the bed to himself. He slept quite well, considering.

20 GET PUSH
Back to Start

'A shambles. A bloody shambles,' Maurice Wagstaff said to Preston. 'I think that just about sums it up, don't you?'

Preston inclined his head and pretended to consider it.

'Equipment smashed, headlines in the press, cameraman in hospital.'

It was only a small headline, in one paper, and the cameraman hadn't been kept in hospital, but Preston didn't think Maurice Wagstaff wanted to know that.

Preston was on the carpet. Actually, he was on a chair, but this, again, was a small detail. He maintained an expression in keeping with the gravity of the occasion, but his mind kept wandering off on odd little tangents of its own. At present it was thinking that the head of network features was remarkably attractive for a man who was almost completely bald.

Preston didn't normally fancy bald men, but it struck him that Maurice Wagstaff was extremely sexy, in an authoritative kind of way. He looked elegant, groomed, successful. Hair would have seemed an unnecessary piece of frippery.

This was interesting to Preston, because Preston had always been obsessively worried about losing his own hair. Once, when he'd thought he was, he had taken a number of pictures of himself in a booth at an Underground railway station and erased his hair with liquid paper to see what he'd look like without it. The effect had not been encouraging and shortly afterwards he had married Polly.

But if he'd been confident of turning out like Maurice Wagstaff, Preston thought now, he might have had the courage to say, Fuck it, and stayed single.

Maurice Wagstaff had a firm, strong chin and a straight, strong mouth. An uncompromising sort of mouth, Preston thought, admiringly. The mouth of a man who had achieved high rank within the BBC before his mid forties. He was clean-cut, handsome and, as Preston had noted, more or less, give or take a few grey patches around the ears, hairless. Not counting the eyebrows of course and obviously Preston couldn't speak for anything below the neck, but if

Maurice Wagstaff hadn't been called Waggy, he could very easily have answered to Kojak.

Interestingly, the bits of hair he did have, Preston observed, were carefully trimmed. Not one hair out of place. Preston thought that if a hair had strayed out of place Maurice Wagstaff would have ruthlessly plucked it out. It was possible this was why he had gone bald in the first place.

But they were not here to discuss the baldness of Preston's head of department. They were not even here to discuss the riot for which Preston was apparently being held responsible. This had just been raised in passing. What they were here to discuss was the word Cunt.

The word Cunt had gone out in its uncut, unblushing entirety on Thursday night's programme and the reaction, so far measured only in complaints calls, had been universally critical. 'An outraged response' was what Maurice Wagstaff called it and Waggy was not a man given to exaggeration. Among the complainants had been two BBC Governors, a former Government Minister, and a Bishop of the Church of England. Preston was tempted to remark that this evidence of a high-profile audience appeal did much to counter the low viewing figures, but he thought it best to keep this observation to himself, like most of the others that had flitted across his mind during the conversation. Apart from anything else, there didn't seem much point. The word Cunt had brought matters to a head. The 'experiment' had been a failure. There would be no subsequent series of *Shrews at Ten* and for the remainder of the current series there would be a new producer.

'We think we need a firmer hand on the tiller, Preston,' Waggy informed him, firmly.

Preston thought he said, 'a firmer hand on Attila,' and thought this was very witty. He smiled but Maurice Wagstaff did not smile back.

'What on earth did you think you were playing at, Preston?' he said.

Preston had not attempted to explain the political, or moral, reasons for letting the word Cunt out on the airwaves in, as Maurice put it, 'such an unpleasant context'. He thought Attila was the best person to expound that particular theory and somehow he didn't think it would make a bundle of difference.

21 MEET ALBERT SCHWEITZER
Go to Back of Queue

'So what has he given you instead?' asked Edward Cartwright when Preston told him about it in the club at Lime Grove.

'God,' said Preston cheerfully. He was cheerful because he had just drunk three pints of bitter and a Screwdriver. When he sobered up he thought he would be very depressed. Consequently he was in no hurry to sober up.

'You mean Religious Programmes?' Edward interpreted, correctly. 'You've been moved to the God slot?'

'I have,' said Preston. 'And in so doing I have made an important discovery. Well, two actually. One: I am not going up the ladder, I am sliding down a snake, and two: in the world according to Maurice Wagstaff and his peers, women rate lower than children and animals but not as low as God. This is interesting, don't you think?'

'I'm very sorry, Preston,' said Edward.

'Don't be.' Preston shook his head emphatically. 'Have another drink.'

He beamed at the barman and ordered a gin and tonic for Edward and another Screwdriver for himself. Preston always drank vodka when he intended to get seriously drunk. In his experience it achieved the maximum effect quickly and painlessly and with the minimum of nausea.

'I wouldn't say it was the bottom,' said Edward.

'What?'

'The God slot.'

'I suppose there's always the duty officer,' Preston agreed.

'No, I mean, it produces some good programmes.'

'Name one,' said Preston.

'Well, I can't offhand. I mean, I never watch it, I never have the time. But lately there've been some good directors on the God slot. You know, bright young things on their way up.'

'I'm not a bright young thing, Edward,' Preston pointed out. 'And the thought of meeting a few on my way down is not a happy one. Cheers.'

Edward shook his head.

'The one good thing about it,' said Preston, 'is I'll be all right when I join the queue.'

'Oh I don't think it'll come to that,' said Edward. 'They don't actually sack people at our level. Spell in the penal battalion and that's about it. Though they did push someone out of a window once. At Bush House. Well, they said it was suicide but we all knew.'

'Thank you, Edward, that's very encouraging, but I don't mean the dole queue. I mean The Queue. The one that waits for all of us.'

Edward looked confused. Preston did his best to explain.

'I've always been a bit worried about who I'd be standing next to. I mean, who's going to be in front of me when we're waiting to see where we're going to go to.'

'Go to?'

'Next.'

'Ah,' said Edward.

'After death,' said Preston.

'Ah,' said Edward, but his face still wore a hunted look.

Preston had first seen a painting of The Queue in the Walker Art Gallery as a child. Probably the same time he'd seen women without willies. He remembered it vividly. A long line of recently deceased mortals outside the pearly gates where they were being divided into saints and sinners. He remembered the stern faces of the angels, who were doing the dividing, and the panic on the faces of those condemned as they were herded down a dark staircase left of frame by demons with big pitchforks, looking jolly pleased with themselves. And the saints, looking saintly, disappearing off to the right in clouds of glory.

'I mean,' said Preston. 'Imagine if you were next in line after Albert Schweitzer.'

Edward nodded understandingly. 'I suppose someone has to be,' he mused.

'But what would you say?' Preston wondered. 'Just imagine, if you had to follow that. "And what did *you* do?" they'd say.

' "Oh, I was a producer at the BBC," I'd say, "I did *Animal Antics* and *Shrews at Ten*." '

'It might not be Schweitzer,' Edward pointed out, kindly. 'He died a long time before you and I shouldn't think they'd keep him hanging around long.'

'True,' said Preston, looking more cheerful. 'I've always hoped

I'd be after the PR man for the firm that makes instant mashed potatoes. I'd be in with a chance then.'

'Or the controller of British Rail Southern Region,' suggested Edward, who lived in Surrey.

'But now I can follow anyone. "Did the God slot," I shall say, "for the last thirty-odd years."

'"Did you really," they'll say. "My dear chap. Here's your harp, follow Albert along that corridor."'

It was some time after this and in another place that Preston asked Edward if Edward knew what was the root cause of his problems.

'Carla?' Edward hazarded.

'No,' said Preston. 'Miranda.'

'Miranda,' Edward repeated, nodding wisely, though as far as Preston was aware the name was a new one to him.

'My wife's best friend.'

'Ah,' Edward looked enlightened. 'And you slept with her?'

'I was forced to sleep with her,' Preston told him dramatically, 'by my wife.'

'My dear boy,' said Edward, sympathetically.

'I was drugged,' said Preston.

This may not have stood up in a court of law but it was technically true, in that immediately prior to the event Preston, Polly and Miranda had consumed a quantity of mescalin, in the form of magic-mushrooms picked near Bath, and washed them down with three bottles of sparkling wine.

'Drugged and pressured into it,' insisted Preston. 'Against my better judgment.'

This was also true, though, had he been closely questioned, Preston would have had to admit that he had been curious to see what Miranda was like under all the ethnic fibres – the Afghan shirts, Bolivian waistcoats and skirts hand-embroidered by a Masai goatherd for the Global Village in the basement of Liberty's.

'Miranda and Polly went to school together,' Preston explained. 'They are thick as thieves.' He considered this. 'Or were. And Miranda wanted a baby.'

'Ah,' said Edward. He was having trouble concentrating, Preston thought, after so much alcohol, but he didn't seem bored.

'She was thirty-five years old and she thought it was getting late and she didn't have a Relationship.'

Edward seemed to understand. 'But why you, Preston?' he enquired, politely.

Preston was not offended. 'I've always been considered attractive by the opposite sex,' he said, simply. 'I don't know why. I think it might be because they don't feel threatened.'

'I didn't mean that, I meant why did your wife volunteer *you*? Didn't she mind?'

'No, she did not,' said Preston, sternly. 'That is the point. You have put your finger on it precisely, Edward.'

Edward looked gratified.

'She said it was because she trusted me,' Preston said, curling his lip. 'And because I had clean genes.'

Edward looked confused again.

'Well, the twins proved it,' Preston pointed out. 'And also, Polly thought the experience would not be so traumatic for Miranda if I did it. So she said.'

'Preston, forgive me for being obtuse, but whatever the state of your jeans, I don't see how having a baby can be less traumatic just because it was you who supplied the wherewithal, as it were.'

'I don't mean having a baby,' Preston corrected him. 'I mean starting it off.'

'I'm sorry?'

'Fucking.'

'I see. You mean she hadn't done much?'

'I doubt if she'd done any.'

'At thirty-five? That must be something of a record, surely, in this day and age.'

'Maybe she wasn't a virgin,' Preston conceded, 'but near as damn it. I mean she always acts like one.'

'You couldn't tell when you did it?'

'I didn't.'

'Didn't?'

'Do it.'

'Ah.'

They both brooded on this for a while.

'Drink?' asked Edward.

'I think I'll have another Screwdriver, please.'

'I meant why you didn't do it.'

'Oh. Yes. I suppose so. Well, not just drink. See, it's a funny thing but, well you know the way you look at some people sometimes and you think, you can't imagine them doing it, you know what I mean?'

Edward nodded cautiously.

'Well, sometimes I think that about myself.'

'I see,' said Edward.

He ordered more drinks and some peanuts.

'And I suppose the mescalin could have had something to do with it,' Preston admitted.

'Mescalin?'

'I mean, you know what it's like, you're giggling away half the time and you think everything's absurd and then you suddenly feel very sad and you burst into tears.'

'I've never had it,' said Edward.

'Oh, you should try it sometime. It can be very relaxing. And it's quite nice eating mushrooms. I mean I don't smoke and I don't like shoving things up my nose. I don't do it a lot, mind you, but we were on holiday at the time.'

'You, Polly and Miranda?'

'That's right. And the twins. Last summer. We were eating prawns in this restaurant in Bath and of course we all thought it was hilarious.'

'Eating prawns?'

'Yes, well, have you ever looked at a prawn? I mean, *really* looked at one?'

'I don't believe I have,' Edward admitted.

'Well perhaps it was the mushrooms, but they look like very pompous old men in a club somewhere, you know, all red in the face with whiskers and bulging eyes. We kept picking them up and looking at them and falling about and then I looked at the one I was about to eat and I said, But just think, this was once some little prawn's uncle. I don't know why I said uncle, I mean it might have been a daddy or a grandfather or something, even a woman, but it just seemed to me to be an uncle. And I burst into tears. And then we were all crying and Miranda said, You're so sensitive, Preston, and Polly said, Well, what about it you two? And that was it, really.'

'Good Lord,' said Edward.

'Yes, well, she had been on at me for some time. Polly I mean.

Saying it was the perfect solution and all that. How Miranda quite liked me and I'd be doing her a great favour and *she didn't mind*. But until then I'd resisted it.'

'Well there's obviously something to be said for these mushrooms. Except that – of course, you didn't.'

'No. Well, I can't blame the mushrooms entirely. I think it was mainly the embarrassment when we stopped giggling and crying and found ourselves in bed together.' He reflected on the experience. 'I mean, Miranda's very nice and all that, but she never sort of takes off the ethnic fibres, even when she's naked.'

'I've known one or two women like that,' Edward confessed. 'But didn't pure lust . . . ?' He looked at Preston's face. 'No. I see. Is she particularly . . . I mean, not very . . .'

'She's attractive, but she's not very sexy, you know. Maybe it's me, but she has these trusting brown eyes. I've never really been able to cope with that. You know, there was a line in Wodehouse once about this woman Bertie Wooster had got himself engaged to who thought the stars were God's daisy-chain. Well, that's a bit like Miranda.'

'Well, after a few months of the God slot, perhaps you should have another bash.'

Preston looked reproachful.

'Sorry,' said Edward. 'Let me get you another drink.'

Preston had another Screwdriver.

'Anyway,' he said. 'There'd be no point. Not from Miranda's point of view, now she's pregnant. Or thinks she is.'

'Good Lord,' said Edward. 'An immaculate conception?'

'I prefer to think of it as a phantom pregnancy. But there is always the possibility that she did it with someone else.'

For some reason this made Preston feel depressed.

'Haven't you discussed it with her?'

'God no. How could I? We were both so embarrassed. I mean, there we were and I couldn't do it. I felt awful. She kept on saying she was sorry. It was terrible.'

'But what does Polly say? I mean, she must have talked to her about it.'

Preston shook his head. 'Apparently not. Miranda obviously hasn't told her. She must have wanted to spare my feelings.'

'But you've told her? Haven't you? Preston?'

'I didn't consciously set out not to,' Preston replied cautiously. 'I mean, I didn't tell her straight away, I suppose I thought Miranda would.' He considered. 'I suppose I felt a bit of a failure. See, the trouble with Polly is she always expects me to fail. She doesn't even think I can put up a shelf by myself. She's right actually, I can't. Not straight.

'She thinks I'm an under-achiever. You know, at work and everything. I suppose compared to Cliff Coxhall I am.'

Edward knew all about Polly and Cliff Coxhall. He'd worked for him at the time. Probably knew a lot more about their affair than Preston did.

'She wouldn't say anything. She wouldn't laugh at me or anything. But there'd be that look in her eyes.'

'I see.' Edward looked unhappy, as well he might. 'And is that why, I mean ... you said Miranda was the root of the problem ... is that why, I mean, does that explain you and Carla?'

'I'm not saying it was revenge, precisely. I mean, I was very curious about Carla. She was different. And she ... well, she made the approach, you know. But I suppose why I responded ... perhaps there was an element of *I'll show her*.'

But it wasn't as simple as that, or perhaps not as complicated. For years, certainly since her pregnancy, it had seemed to Preston that Polly had treated him as a piece of furniture. Something that had been around a bit too long and ceased to have any real function, like the tallboy in the front room. A note of irritation had crept into her voice whenever she spoke to him. She was not actively unpleasant but she ceased to regard him as a grown-up person, if, indeed, she ever had. Then there was all that pressure to mate with Miranda. It had begun as a sort of tease, a kind of dare. Then the bullying, thinly disguised as banter. It seemed to Preston that, consciously or unconsciously, Polly was trying to dump him. She didn't need the furniture any more, but Miranda did. Why not lend it out? Why not give it away? And gradually the banter had become more forceful, more personal. 'What's the matter, Preston, what are you afraid of? Scared you won't be able to do it?'

Well, he was damned if he was going to tell her he couldn't.

'I'd have told her eventually,' he assured Edward. 'When it was obvious that Miranda wasn't pregnant. But then she was, or looked like she was.'

'Good Lord,' Edward said again. Then, after a while, 'But when she has the baby Polly is going to think you're the father.'

'D'you think that will matter?' asked Preston, anxiously.

'Well,' Edward seemed bemused, 'I suppose it won't.'

'All the same, I hope it is a phantom job,' Preston confessed. 'I'm in deep enough as it is.'

He told Edward about the natural childbirth classes. Edward took it very well, though his eyes were beginning to glaze over, possibly from the effects of the drink. The vodka didn't seem to be making much difference to Preston, though he'd drunk about a dozen Screw-drivers. He'd been feeling anaesthetised and light-headed from the moment he'd walked into Maurice Wagstaff's office. He told Edward about the Singing Exercise and the Australian Knee-Capper.

'But why do you go?' Edward demanded.

'Polly thought I should. She said Miranda would feel embarrassed about being the only woman without a man. Bit like going to dancing lessons without a partner.'

'Preston, you really must be more firm with Polly,' Edward insisted. 'You mustn't let her push you about so much. She's too strong-willed for her own good sometimes. Don't let her subjugate you.'

'It's not just Polly.' Preston was starting to feel depressed. 'It's the same with Carla. It's the same at work. Sometimes I think it's the same with everyone. I don't mean to be pushed around. But I just can't seem to think of an alternative. And I don't like to be disobliging.'

'Sometimes,' said Edward firmly, 'you have to oblige yourself. You can't go around trying to please everyone. You end up pleasing no one, Preston.'

Now even Edward was starting to sound like his grandmother.

'Look, how about something to eat?' Edward suggested. 'I can't drink any more without something solid inside me.'

The last thing Preston wanted to do was eat.

'Fine,' he said.

'What d'you fancy: French, Italian, Chinese . . . ?'

'I'm easy,' said Preston.

They had a Chinese in Soho.

Halfway through the first bottle of wine, and after the prawns and sesame seeds on toast, Preston went outside to be sick. It was the first time he had been sick from drink since he'd married Polly and it was a strangely liberating experience. It reminded him of how nice it had been being a bachelor. He felt much better physically, too.

'You know what you said about pleasing myself,' he said, when he came back. 'Well I think that's what this Eva Eichler business is all about.'

'What Eva Eichler business?'

Preston reminded him.

'Ah yes,' he said, trapping a small area of seaweed with his chopsticks. 'How's it going?'

'Not very well,' Preston admitted. 'But I'm doing it for myself. I'm not being pushed into it by anyone else.'

'Jolly good,' said Edward. 'But why?'

'I've thought about that,' said Preston.

He thought about it again.

'I think I could fairly claim to be a feminist,' he said.

'Aren't we all,' said Edward, 'these days.'

He sighed.

'Well, at least we try,' said Preston, 'and that's just the point. Do you know any women who try to help us? I mean, who even meet us halfway?'

'Not personally,' Edward admitted.

'I was just thinking about it,' said Preston, 'while I was being sick, and they actually go out of their way to be unhelpful. Polly . . . Carla . . . Mags . . .'

'Mags? I don't think you've mentioned . . .'

'Woman I met up in Liverpool. The one who started the riot.'

'Ah.'

'I mean, I don't expect a pat on the back or anything, but, you know, they might give an inch. Or two. Now and again.'

'Yes,' said Edward, nodding.

'But do they? Do you know any who do?'

'No,' said Edward, shaking his head.

'And you know who I blame?'

'No,' said Edward.

'Eva Eichler,' said Preston.

'Ah,' said Edward.

'And women like her. I mean . . . false prophets, Edward, you know what I mean.'

'I do. Oh yes, I do. You sure you won't have any of this seaweed?'

'No thank you,' said Preston, firmly.

'It's very good.'

'I'll have some tea,' said Preston.

He poured himself some tea.

'Well, I mean, if they know all the answers, and they seem to think they do, what are they doing walking into the sea? That's what I want to know.'

'Splendid,' said Edward, 'but what if it was murder?'

'Yes,' said Preston, sighing. 'That is a worry.'

'No closer to finding out?'

'No. I've spoken to Suffolk Police – the press-office – but they didn't know anything. They're supposed to be contacting the investigating officer, but he was on leave until this week.'

'Where was it – Felixstowe? Have you been there?'

'No. I mean, not since I started this.'

'You should. See where it happened. Talk to people. There must be a local paper. There's probably a journalist who worked on the story. He might help for the price of a lunch. Find out if there were any witnesses. Find out what they did with the body. If they ever found it. Ask questions. It's the only way you'll get any answers. But what are you going to do when you get them, that's the thing?'

This had been bothering Preston, too.

'I don't know,' he confessed. 'I was thinking about a documentary for network features, but I should think that's out of the question now.'

'Hmmm . . .' Obviously Edward thought it was, too. 'Well, what about the God slot?' he proposed. 'They've put out some pretty good documentaries lately, by all accounts.'

'Don't they have to be about God, more or less?'

'Not nowadays. They just have to have a moral angle. Was she a moral person? Why did she kill herself? Was she killed because of what she said, preached, wrote? You know the kind of thing. Did she have a moral standpoint? Were her books about Great Moral Dilemmas Of Our Time?'

He reached for the bean curd and water chestnuts.

'Very loosely,' Preston conceded.

'Well, there you are then,' said Edward.

22 GO BACK TO DOCTOR
Miss a Go

'Felixstowe,' said Polly. 'I see.'

Preston didn't like the way she said it.

'Just for a few days,' he assured her. 'Maybe less. I just need to get away for a bit. To think.'

He didn't want to tell her about Eva Eichler yet.

'I suppose you're taking Your Friend with you.'

'God, no.' Preston was genuinely shocked. 'Why d'you say that?'

'I know you, Preston.'

'Apart from anything else, she's still got the programme.' He took in the last bit. 'What do you mean, *I know you?*'

'What about your job?'

'What job?'

'Preston.'

Preston carried on packing.

'Oh, I think the God slot will survive without me for a few days,' he said.

She sat down on the bed.

'It's not that bad, Preston. At least you're off That Appalling Programme.'

'Yes,' he said.

He knew what she really meant. She meant That Ridiculous Woman.

'Don't worry,' he said. 'I'll finish it tonight.'

It sounded like some household task, long awaiting completion.

'I'm not worried, Preston,' said Polly. 'It's you who's worried.'

She was right. Preston was terrified. The thought of the words he would have to use filled him with panic. He wondered if he could write her a letter and post it from Felixstowe.

Dear Carla,

But he would still have to find the words. And besides, she was expecting to see him tonight. She would have heard he was off the programme. If he didn't turn up she might phone the house. If he went away without seeing her he might even try to speak to Polly and Preston was seriously perturbed at the prospect of Polly and Carla speaking to each other. Discussing him and his many faults, discovering the liberties he had taken with the truth, their characters, what he had said to one about the other.

'Are you really upset about the God slot?' Polly asked him, almost gently.

'It's been my ultimate ambition,' said Preston.

He had heard Polly talking about the God slot when she was on current affairs. He knew what she thought about it, and the people who worked on it.

'I suppose,' said Polly, 'if you wanted, I could always speak to Cliff.'

Preston sat in the kitchen, sulking and pretending to read *Men – the Second Sex*. After a while one of the paragraphs impinged on his consciousness.

'Men,' Eva Eichler had written, 'have been provided with a penis bigger than that of any of their near relatives in the animal kingdom, and far larger than is strictly necessary for the functions it has to perform.'

Preston pitched the book across the room.

Polly came in.

'I'm sorry,' she said. She bent over and kissed him on the forehead. 'I'm going to fetch the twins. Want to come?'

'No thank you,' he said.

Polly shrugged and went to fetch the twins.

When she'd gone, Preston phoned the clinic.

'My name's Moody,' he said, hoping it would trigger some positive response and he would not have to say more.

But it didn't.

'Yes? And what is the problem?'

Preston thought he recognised the voice. It was the receptionist whom Dr Emma Blackwell had briefed while he stood in the waiting-room.

'I was told to phone you whenever I wanted to come,' he said.

'I beg your pardon?'

'I mean, come in for treatment,' said Preston, blushing.

There was a small pause. Then the receptionist said, 'Treatment for what?'

Preston struggled with his emotions. He wondered if there was a delicate way of putting it, but there wasn't. He had looked it up in Roget. The alternatives were: gibbosity, bilge, bulge, excrescency, caruncle, bleb, blain, fungosity and furnuncle.

'Warts,' said Preston.

There was another pause, longer this time. Preston wondered if there was still someone there. He noticed he was beginning to sweat.

When she spoke again her voice seemed to have altered slightly.

'Where are the warts, Mr Moody?' she said.

She knows, he thought. The bloody woman knows.

'On my penis,' he said.

She was laughing at him. She was holding the phone away from her and rocking. She was calling people over to listen.

'You can come right now, Mr Moody,' she said eventually. 'We'll have everything ready for you.'

'Thank you,' Preston said, with quiet dignity, but she'd already put the phone down and was presumably having hysterics on the floor.

'Everything' was a large ribbed bottled containing a black liquid and a small plastic spatula in a hermetically-sealed wrapper. Preston was relieved that it was not the paint-brush. The receptionist handed them over to him when he announced himself at her little window. She didn't look at him directly but there was a suspicion of water in her eyes.

'Where can I go?' he enquired.

It seemed that this problem had not occurred to her.

After some thought she told him to come round the back.

She was waiting for him in the corridor.

'I'm afraid all the surgeries are occupied,' she said. 'But you can do it in here.'

She indicated a small cupboard opposite the waiting-room. It contained a number of coats hanging on a rail, boxes of stationery on shelves, a vacuum-cleaner, two brooms and a dust-pan and brush. There didn't seem a lot of room for Preston.

The receptionist switched on the light.

'Don't forget to let it dry,' she said, 'before you put it away.'

Preston knew he should complain, make a fuss, but he didn't really want to meet the receptionist's eyes. He was beginning to hate the receptionist. She had very bad skin, he had observed.

Dutifully, clutching his bottle and his spatula, Preston entered the cupboard and she closed the door after him.

There was no lock.

Preston tried to wedge one of the brooms behind the door-handle but it wouldn't work. He looked for some string to tie the door with, but there wasn't any. He tried to hold the door and his penis and the spatula at the same time but he needed another hand. Finally he turned his back to the door, placed the bottle on a shelf, and began to apply the liquid. He took great care.

There was a knock on the door.

Preston jumped.

A large drop was shaken off the spatula and landed on the tip of his penis.

'Shit,' said Preston. He looked for something to wipe it off with.

'Have you finished yet?' asked the receptionist.

Yes, but I thought I'd stay here for a while, I like it in here, I don't ever want to come out, Preston screamed soundlessly as he tried to wipe his penis with a large manila envelope.

'No,' he said, 'I won't be a minute.'

He listened with his ear to the door wondering if she was listening on the other side. When he thought she'd gone he put the top back on the bottle and stood there holding his penis out to dry. There was just about enough room for him to stand. If he moved he bumped into the vacuum-cleaner or the coats or the shelves of stationery. He was reminded of one of Carla's off-stage areas where, according to Carla, women exchanged their most intimate thoughts. If another man had been in there with him, Preston knew they would not have exchanged intimate thoughts. He knew the man would have done his best to ignore Preston's presence entirely, penis notwithstanding. He would have pretended they were both fellow travellers on the Underground, and so would Preston. It was the only way to behave, but you couldn't expect women to know that.

He thought he heard a noise and looked over his shoulder, panicking. If someone other than the receptionist came in what would they think? They'd think he was masturbating. He hoped she was outside standing guard but he knew she wouldn't be. She'd *want* someone to come in.

Preston turned to face the door. At least, then, they'd see he didn't have an erection. He picked up the bottle and held it in his free hand.

If someone did open the door they'd see him standing there with his penis in one hand and the bottle in the other and they might think this was very odd but they wouldn't think he was masturbating. Not with a bottle in his hand.

There was a picture on the back of the door.

Preston noticed it for the first time. It showed a man and a woman naked. It wasn't the sort of picture anyone normal would masturbate over but you might not be able to tell at first glance. It indicated all the important parts in different colours: bones, blood-vessels, organs. Preston wondered why they wanted to put a poster like that on the back of the door. Did many people come here for treatment, he wondered, and if so for what? Just warts victims, or people with really serious diseases? People with social diseases?

It all seemed most irregular.

It reminded him of something, too. Something in his past. He thought he had been here before, but a long time ago. When was it?

The lavatory.

The Lavatory At The Dentist's.

Preston felt the sweat break out at the memory. He'd been five years old. His Auntie Ethel had taken him to the dentist's to have a tooth out. His mum must have been too squeamish. They'd been sitting in the waiting-room and he'd been reading a comic when the receptionist – a different receptionist from the one he had now – had come in and asked him if he wanted to sit on the toilet.

Of course, what she meant was: *Did he want to do a big one?* but Preston had not realised that. People in Preston's house did not speak of 'Sitting on the toilet' when they meant 'Doing a big one'. His Auntie Ethel might have translated for him but she was saying nothing. She allowed the receptionist, whom she referred to ever after, with faint contempt, as The Girl, to remove Preston's comic and take him from the waiting-room and deposit him without further explanation in the place that Auntie Ethel normally called The Little Boys' Room. There, surprised but obedient, Preston had obeyed The Girl's instructions to the letter. He sat on the toilet and waited.

After some time he heard her scratching about on the far side of the door.

'Have you finished?' she called.

Preston had been very puzzled. Finished what? he wondered. She had taken his comic away, so she couldn't mean that and there were no others in the room. Preston decided to ignore her. After a while she knocked again, more insistently this time.

'Can I come in?' she said.

Preston saw no reason to object.

He remembered the look of surprise and confusion on her face when she saw him sitting on the lavatory with his pants still on. It still made him groan with embarrassment to think about it.

'Can't you get your buttons undone?' she had said.

Auntie Ethel had turned up then and whispered something to The Girl and The Girl had looked even more confused and then Auntie Ethel had come into the lavatory and whispered to Preston: 'She means, Do you want to do a big one?'

Preston groaned.

'Have you finished yet?' said the receptionist. The new receptionist. The Wart Receptionist. 'Is anything the matter?'

Go away, screamed Preston.

'No,' he said. 'Everything's fine.'

I just hate women, he screamed, that's what's the matter. It is something I have just discovered. I have cause. I have many causes. I have an enormous file of Reasons for Hating Women. You are adding to them by the second.

'Isn't it dry yet?'

'Not yet,' said Preston, adding another.

It was dry but Preston still had something to do. He took from his pocket an empty glass bottle that had once contained an expensive shampoo of Polly's. Into this he poured about an inch of liquid from the Wart Bottle. Enough to keep him going while he was in Suffolk where he intended, Dr Blackwell's instructions notwithstanding, to treat himself.

'Thank you,' he said to the receptionist when he came out, handing her the Wart Bottle and the used spatula. 'Until the next time, then.'

He thought he'd dealt with that very coolly. It was only when he reached the front door that he realised he'd forgotten to put his penis away.

23
TAKE WRONG TURN

Preston moaned quietly to himself all the way to Baker Street. He had two basic moans. The 'Oh' moan and the 'Aaagh' moan, each accompanied by a small gesture.

When he did the 'Oh' moan he put his hands between his legs and squeezed, screwing his face up into a tight ball. When he did the 'Aaagh' moan he brought both hands up to chest level and trembled like a little mouse.

This was noticed by a number of his fellow-travellers but Preston was impervious to this. He was too busy moaning.

The specific cause of his moaning was the thought of what had happened to him at the clinic, but this generated other memories of similar incidents stretching back through his life. A whole history of embarrassing moments starting with him sitting on the toilet at the dentist's and ending with him walking out of the cupboard in the clinic with his penis hanging out.

But it wasn't just the past that troubled him.

The future looked worse.

It was going to be terribly embarrassing telling Carla that Their Affair Must End. The more Preston thought about it and the more he tried to find the words for it, the more embarrassing he thought it was going to be.

Carla, there is something we must discuss ...

Aaaaaaaaaagh.

Carla, in view of my sudden transfer to Religious Programmes I no longer feel I can continue with my present way of life.

Oh, oh, oh, oh.

He stopped moaning at Baker Street because his penis started to hurt.

It was a burning sensation like the first time but much, much worse. By the time he reached the Angel he was in agony.

He sprinted the two blocks to Carla's flat and hung on the doorbell.

'Where the hell have you been?' said Carla.

Preston darted past her and into the bathroom and slammed the bolt shut on the door.

He took it out and examined it in the light. It looked like it had been napalmed.

Preston moaned.

'Preston, what's the matter?'

'Nothing,' said Preston. 'I was just desperate for a pee.'

I'm drowning, he thought. I'm drowning and burning up at the same time. He turned the tap on and held his penis over the wash-basin and ran cold water over it. It felt better like that. He wished he could stay there for ever. He thought if he stayed there long enough all his troubles might go away and there would be no more pain. But he couldn't of course. You could never do what you really wanted to do. Even a simple thing like holding your penis under a cold-water tap for the rest of your life. There was always someone putting pressure on you to do something else.

'Preston, are you trying to slash your wrists in there?'

Preston sighed and turned off the tap and dried his penis on the towel and put it away.

'How are you?' he said, when he came out. He kissed her politely.

'How do you think?' she said.

Preston looked at her for the first time. If it had not been Carla he would have said she had been crying.

'You heard about the row,' he said.

'A row, you call it.'

'Well ...' He tried to think of another way of putting it. While he was thinking Carla fell back against the wall, slid down it and put her face in her hands, emitting the while a long, low keening sound.

Preston watched this process with alarm and confusion. After a few moments he sat down on the floor next to her and patted her on the shoulder.

'Carla?' he said.

Carla rocked her head from side to side without taking her hands from her face. Preston wondered what to do next. Go away? Is that what she wanted? Comfort her? Distract her? Preston, though very good with small children who hurt themselves, was hopeless with women. His normal procedure was to remind them how lucky they were compared to others: cripples, for instance, lepers, the starving millions, people with genital warts. Perhaps he should get his out and show her. That would distract her all right. You think you've got problems, take a look at that. A few days ago it was a minor blemish.

'Carla, what's the matter?' Preston murmured, with sympathy if not understanding. 'Tell me about it, please.'

Carla climbed up the wall and went into the bathroom. Preston remained sitting on the floor, feeling uncomfortable. Also slightly ridiculous. It seemed to him that the bathroom had played altogether too large a part in the evening's entertainment and he'd only been here a few minutes. From inside the bathroom he could hear the sound of running water and also, though he could not be sure of this, sobbing. He wondered what was wrong. He had never seen Carla crying before and it was a disconcerting experience. He wondered what had brought it on. Surely it was not simply because he had been given the push from *Shrews at Ten*. Or that it had been made patently obvious to everyone in the department that Preston Moody was *persona non grata*, a failure, bad news, fitted only for the God slot. If anyone should be crying over that it should be him, and he was not crying. He was sitting on the floor outside a bathroom feeling ridiculous.

He was wondering about getting up and sitting somewhere else when Carla came out.

He looked up at her. She was no longer crying but her eyes were very red.

'Where do you think you've been for the past twenty-four hours?' she said.

Twenty-four hours, Preston thought. Was that all it was? It seemed longer than that.

'I didn't know where you were or anything.'

Preston stood up.

'I've got some leave owing,' he said. 'You heard I'm off the programme?'

'I would have preferred to hear it from you.'

'You'll be better off with someone else,' he said. 'I mean a different producer,' he added hastily in case she got the wrong end of the stick, even if it was the right end.

'I won't be with someone else,' she said. 'I'm not doing it any more.'

Preston stared at her.

'I resigned,' she said.

Preston sat down again.

'But why?' he said.

'Why? Well, what did you expect me to do? It was me who insisted it went out the way it did. I told him if you went, I went.'

Preston heard this with mixed feelings. He was touched, impressed, also slightly alarmed.

'You shouldn't have said that,' he said.

Carla stamped her foot.

'I didn't expect him to accept,' she said.

But he would. Of course he would. Preston could have told her that. The viewing-figures were terrible. The Carla Experiment clearly hadn't worked. It hadn't been Maurice Wagstaff's idea anyway. He'd be glad to get rid of her. There'd be repercussions – stories in the press and so on – but they wouldn't do him any harm, or the Corporation. It would look like they were putting their house in order. But even so, it was a shock. He stood up again.

'Fight back,' he said, surprising himself. 'Talk to the press. You've got nothing to lose.'

'Oh I will,' she said. 'Don't worry, I will.'

She hugged him.

'I was worried about you,' she said.

Preston was now seriously alarmed. He'd never seen Carla like this before. He didn't know how to handle it.

'What are you going to do?' she said.

Preston told her what Maurice Wagstaff had in mind.

'You're too good for that, Preston,' said Carla.

Preston wondered what it was about God that made people say things like that.

'It's possible they won't have me,' he said.

This had not seriously occurred to him until now, but *what would he do if they wouldn't?*

'Perhaps I'll resign,' he said.

Carla looked thoughtful.

'I shouldn't do that until you've got something else to go to,' she said. 'You'll need a job if you're going to leave Polly.'

Preston reeled. Had this possibility ever been mooted? He tried to remember. He was sure he had never said anything so categoric, but perhaps his whole manner had implied that this was what he had in mind. Oh God, he thought. Aaaagh. Oh, oh, oh, oh.

She was off the programme. She had resigned because they gave him the push. There were no words for dealing with this. He decided to put it off, at least for a few days. Until he came back from Suffolk.

'I thought I'd go away for a few days,' he said. 'Have a bit of a break.'

'Away?' She looked startled. 'Where to? With your wife?'

'No, of course not,' he said, before he realised it might be much easier if he said he was. 'I'm going to Felixstowe. To think.'

We've had this conversation before, he thought. But they hadn't. It was just something similar, with Polly.

He felt a moan coming on but suppressed it.

Carla took him by the hand.

'Come to bed,' she said.

Preston followed her into the bedroom and they sat down together on the bed.

'I have missed you,' she said.

She put her hand on his crotch. Preston stared at it in amazement. He had an erection.

Perverse *bastard*, he thought. It knows. The bloody thing knows I can't do a damn thing about it.

Carla began to unzip him.

'I'm a bit sore,' he said.

'Why? What's the matter?'

He told her about the wart treatment.

'Oh you poor thing,' she said.

This is not Carla, he thought. *This is not Carla*. This is a substitute. This is an alien. This is Miranda.

She zipped him up again and gave it a friendly pat.

'Have you eaten?' she said.

'No,' said Preston. It came out like a sob.

'I'll make us something.'

She made them omelettes and a salad and later they went to bed to watch an old Hitchcock movie on the video. Preston had an erection through most of it. It wouldn't go down. He desperately wanted to make love.

'It's not that they put me off,' Carla said, 'but I know how sore you must be.'

Later still, with the mystery solved and Cary Grant having it off with the heroine in a railway tunnel under the end credits, Carla snuggled up to him and said, 'Preston, can I come to Felixstowe with you?'

24
GO TO FELIXSTOWE

They drove to Suffolk in Carla's car. Neither of them spoke much. Preston did not speak because he was driving and having to struggle with the early-morning traffic and his conscience. He did not know why Carla was not speaking. He thought it might be because she was already regretting her brief, extraordinary lapse into vulnerability.

Preston had always equated vulnerability with weakness, with Being Taken Advantage Of. Once, during his previous existence as producer of *Animal Antics*, he had produced a programme about the peculiar family life of crabs. One peculiarity which Preston had noted with interest, but not used in the completed programme, was that the breed known as Soft-Shelled Crabs, which were particularly vulnerable to predators, only became soft-shelled while mating. At all other times their shells were hard, and hence indigestible. In the course of setting up this programme Preston had walked along a beach in North Wales with the researcher and a zoologist from Bangor University, turning over stones in the hope of finding a pair of these creatures during the mating act, and it had occurred to Preston that it must be one of the most poignant and tragic aspects of a Soft-Shelled Crab's life that the precise moment of reproduction, when it is at its most vulnerable, is also the precise moment when it is worth eating. Perhaps Carla knew this.

At any rate, when he had arrived at her flat in the morning he had noted a distinct hardening of the shell. She had handed him the car keys with a curt request for him to drive. She couldn't stand traffic jams, she said.

She had said very little else since. Her manner towards him was cold and aloof. This did not disturb Preston in the least. He was, in fact, relieved. If Carla was regretting her moment of weakness it could be nothing to the regret Preston was feeling about his own weakness in agreeing that she should accompany him to Felixstowe. He told himself that he had no choice, that it would have been callous for him to spurn her, to bring his foot down on the soft shell. He told himself that it might turn out for the best and that a few days in each other's company would only confirm their total incompatibility and make it that much easier to part.

At the same time he could not help wondering if those same few days might provide the opportunity to finally consummate their long and strained relationship. To end it, as it were, with a bang.

The trick would be to achieve this objective while emphasising their total incompatibility.

This was partly the reason for Preston's taciturn and withdrawn manner through the endless traffic jams of the endless north London suburbs.

That and the problem of Polly.

Preston had lied to Polly. It was not the first time he had lied to her, but it was almost certainly the biggest lie. No one, not even Preston, could call it a fib. It was a Lie. It was a whopper.

Polly knew that Carla was no longer presenting the programme. Preston didn't know how she knew, but she knew. The lines that linked BBC secretaries past and present doubtless continued to jingle with good and bad tidings and they had lost no time in jingling.

So, she had said, when he came down from reading the twins their bedtime story, what's she going to do with herself, then?

And that's when Preston had told her she was going to Nicaragua.

He didn't know why he had made up such an awful fib. Lie. It wasn't just the basic lack of integrity. It was the fact that it was such a Silly Lie. It was open to so many pitfalls.

Question: Why is Carla going to Nicaragua?

Answer: Because Carla has always wanted to show solidarity with the women of Nicaragua in their hour of need.

Because Carla has always been interested in the Women's Role in the Revolution.

Preston had babbled, sweatily, veering into a mine-field of truths and half-truths and ... Lies. Trying to make notes as he went along. Wishing he could have said she was going to visit her grandmother in Totnes.

Question: Why is Carla going to Nicaragua?

Answer: Because Preston, either from too much or too little imagination, because he was feeling awful after settling the twins down for the night while contemplating an illicit trip with his mistress to Felixstowe during which any manner of evil might befall them, had suddenly and disastrously felt the need to remove Carla to the furthest ends of the earth.

Because, caught unawares by Polly's question, thinking on the spur of the moment, Preston had instinctively felt that anything less dramatic than Nicaragua simply would not do. Might seem a bit weak. Might succeed in arousing suspicions previously dormant. Might just incline Polly to the ludicrous belief that Carla was going to Felixstowe with Preston.

Why Nicaragua?

Because not even Polly, who knew Preston as well as any woman, or thought she did, could possibly imagine that he could invent a story like that.

But the complications. Oh God.

What if Maurice Wagstaff had a change of heart and persuaded her to come back?

This was not likely.

But what if she was interviewed in the press?

What if she was interviewed on TV?

WHAT IF THE AMERICANS INVADED?

This new thought laid its clammy hands on Preston's soul when he switched the radio on for the ten o'clock news and heard reports of 'heavy fighting' on the border between Nicaragua and Honduras. New warnings from the White House. Our Own Correspondent lobbing 'tensions' and 'threats' and 'worst scenarios' into the bulletin like so many hand-grenades while Preston cowered in his bunker and tried to assess his personal position in relation to this emerging world crisis. A new horseman had galloped up to join Death and Mutation and Perpetual Twilight in his individual vision of apocalypse. Its skull features were twisted into a knowing smirk and it was called Being Found Out.

Perhaps he could have Carla turning back at the airport.

But this would imply some communication between them. Better plead ignorance of her movements; ignorance and mild concern. On the other hand, if he let her press on regardless and Nicaragua went to war with Honduras and the Marines went in, what would he do with her? Airlift her out, have her fighting with the Sandinistas, get her shot by the Marines?

'You can go a bit faster now, Preston,' said Carla, sitting beside him, ignorant of this life-or-death struggle over her fate, 'or is this your idea of a safe speed?'

Preston saw that the traffic had mysteriously cleared and he was still poddling along at thirty. He put his foot down.

What if Polly rang Carla's number while they were away and she'd left a message on her answer-phone to say she'd gone to Suffolk?

'For Christ's sake, Preston,' said Carla.

Preston had just gone into a corner at sixty.

'Sorry,' he said. 'By the way, did you leave a message on your answer-phone?'

Carla looked at him.

'A message? On my answer-phone? Well, what a cute idea.'

'What did you say, exactly?'

'What did I say?'

'Yes. What sort of message did you leave?'

'I don't believe I'm having this conversation, Preston, but in the interests of scientific research I think I said, "I'm sorry I'm not in at the moment but if you want to leave a message speak after the beep." Is that all right with you? Or would you rather I'd said something else?'

'No, I just wondered if you'd said where you were going. Left a contact number or something. You know, in case someone offers you a job.'

'I see. Well, I didn't.'

'Oh.'

She wouldn't of course. Silly. But it wasn't silly to think Polly might phone. Polly was definitely suspicious. She had watched him packing and he had sensed it. It had made him very nervous. For some reason he had completely filled the hold-all full of under-pants.

'How many pairs of underpants do you need, Preston?' Polly had said and he'd had to take most of them out again while she watched curiously.

Why did he get himself into these situations? Never mind the excuses, why?

He supposed he'd just been taken unawares while he had a lot on his mind. Carla's miraculous change of character, her resignation, his warts, his erection. He hadn't been thinking straight.

And why did she want to come?

Because, surprising as this may seem to you, I quite like being with you, Preston, she had said, when challenged on this very subject. *Don't you want me to come with you?*

Oh yes, he'd babbled, *it isn't that.*

Just get me through the next few days, God, he prayed, a few days of mindless passion and then . . .

Then what?

Well, thank you very much, Carla, it's been wonderful but we're basically incompatible.

Oh God.

But I need a second mortgage to mend the latch on the gate.

But if I don't go back to Polly I'll only see my children at weekends.

But if I don't go back to Polly God might make my warts bigger.

And that was another thing. What passion? He was in no fit state even to consider the possibility of passion, mindless or otherwise. The pain had stopped but most of the skin was gone from one side. Only the warts looked undamaged.

Yet he kept getting erections. He only had to think of Carla and it started.

It was starting now.

Miranda, he thought. Quickly, think of Miranda.

Miranda, he had discovered the previous morning, was an antidote. The opposite of Mrs Gladrags. Strangely it was Miranda, and not Polly, who made him think of his responsibilities.

'And what about Miranda?' Polly had said, when he'd taken the underpants out of his hold-all and started to fill it with socks. 'Have you told her you're going?'

'No.' Preston had been puzzled. 'Do you think I should?'

'You'll miss NCT classes.'

Preston tried to look devastated.

'She won't have a partner.'

'She can use a chair,' said Preston. 'I'll phone her and explain. I'll ask her to take notes.'

What was he talking about? Take notes for what – the birth? But even if it happened he wasn't going to be there.

'Are you still with us, Preston, or on a different planet?'

'I'm sorry?'

'I only ask,' said Carla, 'because that truck driver in front has been trying to wave you on for the last five minutes. Would you care to overtake, or perhaps you'd like to wave back, only do something please because it's making him and me very tense.'

'Sorry,' said Preston. He pulled out just as they went into a bend and missed a car-transporter by feet.

180

'Sorry,' said Preston.

'You have passed your driving test, I suppose,' said Carla after a few moments.

'Of course I have,' said Preston. 'Ages ago.'

'Where did you take it? Alderney? Sark?'

'I was thinking,' said Preston.

'Well please try not to, as it obviously gives you so much trouble.'

Why, Preston agonised. Why are these two people doing this to each other? What are they trying to prove?

Why does she want to come with me to Felixstowe?

Just a few days, God, he prayed. Forget the passion. Just do not let the world end, just do not let me be caught.

25
THE NINETEENTH HOLE

Carla had a friend who lived near Felixstowe. Her name was Cristobel and they had been best friends at school. They had little in common besides above average intelligence and the oddity of their names. They were Carla and Cristobel in a form full of Sharons and Susans and Cindys and Mandys. And at a small Wiltshire primary school, this was enough. More than enough to compensate for minor differences like class and culture and appearance.

On all three counts Cristobel had natural advantages. Cristobel's father was a writer and her mother a musician. They lived in a big house outside Calne which they'd inherited from Cristobel's grandmother. They were comfortably off and they were smart and they voted for the Labour Party. That was why Cristobel went to the local state school instead of a private boarding school. Like them, Cristobel was rather posh. She was also very beautiful. One of those assured, watchful, fey children with a mass of long brown curls and big brown eyes. Carla was not posh, or beautiful, or assured. No one would have called her fey. She was awkward and freckled and brash. An ugly duckling waiting, without much confidence, to turn into a swan. She lived in a council house and her father and mother had both worked in the pork-pie factory in Calne until it closed, making them both redundant. Carla thought it was amazing they had called her Carla instead of Susan or Cindy or Mandy or Sharon. Her mum said it was because Carla sounded like Calne. *But why did you want me to sound like Calne*, Carla asked? But her mum couldn't tell her.

Calne was the original one-horse town, except that the horse was the pork-pie factory. The reason that Calne had the pork-pie factory was that several centuries ago there was a lucrative trade in Irish pigs. The pigs were landed in Bristol and herded to London where they were sold for slaughter. The only problem with this trade was that on the walk to London the pigs lost a lot of weight so the swineherds used to stop on the way to fatten them up. The place they stopped happened to be Calne. Something to do with the grass, or the acorns, or the local beer. And then one day someone had the bright idea of slaughtering the pigs in Calne and turning them into pork-pies and then sending them to London. That way they wouldn't lose any more weight between Calne and the capital.

So the Calne pork-pie factory was born. And around the factory the little village thrived. It became a town. And practically everyone in the town worked in the pork-pie factory. Then the pork-pie factory was sold to a bigger business with lots of pork-pie factories and then the bigger business was sold to an even bigger business in the convenience-food industry and the bigger businessmen who ran the even bigger business looked at their chain of pork-pie factories and said, Why have we got one in the middle of Wiltshire? And no one knew. Or if they did, they were keeping quiet about it because it was daft to have a pork-pie factory in a place just because a load of Irish pigs had stopped there two hundred years ago. So they closed the pork-pie factory at Calne and Calne no longer had any reason to exist.

But the people didn't go away. Unlike the pigs, they had nowhere to go to, not even to be slaughtered. They stayed and they drew the dole and their children went to the local schools and when they left school most of them stayed and they drew the dole too.

Except the bright ones.

Carla was one of the bright ones. At the age of eleven she went up to St Hilda's High School for Girls at Chippenham. And so did Cristobel.

St Hilda's was a Church of England school and they were very choosy about who they let in but technically it was part of the state system, so it was all right by Cristobel's dad, the Socialist, and you didn't have to pay fees so it was all right by Carla's dad, the redundant pork-pie pastry-maker. It was a half-hour journey by bus from Calne and they were the only girls from the junior school to go up together. And together they stayed.

Carla wasn't sure why they stayed together. It wasn't their names any more – there was at least one other Carla at the High School, a few Emilys and Sophies, even a Natasha – and it wasn't the fact that they had known each other in the previous school. They stayed together because they were in competition. To the death. No quarter asked or given. First one who gives in is a cissy.

At first they competed for results. Exams, homework, essays, netball. Anything that had a percentage, or a mark, or a score. Then it was clothes. Then boys. Other things came into it from time to time. One summer it was swimming, and diving from the high board. For a whole year it was ponies. Once, for a weekend until Authority intervened, it was punk hairstyles. But the front runners swiftly emerged and stayed way ahead of the field. Exams and boys.

Here again, Cristobel had all the advantages. Cristobel grew up in what Carla later learned was a cultural environment. Her home was full of books and paintings and flowers and music. Her father and mother believed in quiet encouragement. They talked to her a lot. They took her up to Bath and Oxford and London. They took her to restaurants and theatres and cinemas. They took her on foreign holidays.

Carla grew up in a council house with her mum and dad and two younger brothers. The only books they had were school books and children's books and a medical dictionary. There were no paintings. Instead of paintings there were ornaments. There were ornaments on every surface. On the mantelpiece, on the window-ledge, even across the top of the pelmet that covered the curtain rail. And instead of music there was the television.

The television was on from the moment her dad got out of bed to the moment after he said, *Well, that's it for one evening, then,* and switched it off and went back to bed. The television was Carla's cultural environment. The television brought Carla *Coronation Street* and *The Liver Birds* and *I, Claudius* and the Vietnam War. The television lived in a corner of the living-room between the window and the fire-place and it, too, had its quota of ornaments. A black cat with a long neck, a donkey pulling a cart full of some kind of fungus that was supposed to change colour when there was rain on the way, and an ash-tray with A Present From Ilfracombe written on it. Ilfracombe was where they usually went on holiday, or Weston-super-Mare, or, after Mum and Dad were made redundant, Granny's house in Totnes which wasn't much different from theirs but was close to Dartmoor and to the beaches at Torbay.

Carla's mum and dad did try to encourage Carla – they believed she should Get On – but they had no clear idea how to go about it. All they knew was that she should Keep Her Nose To The Grindstone. That was how you Got On. But Carla didn't need any encouragement to keep her nose to the grindstone, not when she had Cristobel. Cristobel might have her cultural environment but she didn't have Carla's will to succeed and she didn't work as hard. By working hard Carla kept in the race.

For the first few years, she was just a close second, a few marks behind Cristobel in everything except English and History. Then she began to pull ahead. By the fifth form, Cristobel was only better at science and maths and Carla was top of the class.

But boys were a different matter.

It was apparent from early adolescence that Cristobel could have any boy she liked for the asking. But she didn't like any boys – not any local boys, anyway – and she never asked. She treated her many admirers as a fickle queen with her courtiers. She expected them to dance attendance on her for scant reward save an infrequent smile. She expected her little coterie to hang around the school gates every evening and to follow her to the bus-stop and to show off and to compete for favours, but her manner was always distant, and the favours were never granted.

Carla was also in attendance on these occasions. A sort of duenna/ companion with sour face and sharp tongue. Cristobel prattled happily away to her while the boys romped like squabbling puppies at their heels and Carla kicked out at them from time to time. They tolerated her because she was Cristobel's friend. Otherwise they scarcely noticed her.

The boys didn't notice Carla until she fucked one of them. It was an act of calculated vandalism. His name was Lol, short for Larry, Carla guessed, though she never got around to asking. He was a gangling, grinning, lolloping sort of boy – perhaps it was Lol for lolloping – and he was in the sixth form at the comp. Carla fucked him at a party one Saturday night in June shortly before her fifteenth birthday. His eighteenth.

She didn't enjoy it but it satisfied a vague curiosity on the subject and contrary to popular myth it didn't hurt much. Lol must have thought it was Christmas.

There was a different attitude to Carla at the bus-stop the following Monday. It wasn't respect and it wasn't contempt. It was something between the two, not altogether satisfying, but better than not being noticed. Carla built on this small, uneasy platform. She established a reputation for wit and eloquence – or sarcasm, which in that company passed for the same thing. There was a predictable attempt to brand her a slag, although she never repeated the experience, not while she was at school. Not with Lol, not with any of his friends, not with anyone. Christmas had come and gone and it wasn't going to happen again in a hurry. The ice-queen ruled, OK?

When this became apparent there was an attempt, also predictable, to brand Carla as a prick teaser. Carla took this at its face value, which was dirt cheap. She had learned to recognise the double standards of the male sex from an early age, observing the way her father and mother treated her younger brothers and the way they treated her. But there was some truth in this particular allegation. From time to time Carla felt the need to top up her credit with Lol's mates, to stick the odd crocus up above the ice and wave it about, but she never went as far as she had with Lol and she got the impression, though she might have been mistaken, that the boys were rather more relieved than not. It was not long before she became aware that she had a nickname. The Nineteenth Hole. The hole that wasn't there. This did not please her, but she conceded that it displayed a greater degree of wit than she had come to expect from Wiltshire boys.

And it had an interesting effect on Cristobel. There had always been an edge to the relationship, now it drew blood. It was clear to Carla that Cristobel very much resented Carla's new popularity with the boys. She considered that it had been secured unfairly, improperly even. It was, so to speak, under the belt and she told Carla so. Carla, for her part, considered this to be bullshit. It was the equivalent of the Americans telling the Vietcong to come out in the open and fight clean and she told Cristobel so. Cristobel did not like it. They were both, at this stage in their lives and world history, rooting for the Vietcong. For a while they did not speak.

This was the summer they were competing for causes. As well as boys and exam results. They supported the same causes, but in different degrees. That was where the competition came in, the competition for who could be the Most Extreme. Being extreme, Carla quickly discovered, was like fucking Lol. It got you noticed.

It was her extreme views on Feminism that got Carla noticed by Cristobel's father.

Cristobel's father was exactly the sort of father Carla wanted for herself. Cristobel's father was called Jonathan. He had long hair and a beard and a voice like brown gravy. Or hot chocolate-sauce poured over ice-cream. He dressed in leather jackets and frayed Levis and hacked-off denim shorts. He sprawled about the place, tall and angular and benign, except when he was writing when he locked himself up in his study or was seen, pacing the lawns, preoccupied and intense. He wrote thrillers which weren't Carla's cup of tea and didn't sell very well but he was Carla's ideal as a father, or a lover. And he was interested in her. Not sexually, but really interested. Interested in her opinions. He argued with her. He took her seriously. He approved of her. Carla knew that all this made Cristobel furious. This was an added bonus.

Carla's own father was a disappointment to her. He was amiable and podgy and ineffectual. They said he was the best pork-pie pastry-maker in Calne, but what was that to Carla? What was it to Carla's father, or Calne, once the pork-pie factory had gone? Carla's father horsed around with the younger brothers and took them fishing and ratting and trapping rabbits. Carla's father was worried about the pressure Carla's mother was putting on Carla to Get On. He thought it would be a good idea if she got a couple of 'O' levels and went to secretarial college.

'They always need secretaries,' said the redundant pork-pie pastry-maker.

Sitting next to Preston on the way to Suffolk to see her old friend Cristobel, Carla worried that Preston was more like her own father than Cristobel's. This was a new thought and an alarming one. If it were true it would defeat the object of the exercise.

Since leaving school Carla and Cristobel had gone their separate ways, Carla to Bristol University, Cristobel to Sussex. They saw each other on rare visits home. Once or twice, Carla visited her in Brighton. But she continued to compete with Cristobel in her absence. She competed with Cristobel for impressive jobs and for impressive men. These were the equivalent of exam results and the boys at the bus-stop. But Cristobel didn't want to play any more. Cristobel had stopped competing. She'd never taken it too seriously. Now she'd stopped altogether. It was almost as if, with the disappearance of Carla, she'd lost the incentive.

Cristobel was now a medical social worker at Ipswich General Hospital. She was going out with one of the doctors, a junior house-man. She and Carla corresponded infrequently and once Cristobel had been to stay with her in London. Carla gathered that Cristobel was vaguely dissatisfied with her life but didn't know what to do about it. She was applying for a course in social administration at London University but didn't think she'd get in. She seemed to be in a backwater with life passing rapidly by.

While Carla was busy riding the rapids.

When she lost *Shrews at Ten* and hit the water and came crawling out like a half-drowned rat, it was the purest instinct for her to seek out Cristobel to remind both of them How Far She'd Got. Compared to Cristobel, administering to the halt and the lame and the dying at an Ipswich hospital – not even a London teaching-hospital, for God's sake – it seemed to Carla that she'd got rather a long way. She'd probably have sought out Cristobel even if Preston hadn't been going that way. But as he was she could put him to good use.

Preston was the sort of man Cristobel would be impressed with. He was presentable (in a floppy sort of way), he had a high-status job (never mind the God slot, they needn't talk about that), and he was interesting (or at least, he had a wife and children, which made him interesting). He was definitely an advance on the boys at the bus-stop.

Or was he?

In the cold light of morning, the morning after her binge of sentiment and self-doubt, Carla could not be sure.

Preston was not successful. He was of average height and he was not interesting. In fact he was really quite boring, apart from having a wife and children, and Cristobel might not consider that to be a Plus. If Cristobel wanted to look at it in a certain light, Carla might be considered to be his bit on the side. Carla didn't like the sound of that at all. It was possible that she would have to rescue the situation by treating Preston as a bit of a joke, a not very serious problem she could talk to Cristobel about, the way she'd talked to her about Lol, as if he was something of an embarrassment.

Preston was, after all, the latest in a long line of Lols. And that was another thing. For the first time it began to dawn on Carla that the Lols had had their time. They were obsolete. Worse than that, since AIDS, they were dangerous. Besides, Cristobel wasn't interested in Lol or his many surrogates. She didn't care. Cristobel didn't care what Carla did, or what jobs she had, or what men she had. Cristobel had stopped competing. Perhaps she'd never really started.

Carla took this badly. It seemed to rob her life of meaning. She felt like Calne after they'd taken away the pork-pie factory.

But like Calne, life had to go on.

'What do we do after Ipswich?' asked Preston. 'Can you look at the map?'

Carla got the map out of the glove-box and looked at it. It was only then that it occurred to her that Felixstowe was a very curious place for Preston to go to because he wanted to think.

26
A SILLY PLACE TO DIE

The termagant had emerged from her den, cross and spitting after a short nap and looking for someone to gnaw.

'Why are we here, Preston?' she said. 'What are we doing here?'

Preston, in his quiet way, had been wondering much the same thing. He stood at the hotel window with his back to her looking out to sea.

This was the precise patch of sea where Eva Eichler had drowned, or been drowned, depending on how you looked at it. *They took her woman's body and dumped it in the sea.* The gospel according to the Gang Band. Preston had the event clearly fixed in his mind, or rather, two versions of it, both painted in the lurid colours of a pulp novel. One: Moonlight. Two thuggish men, Neanderthal, brute-featured, dragging body of naked woman through surf. Beyond on distant headland, the dark shape of her hotel with a single square of light in an upstairs room. Perhaps a solitary figure outlined in the window, watching. Two: Same moonlight, same beach, but no men, thuggish or otherwise. Just the woman, still naked, walking slowly towards the sea, perhaps discarding the last of her clothing as she walked and the sea waiting for her like an open mouth.

The trouble was he couldn't imagine either of these scenes happening in Felixstowe. It was all so dismally mundane. It was all so humdrum.

There, beneath him, was the beach where it had happened, in whatever form. A grey strip of shingle with wooden groynes running out into the sea. A couple of hundred yards to the right was the conference centre, slick and forgettable in sixties' concrete and glass. Beyond that, The Front, which was a good bit older and not at all slick and totally forgotten.

The Front had probably had its heyday around the turn of the century and had been fading ever since, along with Clacton and Frinton and all those other sad Edwardian resorts, slowly expiring on their deserted beaches with an injured air of betrayal, like prim old ladies who'd once, in their youth, been tempted out of respectable obscurity by a Knees-up Mother Brown, dirty post-card, tuck your skirt in your knickers, what the butler saw, wink wink, flashy salesman with his fancy woman bit of a slap and tickle in the where-were-you sun, and didn't know whether to live on the memory or be embarrassed by it.

And who were now the victims of plausible PR men with their schemes for Conferences and Marinas and Exhibitions as if they hadn't made enough of an exhibition of themselves already and might reasonably be allowed to die in peace along with their piers and their esplanades and winter gardens and foolish memories.

Except that there was another side of Felixstowe, almost another entity, tucked out of sight on the far side of the headland in case it upset the non-existent tourists. This was the new container-port which Preston had glimpsed briefly on his way in, a productive, highly-profitable enterprise with all the character of a multi-storey car-park, a clinical exercise in time and motion where lorries and cranes moved bright orange Lego bricks in controlled harmony across a vast expanse of concrete with no nonsense and no mess and no apparent intervention by people. Preston's grandad, the deceased Liverpool docker, would not have survived a morning in the Port of Felixstowe. They probably wouldn't have let him through the gates.

The two Felixstowes went about their separate businesses with their backs turned, one tight-lipped and mealy-mouthed, the other whistling jauntily, and each pretending the other did not exist. For Preston neither of them seemed real. Neither of them lived up to his image of the Death Scene On The Beach. Eva Eichler had obviously made a mistake. She had come to the wrong place. This was not the sort of place you came to kill yourself, or to be killed. It was a silly place to die.

And what was he doing here? That was what really bothered him. It seemed as if it was the final wrong move in a game which he'd been playing desperately badly since the moment of his conception in Mrs Munster's boarding-house in Blackpool. He'd come to a crossroads and taken another meandering route to Nowhere. And here he was, Nowhere, wondering how he was going to get back and whether he should even bother.

'I mean,' said Carla, 'if you'd wanted to think, whatever that means, I could have suggested a million places better than this. It isn't even depressing. It's just ... shabby.'

Carla didn't like the hotel, that was the trouble, and Preston could hardly blame her. It was a truly appalling hotel, the sort of thing the

English do really well. With very little resources, no imagination, and no help from the government, the owners had created an institution that was a model of its kind. From the moment you entered the deserted foyer with its dead and dying pot-plants and its faded chintz, you knew you were here to be punished.

The process had begun with lunch.

It was the kind of lunch that, had they been in a better mood and less hungry, might have afforded them some amusement and provided an endless source of stories for future dinner parties. The 'fresh lemon sole', fresh from a deep-freeze and still frozen in the middle – frozen fish in Felixstowe with all that sea to drown in – the 'salad bowl', like seaweed washed up on a beach and left all day to dry, and a 'cheese board' consisting of a small hard lump of Cheddar and a piece of brie too tired to walk away. And so they retired, cross and grumpy, to their bedroom for a nap, it having occurred to both of them, more or less simultaneously, that there was very little else for them to do.

Preston would have liked to pursue his enquiries relating to the mysterious, vanishing Eva Eichler, but he still wasn't quite sure how to go about it and he was reluctant to let Carla know what he was up to in case she interfered. Which, being Carla, was only to be expected. So he brooded by the window and she brooded on the bed until, after a long silence, she said, 'Why did you want me to come with you, Preston?'

This more sinister version of 'What are we doing here?' caused Preston considerable anguish. It reminded him of those banal questionnaires drawn up for a women's magazine by some pseudo psychologist which begin with a statement and then attempt to elicit your views without giving you the chance to challenge the basic premise. As in, You ask your girl-friend to come away with you for a few days. Is this because, A: you think it might be fun; B: you think she might let you have sex with her; C: you think it might be so awful for both of you she won't have any further objection to you going back to your wife; or D: you've just poured some unnamed acidic substance over your penis and have a masochistic desire to maximise the pain?

You had to answer A, B, C or D. It was no good pointing out that you hadn't asked anyone away for a few days; they'd asked you if you'd mind if they came with you. And if you couldn't see what difference that makes you should be designing crossword puzzles for Kiddies' Korner, the comic sensation for the under-threes.

However, there was no point in pursuing this line of reasoning with Carla. In the circumstances there was really only one answer.

'I thought it might be fun,' Preston said, hating himself, but going for the full ten points.

'Ha,' said Carla.

Preston sighed and turned away from the window and came and sat down on the bed next to her.

'I know,' he said, brightly. 'Let's go for a walk.'

'Whoopee,' she said, turning her back on him. 'Where to? Into the sea?'

Preston stood up.

'Well, *I'm* going for a walk,' he said. 'You can please yourself. I shall see you later.'

Before he went out he rang the bell on the reception-desk. Surprisingly, after only a minute or two and three or four rings, a door opened in a dim recess of the foyer and a man emerged. Preston had never seen him before but he recognised him immediately. It was Mr Studge.

'Er, yes? Can I help you?' he said.

He wore a brown cardigan over a white shirt and tie. He was clean-shaven and his thin dark hair was combed carefully over his forehead where it had started to show through. His features were sorrowful, almost grieving. They looked as if they had been trodden on some time past and not succeeded in springing back into place. His eyes had looked briefly startled when they encountered Preston's as if he, too, had met someone he recognised. Now, as he approached, they were guarded, as if they were preparing to flinch from a blow, or a request.

'I was looking for the manager,' said Preston. 'Or the owner.'

'Ah,' said Mr Studge. Then, after a moment, 'Erm, I'm the manager ...' He left the sentence in the lurch as if it was altogether too absurd for a full stop, as if it needed some qualification, some excuse, but he couldn't think of one. Yet it was not entirely fantastical for Mr Studge to be managing a small hotel in Felixstowe. In fact it showed a certain degree of imagination on the part of the absentee owners, a sense of moral justice. Whatever else he had been in life, schoolmaster, abandoned husband, shopping-bagged trudger of dismal streets, Mr Studge had clearly been heading for Felixstowe all along. The small hotel had been waiting for him.

'I see,' said Preston, sternly. He had not, until now, thought of complaining about the hotel's many deficiencies. His object in searching out the hotel manager had been to elicit information about Eva Eichler and the last night she had stayed here, but, seeing Mr Studge, he was at once moved to complain. Mr Studge invited complaint as a small fat boy without glasses invites someone to tread on him.

'There's no hot water in the taps,' said Preston.

Mr Studge flinched.

'In fact,' said Preston, 'the rooms are very cold. I wonder is there any chance of having any heating on.'

Mr Studge looked injured, as if this was a blow below the belt. He had probably, Preston thought, come to the hotel as a guest, out of season, and been prevailed upon to stay and run the place. He might have hoped, at the time, that it might presage a change of fortune, a sudden change of direction that would make a new man of him. But it had been a cruel joke.

'I'm afraid,' said Mr Studge, 'that the heating is switched off for the summer.'

'In April?' said Preston, unbelievingly. 'In England?'

'I'm afraid I can't do anything about it,' said Mr Studge.

And that was why Mr Studge was such an excellent choice as manager, Preston reflected. Mr Studge would never be able to do anything about anything. It was far too big a problem for one man to solve, especially a Mr Studge. *But he would not run away from it.* He would persevere in his inadequacy. He would continue to be bullied by the guests and by the rest of the staff. He would continue to be responsible for unspeakably bad food and cold rooms and no hot water. He would keep the wreck afloat to the bitter end and then, probably, elect to go down with it.

Perhaps, after all, Eva Eichler had chosen wisely. A night at Mr Studge's small hotel would preclude any last-minute change of heart, any eleventh-hour ray of optimism.

'I see,' said Preston, again. 'Then perhaps a hot water-bottle, or one-bar electric fire?'

Mr Studge said he would see what he could do. Was there anything else? he asked, bracing himself for the tirade.

Preston briefly considered a complaint about the food but realised he was going over the top. People who came for the food did not stay at Mr Studge's small hotel. Instead he broached the real purpose of his visit. Yes, there was something else. There was a woman, a guest of the hotel, who had died.

Mr Studge looked wary, but his expression was not difficult to read. Only one woman, he seemed to be thinking, only once? And was it my fault?

'Her name was Eva Eichler,' said Preston. 'About eighteen months ago. In the sea. Were you here? Do you remember?'

Mr Studge had been there. He remembered. Such an untoward event in the hotel calendar. So out of season. A guest dying in the night and not in bed, not of food poisoning, nor hypothermia. Not his fault. Or, at least, no one blaming him for it, not yet. While his spaniel eyes begged the question: And have you come, at last, to accuse?

'I want to make a documentary about it, about her, rather,' said Preston, the man from the God slot, accusing nobody. And Mr Studge, relieved perhaps, told his tale.

'The American lady' had come on a night in June with a companion, 'a coloured girl, very tall', having previously reserved two single rooms, with bath or shower, facing the sea.

'Which rooms?' Preston enquired, wondering if one of them was his.

Mr Studge consulted the books. Miss Eichler in Number Ten on the first floor, Miss McCarthy in Number Eleven, next door to it.

'The room you're in,' said Mr Studge.

'How long for?' asked Preston.

One night only. They were touring. In a silver-grey BMW, said Mr Studge, 'C' registration, noticing such frivolous detail as a Studge notices a Fischer.

And what did he make of them, asked Preston, made so bold.

Too bold altogether for Mr Studge, who would never presume to make anything of anybody.

'I didn't see much of them,' he said, by way of an excuse, if it were needed. 'They arrived quite late. After eight.'

'They didn't eat?'

'We stop serving at eight fifteen.'

Naturally. Not a moment later. 'And they didn't come into the bar for a drink?'

'They asked for it in their rooms.'

No! *The sauce*.

'The coloured girl came into the bar and asked for a bottle of champagne.'

In Mr Studge's small hotel?

'Champagne?' said Preston.

'It's not something we keep in stock,' said Mr Studge. 'Except for special occasions, of course.'

'Of course,' said Preston, wondering if it had been a special occasion, or just something they normally had for a nightcap.

'What did she have instead?' asked Preston of Mr Studge.

'Dry white wine,' said Mr Studge. 'Two bottles.'

'How many glasses did she take up with her?'

'Two. That's what the police asked.'

'And did they come down again? I mean, did you see them again?'

'Not until the girl rang the bell. At two o'clock in the morning, she rang the bell on the reception desk.'

A sensation at the Hotel Studge.

'Who answered?' asked Preston, curious, off on a tangent into the realms of Studgery.

'I did,' said Mr Studge, with a sigh. 'I answered the bell.'

And this was what Bernadette had to say:

They'd had a few drinks in Eva's room while working together on the draft of an article for an American magazine.

At around midnight, wilted and in need of a break, Eva had suggested taking a walk along the beach. Bernadette had declined to accompany her.

No, she had said, this companion, cum secretary, cum bodyguard, who had let her walk alone and then fallen asleep and woken some time after two and started to worry because she had not returned and had rung the bell on the reception desk.

'I went down with her to the beach,' said Mr Studge, 'with a torch. And we found some of her clothes.'

A new title for the paperback. *Mr Studge Has An Adventure*.

'And I decided to call the police.'

Enter the police. Exit Mr Studge. End of adventure.

'There wasn't much I could tell them,' said Mr Studge. 'Apart from what I've told you. They stayed around for a while, asking questions, trying to find the body. Then they went away and everything went back to normal,' said Mr Studge, grieving, and Preston had a new cover for his paperback, not so dramatic as the Neanderthal men but more poignant and more mysterious: Mr Studge with a torch on the beach, holding up a pair of knickers and looking ... what? Quizzical? Perplexed? Worried or excited? Shocked? Or just resigned? Expecting to get the blame.

'And what about the ... Bernadette? Did she stay or what? Did you see her again?'

'No,' said Mr Studge. 'She left when the police did. I never saw her again.'

Preston went back to his room, where Bernadette McCarthy had stayed, and found Carla asleep on the bed. He closed the door quietly, in case he woke her up, and went into the bathroom.

He was in pain again. It came in waves. For a while he'd forget about it, then he'd feel the acid, eating away. He took his pants off and looked at it. So far, he'd probably lost only one layer of skin, but then, he wasn't sure how many layers there were. And besides the pain, there was the mess. He could hardly believe that a few days ago this had been a normal healthy penis with a few tiny bumps on the bottom. Now he could hardly bear to look at it. His eye fell instead on Carla's cosmetic-bag lying near the wash-basin. He opened it cautiously. He was looking for one of those stick things you used to cover up spots, but there wasn't one. The nearest thing was a kind of beige-coloured lipstick. Carefully, he began to apply it to the red areas. There was some improvement but it didn't do much for the black bits. He was experimenting with a mixture of talcum-powder and something called pan-stick when a voice said, 'What about mascara, or do you think that would be going over the top a bit?'

Preston stood up quickly, knocking the bag of cosmetics into the bath. He stooped to pick them up, babbling apologies.

'Preston, you can help yourself to my make-up any time you like,' said Carla. 'You can wear my pants if you like, or would that spoil the effect?'

Preston cringed.

'I'm just a little bit puzzled about who it's meant to impress. Me? Or were you thinking of putting it on general display?'

'It just isn't very nice to look at,' said Preston, still scrabbling for make-up in the bath.

'But who wants to look at it? I don't. And frankly, if I did, I don't think Max Factor Number Nine would make a lot of difference either way.'

'I just thought it would boost my morale.'

'Let me see it.'

'Without the make-up,' she said, when Preston showed it to her.

Preston washed off the make-up.

'Don't wipe it on the towel. My God, I have to wipe my face on that.'

Preston showed it to her again, dripping.

'What on earth did they give you for it?'

'I don't know,' said Preston, 'but it doesn't half hurt.'

She picked it up and wrinkled her nose. Preston jerked it away.

'Leave it alone,' he said.

'But it's terrible.'

'It was your idea.'

'But I didn't expect them to do that to it.'

'They're trying to burn them off.'

'Ridiculous.'

'Well, what else did you think they were going to do?' Preston demanded. 'Chant at them under a full moon?'

'I'll ask Cristobel about it,' said Carla.

'Who?'

'My friend Cristobel. I'm seeing her tomorrow.'

Preston was outraged.

'Carla, I will not have you discussing my warts with your friends,' he said.

What friend Cristobel? he wondered. Where?

'Don't be stupid, Preston, she's a medical social worker.'

'What's that got to do with it? It's got nothing to do with it.' Preston knew he was sounding hysterical but he didn't care. 'I don't want you talking about them to strangers,' he said.

'She'll probably advise freezing them off. That's the modern method.'

'*What?*'

She walked back into the bedroom. Preston followed through a mist of rage and fear.

'What do you mean, freeze them off? What do you know about it?'

'I read about it in a magazine.'

'What magazine? *Pig Farmers' Weekly?*'

Carla was putting her shoes on.

'Anyway,' she said, 'Cristobel will know.'

'Carla, I'm trying to stay calm about this. I do not want you to discuss my personal problems with ... this ... this Cristobel. Who is she anyway, what's she doing here?'

'She lives here. Near enough. Works in Ipswich General Hospital. I told you about her.'

'No you didn't. This is the first I've heard of her.'

'Well anyway, I'm seeing her tomorrow for lunch.'

'OK, but I'm serious. Where are you going?'

'I'm going downstairs to phone her up to tell her where we are staying. Do you mind?'

Preston threw himself down on the bed. There would be a bag, he supposed, a plastic bag like you had with a colostomy, only it would be filled with ice-cubes and they'd stick it to his penis with surgical tape.

'I do think it's touching,' said Carla, before she left. 'You trying to make it look nice for me. But don't worry, it doesn't worry me in the least, not aesthetically, anyway.'

27 USE PUBLIC CALL-BOX
Throw Six to Get Out

Preston watched through the window of their room as Carla set off along the cliff walk. There was a fine rain sweeping in from the sea and Carla walked with her head down and her shoulders hunched. This was not because of the rain, or to ward off rapists, but because she was muttering to herself, angrily.

Carla was muttering to herself because the hotel telephones were out of order. Temporarily, they said. Trouble with the exchange. She had been advised to try the pay-phone in the lobby of the conference centre. This had not improved her temper.

'I might see if they'll let me have a shower while I'm at it,' she said to Preston, savagely, 'or a kettle of hot water.'

'Ha ha,' said Preston, who was nervous because he was wondering if she'd take the car. If she didn't – and she didn't seem to like driving – then he might have time to make a call himself.

He waited until she was out of sight and then dashed down the stairs and out the back-door of the hotel to the car-park. He reckoned he had about twelve minutes. Five for Carla to walk to the conference centre, two, maybe more, for her to make her phone-call, five to walk back. Just time, if he was very lucky, to phone Polly and make sure everything was all right at home.

He used up three and a half minutes finding a phone – a public call-box on the coast road – and lifted the receiver in an anguish of hope. Everything was working. Dialling-tone, flashing lights, everything. A minor miracle. He put fifty pence in and phoned the BBC. After the first three words from the switchboard-operator the line went dead. Preston screamed. After a moment he pressed the blue button to get his money back. Nothing happened. Calmly, keeping a very tight rein on himself, Preston rang the operator.

'Operator,' she said. 'Can I help you?'

'I hope so,' said Preston, 'I put some money in and it's not working.'

'What exactly happened, caller?'

'I put in fifty pence and when they answered the line went dead.'

'Did you press the blue button to get your money back?'

'Yes,' said Preston, 'but nothing happened.'

'That's very strange,' said the operator. 'Was it five ten p's or a fifty-pence piece?'

'A fifty-pence piece,' said Preston, feverishly. He looked at his watch. Nearly five minutes and the second-hand still moving. But perhaps Carla was having the same trouble.

'What number did you dial, caller?'

Preston told her. 'That will be eighty pence for three minutes. I'll credit you with fifty pence. Please put thirty pence in the box.'

But Preston didn't have thirty pence. He only had fifteen pence.

'Can't I just have a minute and a half?' he enquired, but he knew the answer already.

'I'm sorry, caller, you can only have three minutes.'

'I'm sorry, caller, you can only have three minutes,' Preston mimicked silently.

'All right,' he said. 'Will you please get me a transfer charge?'

'Do you wish to make a claim for the fifty pence?'

'No,' said Preston, 'you can keep the fifty pence. But would you please get me the number I want and ask them to reverse the charges. My name is Moody. Preston Moody.'

'What number are you calling from?'

Preston told her.

'Please give me the situation of the call-box so I can make a report.'

This telephone is situated at Cliff Drive, said the sign above the receiver, if in need of help phone the Samaritans on Felixstowe 26741. Preston repeated as much of this as seemed relevant. A minute or so later he was speaking to Polly.

'Where are you?' was the first thing she said.

'Felixstowe,' said Preston. 'At a hotel, but the phones aren't working. I'm using a call-box down the road. How are you? Twins all right?'

'We're fine, thank you. What hotel?'

'I'm sorry?'

'Where are you staying?'

Preston told her, with reluctance, wondering why she wanted to know.

'You sure everything's all right?' he said.

'Oh perfectly. How's the thinking going?'

'Oh fine. Oh well, you know . . .' There was something wrong. She sounded altogether too brittle. 'It's a bit lonely, that's all. Pity you and the twins aren't here.'

'Liar,' she said, conversationally.

'What?' he said. His heart began to beat wildly.

'You've got your friend with you, haven't you?'

'What?' His heart started to take off.

'I've had the press on. She's not in Nicaragua at all, is she?'

'What are you talking about? What press?'

'The *Sun* and the *Mail*. Honestly, Preston, Nicaragua. You must take me for an absolute fool.'

'What did they want? Didn't she go or something?'

'Oh please.'

'I'm sorry, I don't understand. Why have the press been on to you? What did they say?'

'She is with you, isn't she?'

'Why should she be with me? Please Polly, will you tell me what's going on?'

'They wanted to talk to you about the programme and why you both left it. I said you were away and so they asked me if I knew where she was. I said I thought she'd gone to Nicaragua. They thought that was very amusing. They said the office had told them she'd gone to Suffolk.'

'What? But it must be a mistake. They must have got mixed up. It's me who's gone to Suffolk.'

'Yes, Preston, unless you're in Nicaragua. Perhaps that's what's happened. She's in Suffolk and you've gone to Nicaragua. To think.'

'Polly, believe me ...'

'I did, Preston. More fool me.'

'Look, this is just a simple misunderstanding ...'

'So then they came right out with it. They asked me if I thought the two of you were together. This was the *Sun*. The woman from the *Mail* was a bit more subtle – she asked if I thought you would know where she was.'

'Polly, all I can think of is that they've heard about her and me having, you know, and they're trying to stir something up. You didn't tell them anything did you?'

'No. I decided I wanted to talk to you first.'

'Polly, just don't fall for it, all right. Look, I'll come straight back. I don't know what I'm doing here anyway. I'll come back tonight.'

'That's up to you, Preston.'

'I will. Are the twins there?'

'No.'

'Well, where are they?'

There was a distinct pause. Preston's heart belly-flopped.

'Polly, they're all right, aren't they?'

'They're staying with Annie.'

'With Annie?' Annie was their childminder. 'But why?'

'Because I wanted some time to myself. To think.'

'Look, I'll drive back this evening,' Preston said, 'I'll be there about nine.'

'I thought you'd taken the train.'

Aaaagh, screamed Preston.

'I hired a car when I got here. I'll keep it.' But that would mean he'd have to hire one. He couldn't turn up without it. 'No, I'll return the car and catch a train. It'll be cheaper.'

'Well, it's up to you.'

'I'll see you about nine.'

Preston put the phone down.

Oh God, he moaned, oh God. He looked at his watch. Nine minutes, but it hardly mattered now. He picked up the phone again and dialled the operator and asked for a transfer-charge call to his office. The PA answered.

'Who's calling from Felixstowe?' he heard her ask the operator.

'Jane, it's me,' Preston interrupted.

'Yes, I'll take it,' said Jane. 'Preston, what are you doing in Felixstowe?'

'Never mind,' said Preston. 'Has anyone been asking after me?'

'Only the *Mail*, the *Sun*, the *Mirror* and Maurice Wagstaff. I don't suppose you know where Carla is by any chance?'

'Carla? Why d'you ask that? Why should I?'

'Oh I just wondered. They want to talk to her too.'

'Did you speak to any of them?'

'Not really. I said I didn't know anything.'

'What about?'

'Anything.'

Pause. Preston drew breath.

'Did you think they knew anything about, you know?'

'I know what?'

Preston whimpered.

'What did you say?' said Jane.

'Nothing,' said Preston. 'So they didn't say anything else about me?'

'Oh yes. They wanted to know if you and Carla were having an affair and was that the reason you were both sacked.'

Preston whimpered again but louder.

'But we weren't sacked,' he insisted, 'Carla resigned and I was moved to the God slot. Because of cunt.'

'Pardon?'

'I mean because of it going out on air and everything. Never mind. What did you tell them?'

'I told you. Nothing.'

'Oh. Well, thanks. And you didn't tell them where I was?'

'I didn't know where you were.'

'OK. And, er, have you spoken to anybody else, er, lately?'

'What do you mean? Like who?'

'Well, Polly for instance.'

'Oh, I see. No. Some other people have asked for you though.'

'Who?'

'Edward Cartwright and a policeman.'

'What policeman?'

'Inspector Johnston. Suffolk Police. D'you want the number?'

'No thanks, I've got it.'

'And Edward said it was important. Especially if you were in Suffolk. Where's Felixstowe?'

'Suffolk. Listen, you won't tell anybody where I am, will you?'

'No, not if you don't want me to. Preston, what exactly is going on?'

'Nothing,' said Preston, 'I'm on my way home anyway. But you'd better transfer me to Edward.'

'Ah, Preston,' said Edward. 'Hot on the trail I gather. But will you get there before the hounds get you?'

'What hounds?'

'The hell-hounds of Grub Street, my dear. Horror, drama, scandal. Is the chief shrew with you, then?'

'No. Who? Why should she be?'

'Ah. Then they've got the wrong scent. Still, that's not what I wanted to talk to you about. I've had some news about your Eva Eichler. Still interested?'

'Go on,' said Preston.

'Well, the story is she was born in Suffolk. In a little village called Elmer. Elmer in the marsh, no doubt. Sticky for her anyway.'

'What are you talking about?'

'Well if it's true, she couldn't stand for Vice-President, could she? Not an American born.'

Preston tried to concentrate.

'You mean if you're not born in America . . .'

'You can't stand for President. Or any post that makes you eligible for President. Like Vice-President.'

'But surely she knew that? Or, if she didn't, the people putting her up must have.'

'Perhaps she was hoping to keep it a secret. Anyway, the story goes she was taken to America when she was six months old but she's never even been naturalised. I don't know how true it is.'

'But hasn't anyone done anything on it?'

'Not as far as I know, but you've seen the cuttings. The family were German *émigrés*, Jews or Communists, maybe both, fleeing the Reich.'

'The which?'

'She was born in '38. Presumably they didn't think England was safe enough.'

'And you think she was trying to keep this quiet?'

'I don't think anything. But I'm told the story was about to break when she disappeared. Very conveniently, too.'

'How d'you mean?'

'Well, it would have been rather embarrassing for the people who were putting her up, wouldn't it? Liberal wing of the Democratic Party, egg all over face. Mind you, there was a lot of opposition, even within the liberals.'

'Who told you all this?'

'Oh you know me, dear boy. Little birds whispering. Always whispering. Never know what they come up with next. How is dear Carla anyway, bearing up under the strain?'

'Go to hell, Edward,' said Preston, savagely. 'Where is Elmer, anyway?'

'I looked it up for you. About ten miles up the coast near Snape

Maltings. Benjamin Britten country. Don't get lost in the mud-flats will you, m'dear?'

Preston promised he wouldn't.

He put his ten pence in the box and dialled Suffolk Police and asked to speak to Inspector Johnston.

'No answer from his office,' said the switchboard, after it had been ringing a while. 'Can I get you anyone else?'

Preston was thinking about it when the pips went.

He put the phone down and stared at it for a while. Then he phoned the operator.

'Operator, can I help you?' she said. He didn't know if it was the same woman.

'I'm speaking from the call-box at Cliff Drive,' he said. 'It's not working properly.'

'What is the nature of the problem, caller?'

'It doesn't work with fifty-pence pieces,' said Preston. 'It only works with ten-pence pieces.'

'Have you used any fifty-pence pieces?'

'No,' said Preston. 'Well, I used one but it doesn't matter.'

'You don't wish to be credited?'

'No thank you. I just want to know why it's got a sign here saying if you need help call the Samaritans?'

Pause.

'Do you wish to call the Samaritans?'

'No, no, I just wondered.'

Another pause. Then the operator answered in a different tone of voice. Almost friendly.

'Well, there've been a number of people've tried to kill themselves from Cliff Drive. We put the phone-box up at the request of the Samaritans. So people could call them at the last minute.'

'I see.'

'Were you thinking of killing yourself, caller?'

'No. Not at the moment. How many people?'

'I don't know exactly.' She sounded disappointed. 'Now, if that's all, I haven't got all day.'

Preston put the phone down and walked to the edge of the cliff. It was a very small cliff. You probably wouldn't kill yourself jumping off it, just break a leg. But then you might drown. If the sea was in.

Still, there must be easier ways, Preston thought.

He went back to the car. It was five-thirty, nearly half an hour since he'd left the hotel. Carla would have been back long ago. He wondered if the pubs were open.

28
MEET CRISTOBEL

There was only one other man in the bar, so soon after opening-time, and he was talking to the landlord about moral values and the youth of today.

'They stopped joining the Boy Scouts,' he said. 'That's what happened.'

'Dib dib dib,' said the landlord. 'Good evening, sir, what can I get you?'

Preston ordered a pint.

'Of course it's the sort of thing the kids today despise. No sense of duty. No sense of pride.'

He looked at Preston.

'Baden-Powell,' he said.

'How d'you do,' said Preston.

'Baden-Powell, founder of the Scout movement.'

'Oh,' said Preston. 'Sorry. Yes.'

It was a pardonable error. He was the spitting image of his hero, in his sixties, thin and ruddy with a grey moustache and a long bony nose with bits flaking off it. All he lacked was a pair of green garters.

'You ever in the Scouts?' he enquired.

Preston confessed that he had not had that privilege.

'Hmmm,' said the man.

He assumed an expression of civilised disdain and turned back to the landlord.

'I'd spend two hours polishing my shoes for an inspection.'

Preston took his drink away to a far corner and brooded on his inadequacies. He was not being fair to people, that was the thing. He was not being fair to Carla, or Polly, or even to himself.

'No moral fibre,' said the man at the bar. 'No sense of respon-sibility.'

Exactly, said Preston to himself, in his corner. It was time he got a grip on things, put his house in order. He had to tell Carla exactly where she stood. It was only fair. Besides, he'd told Polly he'd be back in London this evening.

He looked at his watch. Twenty to six. It didn't leave much time. He wondered if Carla would want to come back with him. It would be awful if she did. On the other hand, if she didn't, he'd have to catch a train. He'd have to ask her to run him to the station.

Preston imagined what it would be like and groaned.

And what about Eva Eichler? It seemed a bit feeble to give up now, when he was so close. But close to what?

The village of Elmer. A twenty-minute drive away.

But what was he going to find in Elmer?

A diversion. Anything to put off the evil moment when he had to make a decision about himself and his life and Polly and Carla. That's what all this was about. It was nothing to do with wanting to make a documentary.

Preston groaned again.

No. He'd made a decision. He was going back to Polly. All he had to do was find the words to tell Carla. No more prevaricating.

'It's no good beating about the bush,' said the man at the bar. 'You've got to grasp the nettle. They don't belong here, they'd be better off where they came from.'

Exactly, thought Preston.

She was waiting for him back at the hotel, but she was not alone. There was another woman with her and they were sitting at a table in the bar with their heads together. Preston paused, taken aback. For a moment he had an irrational desire to run, but they turned and saw him.

'Hello there,' he said, cheerfully, crossing the room towards them, 'I went to pick you up.'

Carla regarded him thoughtfully.

'I've been back here an hour,' she said.

'I got lost,' said Preston, with a laugh. Ha ha.

'You can see it from the hotel,' she said. She didn't seem angry, only curious.

'I know,' said Preston. 'Ridiculous.' He laughed again.

Carla looked at the other woman and the other woman smiled, very slightly, as if to acknowledge a confidence.

'This is my friend Cristobel,' said Carla.

He thought it would be. Cristobel was not unlike Carla, in a way. She was prettier, more petite, dark-haired, but they had the same front of cool self-possession, the same air of knowing something you didn't. He was reminded of two school-girls, fifth-formers perhaps, out for a lark, smoking and drinking and trying to appear relaxed about it. They used their cigarettes like a prop, averting their faces exaggeratedly to exhale, waggling their fingers constantly over an ash-tray, even when there was no ash. Preston sat down next to them, feeling alienated, but this was no new thing.

'How long have you been living in the area?' he enquired, politely, while his mind screamed for more precise information. Like, what are you doing here? When are you going to go? What am I going to do if you don't?

And what have they been talking about?

Whenever Preston encountered two women together – his wife, say, and a friend, in the kitchen – he suspected that they had been talking about him only seconds before. They always had that kind of expression on their faces. The one who'd been doing the talking would look crafty, slightly pleased with herself, the other measuring, judgmental. Polly said this was rubbish, of course. She said women had far better things to talk about, but Preston was haunted by the fear of what they could have been saying. What sexual failings, what unreasonable demands and private aberrations, what doubts and fears and insecurities, what family skeletons might have come crawling out of the fridge with the cheap Sainsbury's muscadet and the Bath Olivers.

'I asked Chrissie about your warts,' said Carla, 'and she says you should have them frozen off.'

Preston stared at her.

'They use a kind of blow-torch thing,' said Carla, 'only it blows a stream of cold air at them and a couple of days later they fall off. It's quite painless.'

A mist seemed to have risen very suddenly in front of Preston's eyes, a cold, wet haze like the ones Suffolk was famous for, or it might have been tears.

'You can go into the Lydia ward at St Thomas's,' said Cristobel, 'and have them done on the spot. You don't even need an appointment.'

He couldn't believe it. It was outrageous. This woman, a total stranger until a moment ago, knew about his warts. Preston was stunned. His most intimate secret had been casually imparted as a piece of happy-hour chitchat. It was unthinkable. It was infamous. Even for a woman. He was now expected to sit here, nodding and smiling and making polite conversation, with an unknown woman who knew he had warts on his penis.

'We thought we'd go out to dinner,' Carla was saying. 'Chrissie knows a decent restaurant about twenty minutes away. What's the matter?'

Preston stood up.

'I've just remembered something,' he said. 'I won't be a minute.'

Twenty minutes. A twenty-minute drive up the coast. Of course it's a complete waste of time, he thought, as he got into Carla's car. I don't know what I'm expecting to find there, he thought, as he drove out of the car-park and took the coast-road out of Felixstowe.

I don't even know why I'm doing it, he thought, as he followed the signs for Snape Maltings where Benjamin Britten had built his fantasy opera-house in the marshes and where, if Edward Cartwright could be believed, there was a little village called Elmer where Eva Eichler had been born to a family of German refugees.

29 FIND A GRAVE
Throw Again

But there wasn't a village called Elmer.

Preston couldn't find it on his map and when he stopped at Snape and asked, no one had ever heard of it.

'You're sure you're in the right county?' asked the man in the craft-shop at the Maltings, the third person he'd asked.

Preston walked out on to the bridge over the river and leaned on the parapet and looked out over the marshes towards the sea. The drizzle had cleared and the last of the sunlight poured through a wedge in the clouds. It was a wonderful filming-light, the magic hour at the end of the day, all golden green and shadow, and Preston, who despised Chocolate Box and Pretty Pictures, longed to be filming it. To be on the road again with a film-crew and no other responsibility than to capture those last few minutes on film before they wrapped-up for the day and went off to find a pub.

He lingered, drinking it in. Swans and ducks on the river, the sunlight striking sparks off the water and stippling the reed beds with shadow, the spritsail of an old Thames barge in the distance. He wondered why he had never appreciated this when he had the chance, when he'd just started directing and he was working on film and could have shot anything he liked, just for the sake of it. But he'd been too ambitious. In too much of a hurry to come off children and animals and shoot something important, something Serious. But there was nothing wrong with filming children and animals. You could do an awful lot with children and animals, as a film-maker and in a light like this.

A passing seagull, passing into the sun, shat on his hand.

Preston wiped it off.

If he drove straight to Ipswich he could still catch a train to London. He could leave the car in the station car-park and the keys with the station-master. He could phone Carla and say one of the children was ill and he'd had to rush back. Later he could talk to her properly. He could say the incident had made him aware of how badly he was behaving and that it must stop.

'Excuse me, but were you the gentleman who was enquiring about Elmer?'

Preston turned to confront an elderly man wearing a linen suit and a panama hat. He carried a walking-stick, though he looked sprightly enough not to need it, and a dog of the spaniel sort lolloped obediently at his heels. He looked like a retired vicar, or a poet laureate.

'That's right,' said Preston. 'D'you know where it is?'

The man smiled, as at some small private joke.

'I know where it was,' he said.

Preston parked his car outside the church where the road ended and walked through the graveyard until he found the stile and the sign that said Public Footpath, pointing a gnarled finger vaguely across the marshes. It was a bleak, lonely place, the raised footpath the only distinction between earth and sky and Preston the only person on it. He disturbed a heron fishing in the ditch below and it took off with a startling slap of its heavy wings and a single harsh cry. Preston stopped and watched its slow, ponderous flight, low across the reedbeds, and saw in the distance the steeple of the old church that marked the village that had once been Elmer.

Elmer in the Marsh.

'It sank,' the old man had said, 'over the years, like Venice, but not quite so magnificently.'

No. There was nothing magnificent about Elmer, thought Preston, when he came closer and surveyed the ruins. A few derelict cottages, open to sky, ragwort and other marsh weeds running riot over what had once been their gardens. A slightly larger ruin which might have been a school-house or hall. And the wreck of the church, standing on more solid ground but raddled and holed, like some grim old relic of the Somme.

'They moved the last of them out during the war,' the old man had said, 'and the Navy used the old church for target practice – from the sea.'

It was too flat for Preston to see the sea, too still for him to hear it, but he knew it was there, at the edge of the mud-flats, lying low, ready to slink up on the land through a thousand little creeks and channels until it was close enough to pounce.

There was nothing for him here. The graves were old and they, too, were sinking, their inscriptions with them. Those he could still read were old, belonging to a different world from that which had spawned Eva Eichler. He'd reached a dead-end. It was time to go back.

Then he saw the flowers.

A vase of roses and ox-eye daisies, red, white and yellow, startling to the eye against the green and the grey. A vase of flowers in an empty graveyard like a splash of blood on a shroud and the weeds stripped back from the stone cold slab to expose the name and the basic facts of its brief existence:

Eva Eichler
Beloved wife of Aaron
Born Leipzig 1912
Died in exile 1939
RIP

It was a moment before he realised it was not his Eva. It was her mother. It had to be. And the flowers had been here considerably less than forty-seven years.

He turned, startled, as if he had heard something, or become aware of someone watching, but there was nothing, no one. Still, he walked back more quickly along the causeway to where he had left the car and there was something in the atmosphere of the place, a loneliness, a Peer Gynt sense of despair and desolation and death, that made him want to quit the place fast, to seek the comfort and companionship of people – Carla, or Cristobel, or even Mr Studge. And yet someone had placed fresh flowers on the grave of Eva Eichler's mother and he had to know why. Or who.

So he stopped when he saw the house.

Not the house. A gate, leading to a house, hidden behind trees. A sign beside saying Private Property. No Trespassing.

Preston opened the gate and walked up the drive.

The gravel crunched expensively like five-pound notes.

Around a bend he reached another sign that said, Trespassers Will Be Castrated.

The bend continued, and so did Preston, compelled now by a force that defied reason, even the fear of castration, and around the bend there was a house and around the house there were flower-beds of roses and ox-eye daisies, red, yellow and white, and kneeling next to the flowers was a woman wearing a candy-striped frock and a straw-hat. And then Preston remembered what Mr Studge had said and wondered why he had not thought of it before.

They stayed around for a while asking questions, trying to find the body. Then they went away and everything went back to normal.

But he never said they *found* the body.

The woman was walking towards him with the secateurs still in her hand but the dog reached him first. It came swift and unseen and didn't bark until it was within striking distance.

Preston leaped, his heart leaping further, his mind full of Dobermans and slavering jaws.

But it was only a Dachshund and its teeth barely broke the skin of his ankle.

'Cleo, stop that, you naughty dawg,' said the woman, in an accent which, even at a distance and in his current state of anxiety, gave Preston a clear guide to country of origin.

But the dog didn't stop. Preston shook his leg feebly but this seemed only to enrage it. It began to worry, issuing growling noises.

'Kick its balls,' said the woman.

It was not a very English thing to do but like most American solutions it went straight to the heart of the matter. Preston drew back his free leg and kicked. The dog yelped and let him go.

'You shit,' said the woman. 'You kicked my dawg.'

Preston was perplexed.

'But you told me to,' he complained.

'I meant its toys,' she said. 'On the lawn.'

Preston stared foolishly and then saw the much-chewed remnants of a tennis-ball, just a few yards away.

'Oh God,' he said.

Then the other woman came up behind him, faster than the dog and more lethal, and he did not turn until much too late.

30
THE COTTAGE OF CONTENT

Well, you've only got yourself to blame, his gran was saying, with satisfaction, looking down at him, and Preston swinging there, snivelling. It was what she always said, as if it was some sort of consolation whenever something went wrong in Preston's life, if he hurt himself playing in the street, or caught a cold playing in the rain, or burned his fingers playing with fire. But Preston didn't want himself to blame. He wanted it to be someone else's fault.

The only time he could remember his nanna blaming someone else was when Preston had fired an arrow and it had hit Jimmy Blackett in the nose, just missing his eye, and when Jimmy Blackett's mother had come round to complain Preston's gran had said that Jimmy Blackett was accident-prone. But later she'd taken the bow-and-arrows and broken them in two and thrown them on the fire and sent Preston to bed without his tea. His gran was always doing things like that to him.

Perhaps that was why Preston was snivelling. He'd got all tangled up in the netting under the bow of his ship, where he went to get to sleep, and his gran was towering over him, a huge, remorseless bowsprit, the Goddess of Retribution, with a chin like Desperate Dan and eyes like King Kong and his broken bow-and-arrows clutched in one mighty fist. And then he was running, his feet sinking in mud or water, and they were all after him, like the witches in the poem by Robbie Burns that had terrified him as a child. No Cutty Sark but his gran and Polly and Carla and Cristobel and Miranda and Dr Emma Blackwell and the Wart Receptionist and the Australian Knee-Capper and the Woman on the Switchboard at the Telephone Exchange. All in it together, all out to get him.

And then, just as they were reaching out for him, he was back in his netting and all was peace and calm aboard the good ship Male Order and the bowsprit had turned into Neptune and Preston was captain of his ship with no women aboard, just him and the lads who were rolling dice on the deck above, the noise drumming slightly in his head.

Suddenly awake, as though stunned into consciousness, he was staring at a white ceiling, patterned with sunlight. He was lying on a bed, covered with a duvet and it was daylight and he had a head-ache and a sore head and a terrible itch in his groin.

He put his hand down to scratch it and remembered at once what had happened. He stopped scratching and felt behind his right ear and there was a lump there, a quite painful lump. God, he thought, the bloody woman, she hit me.

He sat up. He was alone in what appeared to be a bedroom. He looked at his watch. Twenty past eight. He lowered his feet carefully on to the floor and discovered he was without shoes and socks. Otherwise, dressed as before.

Perhaps he was in hospital.

He twitched the curtain aside, wincing from the sudden glare. He was on the first floor, overlooking a garden. He could see nothing beyond that, no other buildings, no road, and it was very quiet.

Not a hospital.

He let the curtain fall back and thought about it. He had been hit on the back of the head. This was a shock. So, too, was the knowledge of who had hit him, because although he'd caught the merest glimpse of her when he turned, it was enough to give Preston a reasonable clue to her identity, unless there were two women like that walking around the region of Felixstowe. And this raised other questions, at least as troubling.

Like, who was the woman in the straw-hat?

He looked around for his shoes and socks but before he could find them the door opened and she walked into the room, without the hat, but carrying a tea-tray.

'So. We're awake,' she said, brightly. 'How's the head this morning?'

Preston looked at her, thinking about this. How's the head? As if he was a weekend guest who'd had a bit too much to drink the night before. She put the tray down by the bed and looked at him, politely enquiring.

'Oh, the head,' he said. 'Oh, there's a bit of a lump but, erm ... how's the dog?'

What was he saying? A bit of a lump. How's the dog? He'd been mugged in broad daylight. Done over. Assaulted by a female karate champion from Toxteth, the women's movement's answer to Rambo. He could sue.

'Oh the dawg's fine. Just fine. It's you we were worried about. You went out like a light. Let me look at you.'

Preston allowed himself to be looked at.

'What exactly happened?' he said, because he didn't know what else to say and it would be interesting to hear what she had to say about it.

'You don't remember?'

'I remember being hit.'

He hoped that wasn't too pointed. It was difficult to know how to behave in the circumstances, to strike the right social form. It hadn't happened to him before.

'You were concussed. Not quite out but dazed.'

She was rolling his eyes back, peering into the pupils.

It occurred to him that she might have been a doctor before she became a professional feminist. This figured.

'Look up to the ceiling. That's right. Now down.'

'But it's morning. I must have been out all night.'

'I gave you something to help you sleep.'

'Ah.'

Now she was peering in his ear.

'Well, I wondered about getting you to hospital but it seemed a little unnecessary, so we thought we'd just let you sleep it off. You seem all right, how d'you feel?'

She stepped away from Preston and they looked at each other. Preston saw a plump, attractive woman in her mid-forties with dark eyes and a calm, almost serene expression. Her manner was gentle, even maternal, and only her voice, with its New York cutting edge, had the stamp of the writer of *Coming First* and *Men – the Second Sex*.

'You're Eva Eichler, aren't you?' he said at last.

She looked away from him and he couldn't see the expression in her eyes. She was looking at the tea-tray.

'Milk?' she said.

'Oh, yes please,' he said.

She poured the milk.

'Sugar?'

'Oh, no thank you.' He coughed. 'Excuse me.'

His Auntie Ethel would have been proud of him.

'My name's Preston Moody,' he said, 'from the BBC.'

'I know,' she said.

She handed him his tea.

'We looked inside your wallet. In case there was someone we had to contact. I wondered then, if ... ' She frowned and sighed, as if slightly irritated. 'But why?'

Why?

'Well, I was hoping to make a documentary about it,' he said, thinking that would do to be going on with.

'A documentary? About ... It?'

'How you died. Look, I'm sorry, but I am right, aren't I? You're Eva Eichler? And that was Bernadette, who hit me. Wasn't it?'

'I'm sorry about that. She's a little over-protective and when she saw you kick Jessie ...'

Jessie was presumably The Dawg. She had hit him because he had kicked The Dawg. This was, in a way, a relief.

'Everyone thinks you're dead,' he told her.

It was only then, despite what he'd said, that it really dawned on him that she wasn't.

'Can you eat some breakfast?' she said.

She led him outside on to a terrace with a table and chairs. He may have looked nervous.

'Bernie's a late riser,' she said. 'It's her only vice.'

Ha, thought Preston.

'I'll go fix breakfast,' she said. 'Sit down and relax.'

Preston sat down but he did not relax.

It was a brick terrace running the length of the house with steps down to a long garden and the orchard at the bottom. Daffodils and other Spring flowers poked through the lawn in clumps. The sun was warm, even so early in the morning, so early in Spring. It came as a surprise to Preston that it was Spring. He had hardly noticed. From inside the house came the sound of music, it might have been a hymn, and then an electric motor blending his orange juice, grinding his coffee.

And Preston waited, just as he had waited in the garden at the rear of the convent where he went every Thursday evening for his Catechism as a child, while Mother Bernard went into the kitchens to fetch him a glass of milk and a piece of fruit-cake. At the end of his instruction, always, in fine weather, Mother Bernard would lead him into the garden and leave him sitting on a wooden bench near a statue of Our Lady.

'Now you can relax,' she would say, 'while I fetch you your bit of cake.'

But Preston had not relaxed.

He used to sit in the garden with his poor little brain whirring away with questions. Questions about God and Sin and Eternity, this little seven-year-old trying to figure it all out: For ever and For ever and For ever. God, World Without End, For ever and Ever and Ever, Amen. Thinking about Martin Luther terrified in the storm worrying about the tree falling on his head and being suddenly propelled into it, Eternity. For ever and Ever. Inescapable, permanent, for all eternity to be You. Oh God, anything was better than that. Even death was better than that. Better to be a tree. Falling crack, bang, wallop, right on top of mad-dog Martin Luther. And he would press his little fist into the bench until it hurt and the panic subsided and then, when he had thought he had won, along it would come, tripping innocently along in the rear: the question he feared to ask more than any other: What did she mean by Being Tempted in the Night?

Seek and ye shall find, saith the Lord, ask and it shall be answered unto you. But did Preston really want to know?

Why was Eva Eichler not dead?

What did it mean?

What am I doing here?

I have been hit on the head, Preston told himself, I am not myself. I am confused.

He composed himself mentally.

He looked around the garden.

He saw the dog lying under a tree. It looked at him and growled.

What had they done with his shoes and socks?

He scratched his groin.

Why did he have an itch in his groin?

'Here you go,' said Eva Eichler, putting a tray on the table. Coffee, rolls, marmalade, fresh orange-juice with bits in it.

Polly.

Polly had been expecting him back last night.

Carla would have been expecting him back last night.

Preston stood up.

'Is anything wrong? If you need the toilet ... '

'I need to make a phone-call,' he said. 'I wonder ... '

She looked at him thoughtfully.

'Don't you think we should talk first?'

Preston sat down. Too late, anyway, far too late.

'Yes,' he said.

'I have to say it's almost flattering. I thought the media had lost interest.'

How could this be Eva Eichler? This gentle, mild, serene woman. This was not Eva Eichler, the writer of *Men – the Second Sex*, this was Mother Bernard.

You only had to look at her. She had Mother Bernard's passivity. A complete lack of tension in her face, as if it had been smoothed flat. And the look in her eyes, kindly, amused, tolerant. Eva Eichler was not tolerant.

She sat down opposite Preston at the table and put her legs across the spare chair. In this she differed radically from Mother Bernard who had never, in Preston's company, done anything with her legs except keep them firmly planted on the ground under a modest black shroud.

Eva Eichler's legs were not shrouded under anything very much. She wore a cotton frock with buttons down the front just like Dr W. K. Swann but unlike Dr W. K. Swann she wore no stockings underneath. Her legs were bare, a rosy brown in shade with tiny golden hairs on them like the bloom of a peach.

Was it possible, then, that Eva Eichler shaved her legs?

He must get these questions in some kind of order. He must make a list.

Question One: Where are my shoes and socks?

Question Two: Why are you not dead?

The music stopped and a voice announced that this was the nine o'clock news. United States Marines are poised to invade Nicaragua, it said. Meanwhile in Europe forces of the Warsaw Pact ...

Somebody switched off the radio.

'Coffee?' said Eva Eichler.

Preston stared at her. Had she not heard? It was what they had all been waiting for. Do Not Pass Go. Do Not Collect Two Hundred Pounds. Go Direct to Eternity.

But the serene features were undisturbed. The hand that poured the coffee did not tremble.

They were all going to die.

He was going to be sitting here with this bloody woman who was supposed to be dead, drinking coffee and passing the time of day while they started World War Three. This was how it was going to happen.

Eva Eichler was not Mother Bernard. Eva Eichler was the Angel of Death.

'Black or white?' asked the Angel of Death, poised with her coffee.

'Black,' said Preston. And that was another thing. Somebody had switched off the radio and it probably wasn't the cleaning lady. The odds were it was the same woman who'd laid him out for the night, the Toxteth Terror creeping through the house towards the french windows with her fingers edged for the killer blow. As if it wasn't bad enough waiting for the missiles to land.

He didn't have much time. He had to find some answers.

'Nice coffee,' said Preston. 'D'you buy it locally?'

'No, we have it delivered,' said Eva Eichler. 'From Fortnum and Mason's. Only the best.'

Was she laughing at him?

She was smiling, but this seemed to be normal. Smiling serenely. Perhaps, Preston thought, cleverly, she's been drugged. Kept in a zombie-like trance by Bernadette McCarthy. Now knowing the world thinks her dead. Signing massive cheques once a month for Fortnum and Mason goodies, and other things.

'Shopping locally,' he tried again, 'must be a bit difficult for you.'

'You mean, because I'm supposed to be dead?'

This seemed to rule out the drug theory.

'Well, I have to admit I don't go down the village much, but . . .' a small shrug . . . 'I don't think it'd cause me too many problems if I did. My name is Jean Frazer, an American, widowed or divorced, with a private income. I'm over here on a long visit. I like the country. I'm an amateur ornithologist. I want to study the marsh birds, maybe write a book some day. And I got a coloured maid I brought with me. Quaint, huh? This is an English rural community, it's a great place to hide yourself.'

'Really?' said Preston, seriously doubting it.

'Sure. You hide behind the stereotype, like everybody else, and a laurel hedge.'

'But what about the police? The village bobby ... ?'

'Alex, you mean?' Ms Frazer chuckled. 'But he's a dear. Have you met him? He wins first prize every year at the village fête, for his onions.'

But bloody hell, woman. Preston rejected the stereotype, even a village bobby who wins prizes for his bleedin' onions might reasonably be expected to raise his stolid yeoman brows at the sudden appearance in mid-Suffolk of a middle-aged American woman and a six foot tall black Amazon from Toxteth. Even a moron, or a genius beset by graver problems – a sudden blight of greenfly perhaps – might have the nous to connect it with the death-scene enacted a few miles down the coast.

Thought Preston.

And she knew what he was thinking and put him out of his misery.

'The police know,' said Eva Eichler. 'We fooled them a while but there was a young detective. An inspector. Inspector Johnston. Very persistent. But maybe you spoke with him?'

Johnston? No. Wait. Yes.

An Inspector Johnston rang.

And Preston had rung him back, but not spoken to him. Because his money had run out.

'A very strange man,' said Eva Eichler. 'Very, you know, obsessive. I sort of liked him, though. He was ... vulnerable. His wife had left him.'

'Ah, yes,' said Preston. Naturally, he thought. 'For a lion-tamer.'

Eva Eichler was surprised.

'No. No, I think he said he managed a supermarket in Ipswich.'

'Ah,' said Preston. 'Yes, he would. I'm sorry.'

'You sure you're feeling OK? Not feeling dizzy at all?'

'No, no, I'm fine. Do go on, please. Inspector Johnston. He cracked it then?'

'He wouldn't let up. Kept on and on, even when all the others had lost interest.'

Pedalling his little bike, thought Preston, for all his worth.

'But he was a very understanding man. A very gentle man. He just wanted to know the truth. He didn't want to put anyone behind bars. And after all, what had we done? Wasting police time was about all they could have charged us with.'

Preston smiled with her.

Oh yes, he thought, Inspector Johnston, I know him well.

'Well hello, you're up early this morning.'

Preston cowered. She lounged in the doorway, a black-panther in leotard and leg-warmers.

'I was disturbed.'

'Have some coffee.'

'I have to work out.'

The Liverpool accent was still there, modified, not refined, by its transatlantic sojourn.

Preston watched, squealing quietly to himself, little paws raised, as she crossed the terrace and squatted sullenly on the lawn.

'Are you going to do anything with this?' asked Eva Eichler.

'I'm sorry?' said Preston, mind on other things.

'Well, you came here for a purpose.'

'Oh yes.' Preston remembered. 'I don't know. It rather depends on whether there's a moral to it.'

'A moral?'

Preston explained about the God slot.

'There has to be a moral to it. It doesn't have to be Christian,' he added helpfully.

Eva Eichler laughed again. Preston was falling in love with Eva Eichler's laugh. Nor had it escaped his notice that she was almost certainly five foot two and a half.

On the lawn Bernadette seemed to be praying, mantis-like, to the fruit-trees. She turned her head and looked at him. Preston mustn't even think about it.

'I'm not sure I want to be the subject of a documentary,' said Eva Eichler. 'Even for God.'

She stood up.

'Care to take a walk?'

'I haven't got any shoes,' said Preston. 'Or socks.'

'D'you look under the bed?' asked Eva Eichler.

Preston's shoes and socks were under the bed.

'My mother,' Eva Eichler announced formally, when they came to the grave.

They looked at it for a moment in silence.

'She was born in a small town in Austria. On the German border. Blonde, Aryan, just like me.' A cynical little smile. 'But she joined the Communist Party and she married a Jew. Not wise, Mom.' Shaking her head. 'Not there, not then.'

She stooped and tugged at some weeds at the bottom of the headstone.

'It grows so fast. It took a long time finding it.' Preston bent down and tried to help. 'I don't know how they got out or why they came here. Maybe they knew some people. All we know is she died. Having me. And then we went to America and I stayed with these people in New York, good Jewish family, friends of my father, and he came back to Europe to fight. And he died, too.'

'There.' She straightened up and threw the weeds away. 'I don't know why I bother. It'll sink one day, into the bog. Guess the coffin has already.'

Preston had a sudden macabre image of the shells dropping in the graveyard and the bodies flying into the air. How did the Navy get permission? he wondered. Perhaps because of the war.

'And so I grew up a New York Jewish princess and lived happily ever after and might have got to be Vice-President, even President, who knows? Except that they found me out.

'They thought of changing the Constitution, you know, for Henry Kissinger, so he could be President. But he was a man and he had better things to do anyway.'

This was more like it. This was the Eva Eichler Preston knew and did not love.

'So is that why you disappeared?'

'It would have been very embarrassing,' said Eva Eichler. 'Just think about it.'

'But couldn't you have retired gracefully?'

She shook her head, looking at the grave.

'Not gracefully. They don't let you retire gracefully. Not from American politics.'

'So it was for the Party?'

She turned towards him then, smiling at the absurdity, so un-American.

'No, not for the Party. No, I wanted time to think. I wanted people off my back for a while.'

He winced, wondering if she meant it personally, but she wasn't really looking at him. Her eyes looked in.

'I wanted time to think about what I'd been saying and writing. Things about success and power I didn't really understand. I wanted to stay still for a while and think about where I was going.'

She focused on him again and smiled.

'Come on, let's get out of here before we sink with it.'

They walked round the old ruin. Small trees grew inside the nave, sheltering from the wind, rooted in the more solid ground and old bones. Shrapnel pitted the walls and the memorials to long-dead soldiers and other wars.

When they came out she led him down a path towards the sea, chatting easily as if he was an old friend.

'I've always had critics,' she said. 'Men, mostly, and I don't count them, forgive me,' turning towards him with a small smile. 'But in the feminist movement, too. They said I wanted women to be like men. Well, to some extent I do. Or did. I wanted women to grasp the nettle. Power.

'Until they get power they stay victims.' She stated it like a codicil, or a chunk of Mother Bernard's catechism, learned by heart. 'That's what I was saying – and a lot of women agreed with me. That's why they supported my political aspirations.

'Others thought I was on the wrong track.

'They said the real battle was about winning control over your own life, not power over others. Well,' she shrugged, smiled again, 'the debate continues but I'm not part of it any more. I burned my wings. Now I'm resting. Maybe for life.'

So Miranda had been right. Power and control. Good old Miranda, a lot more to Miranda than . . .

'Look.' Eva Eichler was stooping beside a tiny pink flower growing up the bank. 'Ragged-robin. First this year.'

The path was like a causeway now, running through the marshes, the banks sloping steeply into the reeds. Preston looked down at her, at the back of her head, bending over the flower. Her hair was pinned up at the back. It was very blonde, only slightly streaked with grey. Released from the pins it would fall around her shoulders.

'When I first came here I had no idea what I was going to do. This whole thing about where I was born, not being an American, I don't know.' She stood up, shaking her head, and he looked away from her, guiltily. 'I think it just made me realise I didn't really know who I was. I'd forgotten. I needed to find out and it seemed reasonable to start here. But I only wanted to look, I had no idea of staying. Not then.'

They walked on. Ahead, in the distance, Preston could see a single red sail but not the water it was sailing on.

'All my life,' said Eva, 'I've wanted to be a success. Can you understand that?'

Preston nodded and for once he really thought he did.

'For that I'd lie, cheat, deceive my friends, commit mass murder for Chrissake ... and suddenly it was all falling apart and I began to consider whether it was worth holding together, why I wanted it so badly, what was it all about, what was it about me that needed all this.'

Preston wished he had a film-crew with him. He needed to record this. This was what it was all about, what he had instinctively felt it was about from the moment Dr Milton Mahlzeit had told him the story about the woman who walked into the sea. But perhaps it didn't matter. Perhaps it was meant for his ears only. Perhaps only he cared, anyhow.

'And you know, right after seeing that grave I walked back to the church where we had left the car and I saw the realtor's sign up by the house, can you believe that?

'So that's when I decided. I'd buy myself some time. I'd disappear.

'I opened an account in the name of Jean Frazer. This was a teacher I had once, a very solid person, very reassuring. Bernie did all the fixing with agents, lawyers and the rest. She's also a very solid person. Very strong,' she added. Unnecessarily.

'Then when it was all fixed she bought another car so we had two and drove over to Felixstowe. You want to know why Felixstowe?'

Preston agreed that it had been bothering him.

'Because that's where I was born,' said Eva Eichler. 'It kind of appealed to me. You know, a beginning and an end.'

'But I thought you were born in Elmer?'

'We lived in Elmer, but that was the nearest hospital. Getting there, I guess, is what killed my mother.

'We should have gone further. To a different county, a different coast, but we didn't really think it through.

'We booked in at the hotel and had a few drinks. Then I went out with a plastic bag full of clothes and scattered them round the beach and then drove back here and left it all to Bernie.'

They could see the sea now but it didn't look any different from the land. Flat and endless and the mud-flats with the bits of old dead ships sticking up at intervals like bones, or question marks.

It was at this point that the thought entered Preston's head that Eva Eichler had merely postponed the event until now. That she intended to walk into the sea and take him with her.

He didn't know why he thought this. Perhaps it was something in the calm of her manner that alerted him, perhaps it was the idea he'd had for some time that their paths were somehow intertwined and they were both going nowhere. Like the travellers in Right Roads and Wrong Roads who end up in the swamp. But whatever it was he had this sudden sense of foreboding, bordering on panic.

It was this, he later maintained, that explained why he did what he did.

'That's how he traced us, through the guy who sold us the car,' Eva Eichler was saying. 'But by then I wasn't news any more. No one was interested, until you came along. So why you, Preston?' She stopped and looked at him again, seeming more amused than curious or alarmed. 'What's in it for you?'

Preston sat down on the edge of the dyke with his legs dangling above the mud.

'I suppose I thought it was Important,' he said, feebly. 'I mean, you, finding out why you did it. I mean, you were a Serious Person. You seemed to know all the answers, you seemed to know the way, but you went and walked into the sea. Or, at least, I thought you had.'

She sat down beside him.

'I could never have walked into the sea,' she said. 'I'm scared to death of water.'

'So am I,' said Preston, surprised. They both laughed and he looked at it across the mud-flats and stopped laughing and shuddered.

'Anyway,' he said. 'Then I thought you'd been murdered and I'd find out why and who did it and Be Famous. And get where I wanted to be.'

'That's interesting,' she said. 'Where d'you want to be?'

'I don't know,' he said. 'Anywhere, except where I am now, I think.

'Anyway, then it just didn't matter any more. It was just an escape.'

'An escape from what?'

So Preston told her about Polly and Miranda and Carla and *Shrews at Ten*, sitting on the edge of the mud-flats by the sea with the oyster-catchers skimming the surface and whingeing because they weren't catching anything and he told her why he wanted to be a Serious Person and why he was afraid of being Mr Studge.

'She-it,' said Eva Eichler when he'd finished. She had pulled a long piece of grass and was chewing it thoughtfully, not looking at him.

'What a mor-ass.'

Preston agreed that that just about summed it up.

'But I don't see how making a documentary about me is going to get you out of it,' said Eva Eichler.

'Neither do I,' said Preston. 'Not now.'

He felt as if he had run a race and come first for the first time in his life and then looked back and discovered that no one else was running, no one watching, they'd all gone home. But he had forgotten Inspector Johnston, whose wife had run off with a supermarket manager from Ipswich and who had got there ahead of him, pedalling for all he was worth.

'I wish sometimes I could get above,' said Preston. 'Just once and see it all laid out before me and think, Oh yes, that's where I went wrong. And that's where I want to be.'

'We all wish for that,' said Eva Eichler. 'Next thing you'll be wanting to know what's going to happen next.'

'I know what's going to happen next,' said Preston. 'My wife is going to divorce me, I'm going to be in the *News of the World* and I'm going to lose my children.'

Unexpectedly, he began to cry, sitting there with his legs dangling above the mud and the oyster-catchers crying with him and darting suddenly to peck at small creatures as they came crawling out of the swamp.

And Eva Eichler, the author of *Men – the Second Sex* and *Coming First*, sat next to him and put her arm round him and said, 'There, there, things aren't that bad. Think how much worse it could be. The Marines could go into Nicaragua. The Soviets could take over West Berlin. There could be a nuclear war.'

'It's all right for you,' sobbed Preston, illogically. 'You've got your cottage of content.'

'That wouldn't save me,' said Eva Eichler. 'It wouldn't save any of us, but if you think it would, go find your own, only for Chrissake don't go equating it with winning all the time. Christ,' said Eva Eichler, lapsing into type, 'men.'

'Look,' she said, a little later, when Preston had stopped wailing and was looking out to sea feeling foolish, 'it probably won't happen and you'll patch up your marriage or you'll get divorced, what the hell, you'll come to some arrangement about the kids. You won't lose them, don't be so emotional.'

'I know,' said Preston, 'I know. Thank you for being so understanding. I know you're right. I'll see them at weekends. It'll be fun.'

'Then why are you crying?'

'I'm crying because I'm Mr Studge,' said Preston.

But even Eva Eichler didn't understand that.

There was some confusion about what happened next. Preston said he thought she was going to walk into the sea and he was only trying to stop her. Eva Eichler said she thought she could see an orchid growing down the bank, just above the mud, and was just going down to take a closer look at it. Either way, they both agreed that he grabbed her around the waist and pulled her down to the ground.

And it was at this point that Bernadette came crashing out of the reed-beds.

31
HAVE A BATH

'I really am sorry,' said Eva Eichler, again, on the way back to the house.

'I know,' said Preston. 'She's over-protective.'

'She's paid to be, it's her job.'

'Is that why she turned the radio off?' said Preston, unkindly, because he was covered in mud and stinking and feeling foolish. 'So you wouldn't know it was World War Three?'

'She tries to keep the world at a safe distance.'

'But is the world safe from her?'

'To be fair,' said Eva, less sympathetically, 'she didn't physically touch you.'

'If she had I'd be dead.'

'Probably. But she didn't. You threw yourself in that stuff.'

'I did not throw myself into any stuff,' Preston protested. 'I fell. I missed my footing and I fell into the bloody stuff.'

'Yes,' said Eva, soothingly. 'Well it isn't far now and we'll fix you up with a bath and a change of clothing.'

It was while Preston was in the bath that he discovered he no longer had any warts. They'd come off with the mud.

He didn't see them coming off but when he pulled his penis up out of the murky water to see how they were doing, they weren't there any more. There was just a patch of raw skin where they'd been. That was what the itching was, his warts getting ready to fall off and the new skin growing.

Preston sat back in the bath with the glass of wine Eva Eichler had given him and felt strangely close to feeling happy.

Then he remembered Polly and Carla and Nicaragua and the *News of the World* and if the water hadn't been so muddy and his warts floating around in it somewhere he'd have put his head under and drowned.

'What am I going to do?' he asked Eva Eichler when he came out of the bathroom. He was wearing a metallic-blue jump suit of Bernie's with a logo on the front that said, Big is Beautiful. He'd had to roll the legs and the sleeves up.

'It doesn't look too bad,' said Eva Eichler. 'I'm afraid these are all I can find for your feet.'

These were a pair of silver thong-sandals with flat heels.

'I mean with my life,' said Preston, putting them on.

'Oh Christ, Preston, I can't tell you what to do with your life,' said Eva Eichler. 'You have to work it out for yourself.'

'But you've been thinking,' said Preston. 'What conclusions have you come to?'

'I was wrong about Lady Macbeth,' said Eva Eichler. 'That was a stupid thing to say. She was obviously unhinged. All that trouble for Scotland. The woman was clearly in need of therapy.'

'That's all?'

'Well, I've only been dead two years.'

'I don't know where I'm going,' said Preston.

'None of us do,' said Eva Eichler. 'But I honestly don't think making a documentary about me is going to help. Admittedly I'm biased.'

'No,' said Preston, 'I'm not going to make a documentary about you.'

He supposed he'd already made up his mind about that while they were walking across the bog but it was a surprise to hear himself say it.

'I don't want to succeed that badly,' he said, 'I don't have the killer instinct. I don't want to be President. I don't want to be Vice-President. I don't even want to be head of news and current affairs.'

He didn't want to be Mr Studge either, but there were probably other ways of dealing with that. Better ways than being Mr Fischer, anyway.

'Thank you,' said Eva Eichler.

She gave him a plastic bag for his dirty clothes.

'You sure she won't mind about me wearing her jump suit?' he asked. 'And are these her sandals?'

'She won't mind. She helped you out the mud, didn't she?'

This was true. Preston's arm still ached where she'd wrenched at it.

'She was almost smiling,' Eva pointed out, 'when she went on with her run.'

'What shall I do with them?' Preston asked.

'Leave them at the hotel,' she said. 'We'll pick them up one day. It'll be a sentimental journey. We'll see Mr Winner again.'

She giggled. Eva Eichler giggled.

'Mr Winner?'

'The guy who came looking for me with Bernie. The manager. The guy who found my pantyhose. Mr V. Winner.'

Mr Winner was Mr Studge.

'What does the V stand for?' asked Preston.

But Eva Eichler didn't know.

V for Vivian, Preston thought as he walked down the drive to where he'd left the car not much more than twelve hours ago. Carla's car.

What would she have done when he didn't come back for the night, he wondered. What would Polly have done when he didn't come home? Would one of them have called the police? Or neither? Or both?

Perhaps they were hunting for him in several counties.

V for Vincent. V for Valentine.

Valentine Studge?

Carla's car was where he had left it next to the church, the new church built to replace the one in the marshes which was sinking, where Eva Eichler the First was buried.

Bernadette was standing next to the car.

'Hi,' said Preston warily.

Bernadette said nothing.

'I'm wearing your jump suit,' said Preston.

She shrugged.

'And your sandals. Eva lent them to me. I hope you don't mind. I'll leave them for you at the hotel.'

She shrugged again. Then she spoke.

'Sorry you fell in the mud,' she said. 'Sorry I scared you like that.'

'I lost my balance,' said Preston, who had, in fact, jumped but was trying to forget about it.

'Hey, you speak like you're from the North.'

'I'm from Liverpool,' said Preston. 'Originally.'

'No kidding. That's incredible. Whereabouts?'

'Old Swan.'

'No kidding. Incredible,' said Bernie. 'I'm from Toxteth.'

'I know,' said Preston.

'D'you support Liverpool or Everton?'

Preston took his life in his hands.

'Liverpool,' he said.

'Hey, so do I.'

'No kidding?' said Preston.

'What about Kenny Dalglish, then, eh? And after one season.'

'Yeah. And over Everton, too.'

'Fantastic, yeah. That Rush.'

'Yeah, and now they've sold him to the Italians.'

'Yeah. Well, he gave us something. And there'll be others. I always wanted to play football for Liverpool. I wanted to be the first woman striker.'

'Me too,' said Preston. 'I mean ... '

They both laughed.

'I guess it won't happen for either of us,' said Bernadette.

She put her hand out. Preston took it, bracing himself.

'Well, take care how you go. Mind you don't go stepping into no more swamps.'

'I'll try not to,' said Preston.

He got into the car and it started first time.

V for Victor, he thought.

Victor Winner.

32 SEE THREE WOMEN
Throw Again

They were waiting for him back at the hotel. The three of them.
Polly and Carla and Cristobel.

Preston saw them through the window where he'd gone to rec-
onnoitre after seeing Polly's car, *their* car, in the hotel car-park.

He hadn't been too surprised.

He was surprised when he saw Cristobel with them, but then,
when he thought about it, not really.

Cristobel *would* be there. She was that kind of woman. They'd
only met twenty-four hours ago and she knew everything there was
to know about him. She was an integral part of his life.

Preston didn't think he'd bother to join them. There wasn't
anything he could say. They'd have it all sorted out by now. They
were sitting back on their tails disembowelling him.

'Heard the news?' said the travelling-salesman who picked Preston
up on the slip road out of Felixstowe. 'There's going to be a peace
conference. I knew that's how it'd pan out.'

The travelling-salesman was an optimist. He'd just sold twelve
gross of plastic disposable razors to a chemist's shop in the town.

'The rate they go through them,' he said. 'They reckon it's because
the women use them, to shave their legs. Another six gross and I'll've
hit my target for the month,' he said, 'with two weeks still to go.
You've got to keep ahead in this game,' he said. 'What you do for a
living?'

He couldn't help glancing down at Preston's silver sandals. Preston
didn't think he'd seen them when he'd stopped to pick him up.

'I box kangaroos,' Preston told him.

33 DEMAND AN EPIDURAL
Go Back to Classes

'I don't think I want to do the Singing Exercise,' said Preston, 'if it's all right with you.'

'It's all right,' said Miranda, 'I'm glad you're here.'

They had broken the waters and left her in a small room by herself, wired to a machine that measured the baby's heartbeat. She looked very pale and tired and frightened.

'I brought along a book of poetry instead,' he said. 'I thought I could read them to you. If you think it'll help.'

'It's all right,' said Miranda. 'Just talk to me.'

'But it's Dylan Thomas,' said Preston, who knew she liked Dylan Thomas.

'I'd rather you talked to me,' said Miranda. 'Tell me what you're doing with yourself. It will distract me.'

'Well,' Preston closed the book. 'We've come to an arrangement about the twins and I'm looking for a garden-flat somewhere in Fulham.'

'Do you still see much of Polly?'

'Oh yes, we get along fine, actually, now we're not living together. Do you?'

'Oh, oh, oh,' said Miranda.

'Breathe,' said Preston. 'Quick. In, out.'

'Ah, ah, ah.'

'Is it contractions?' Preston began to panic. 'I'll sing if you like.'

'No. Cramp. In my leg. Ah.'

Preston jumped on the bed and twisted her foot.

'Aaaaagh,' screamed Miranda.

'Push,' said Preston. 'This is what we used to do playing football.'

'It's all right now. Ah. Thank you.'

'You're sure?'

'Sure. Ah. Please let go of my leg.'

Preston let go of her leg.

'Oh. Thank you. That's better. Go on. Tell me about your work.'

'Oh, work's fine,' Preston said, cheerfully. 'They wouldn't have me on the God slot.'

'No? But Preston, why ever not?'

'They didn't say. I'm doing animal programmes again.'

'Is that awful for you?'

'Oh no. It's not so bad. It's a new series about garden animals. You know, earthworms and snails and slugs and butterflies and things. It's all on film.'

'And are you happy?'

Preston winced, but you had to be ready for questions like that from Miranda.

'I'm all right,' he said. 'It's not going to get me anywhere, but it's nice working on film again.'

'Good,' she said. She took hold of his hand and squeezed it. 'I'm glad you're happy.'

This was going a bit far but Preston thought in the circumstances he'd let it pass.

'I've stopped worrying about getting anywhere,' he said. 'I mean, I've decided you've just got to carry on and try to do the decent thing from time to time.'

'And is that what you're doing now,' she said, 'doing the decent thing?'

'No, not at all,' Preston assured her hastily. 'I mean, I feel I've got a kind of vested interest in this baby, even if, well, we didn't exactly ... I mean, it's not mine.'

'No. I'm sorry.'

'Oh, that's all right. I don't mind at all. Who did exactly? Do it, I mean. You don't have to tell me if you don't want to.'

She smiled.

'It was a man I knew at college.'

Preston was puzzled.

'I met him again when we came back from holiday,' Miranda explained. 'He was going back to Australia.'

Preston was shocked.

'You did it with an Australian?'

'I'm sorry,' said Miranda, 'but he was quite a nice man. And he'd just had a blood test.'

'Did he know you wanted to, you know ... ?' He gestured at the lump under the bed clothes.

'Yes. He didn't mind. He thought it was quite funny.'

'Funny?' said Preston.

'You're not angry are you?'

'Me? No. Why should I be? I mean, it's got nothing to do with me.'

'You were the first choice.'

'Yes. Honestly, Miranda, it's really not ... It's just ... I mean, you are amazing.'

'It was just the right time for me. My stars said.'

Preston winced again.

'Preston,' she said, a little later. 'How do you know what's the decent thing?'

'You don't,' said Preston. 'I thought about that. You just have to guess. It's a bit like trying to please women. You know. They never make it easy for you.' He qualified this. 'I don't mean you personally.'

He noticed she was crying.

'I'm sorry, Miranda. Stupid of me. Please don't get upset.'

'It's not that,' she said. 'It's the baby. Something should be happening.'

Preston tried to remember what the Australian Knee-Capper had told them in classes.

'Perhaps you should push more,' he suggested. 'Do you want to climb on a chair?'

'It's because I'm frightened of the pain,' said Miranda, crying louder.

'It's all right,' Preston soothed her. 'Everything's going to be all right.'

'My baby's going to die,' sobbed Miranda.

Preston called a nurse.

The nurse thumped the machine with her fist. She manoeuvred Miranda on to her side and thumped it again.

'The heartbeat's stopped, hasn't it?' said Miranda.

'I don't think so,' said Preston, 'there's a little red light flashing.'

'It shouldn't be, should it?' Miranda asked the nurse.

'I think there's something wrong with the machine,' said the nurse. 'Don't worry.' But she sounded worried.

She went to fetch the doctor.

'I think she should have an epidural,' Preston told the nurse while the doctor examined her. 'She's afraid of the pain. That's why she's not trying.'

The nurse ignored him. The doctor gave Miranda an epidural.

'My body just won't do it,' complained Miranda, close to tears again an hour or so later.

The red light was flashing again.

'Perhaps we'd better try singing,' said Preston, at his wits' end, 'or I could massage your feet.'

But the doctor had another solution.

'The baby's in some distress,' he said. 'I think we should do a caesarian section.'

The doctor was male, about Preston's age. He had grown a moustache to make him look older. Preston thought that in the circumstances he would have grown one, too.

'I feel I've let her down,' said Miranda.

Preston thought she meant the baby.

'It might be a boy,' he said.

'I mean Barb. All that training.'

Preston was cross.

'Miranda, this is not a competition,' he told her. 'You are not trying to win a race.'

'Will you come in with me?' she asked him.

The doctor said he didn't think this was a good idea.

'I want him to cuddle it,' said Miranda. 'I might not be able to. It's very important for a baby to be cuddled when it comes out.'

'We can cuddle it,' said the doctor.

'It's a rather messy business,' he told Preston quietly. 'You might not be able to stomach it.'

'We could put a screen across her abdomen,' said the nurse. 'So he doesn't have to look.'

So they put a screen up to cut off the bottom half of Miranda's body and Preston cowered behind it in his green mask, holding Miranda's hand.

'I can feel them cutting,' said Miranda.

'It's all right,' said Preston.

'Tell me something to distract me.'

But Preston's mind was a blank. He wished he'd brought Dylan Thomas. Desperate, he recalled a little-known fact from his latest series on garden animals.

'The male snail has a penis four times the length of its body,' Preston whispered. 'Also a kind of barbed spatula to hold the vagina open during insertion.'

'It's going to be all right,' said the nurse. She was standing behind Miranda's head, rolling her eyes at Preston above her mask. 'We're nearly there.'

'Cuddle it, Preston,' said Miranda, 'whatever it is.'

Preston was alarmed.

He wasn't entirely convinced by this Australian.

What did she mean 'whatever it is'? The Anti-Christ?

'It's hurting,' moaned Miranda.

'It can't be,' said the nurse.

'It is,' said Miranda. 'Preston, I can feel them doing things.'

'What can I do?' said Preston.

'Hold my hand,' sobbed Miranda. Then, hysterically, 'Sing.'

Hesitantly, with an apologetic glance at the nurse, Preston began to sing.

The nurse looked at him with an expression of shocked incredulity.

'. . . Of Hector and Lysander and such great names as these . . .'

He held tight to Miranda's hand and risked a glance over the screen. The doctor and his team had stopped what they were doing and were staring at him in astonishment.

'. . . With a ta-ra-ra-ra-ra-ra-ra . . .'

He looked down and his voice died.

The top half of the baby was emerging from a large slit in Miranda's lower abdomen. They'd got it halfway and then stopped and it began to yell at them indignantly. Then it saw Preston, peering over the screen.

It might have been a trick of the light or the way they were holding it but Preston could have sworn it swivelled its head to look at him.

It came out of Miranda's womb like The Alien out of John Hurt's stomach and it swivelled its head and it opened its eyes and it looked at him *irritably*.

An alien being, thought Preston, seeing me for what I am. The enemy. The species it is designed to replace.

'There you are,' said the doctor, pulling it out and handing it to him, 'a lovely baby girl.'

A NOTE ON THE TYPE

This book was typeset using Ehrhardt, a typeface based on a design by the
Hungarian Nicholas Kis (1650–1702) who worked as a punchcutter in
Amsterdam from 1680 to 1689 at the height of the Dutch Republic. A set of
his matrices was acquired by the Ehrhardt foundry in Leipzig, hence the
name adopted when the modern face was cut.
The type has all the sturdy Dutch character of the *Gôut Hollandais*, the
characteristic type-style of the latter part of the seventeenth century. The
relatively narrow, densely black letters also show the influence of German
Black Letter type.